Frederick Stonehouse

Haunted Lakes

Great Lakes Ghost Stories, Superstitions and Sea Serpents

Lake Superior Port Cities Inc.

First Edition: October 1997

5   4   3

 LAKE SUPERIOR PORT CITIES INC.
P.O. Box 16417
Duluth, Minnesota 55816-0417
USA   888-BIG LAKE (244-5253)

Publishers of *Lake Superior Magazine* and
Lake Superior Magazine Travel Guide

Library of Congress Cataloging-In-Publication Data

Stonehouse, Frederick.
    Haunted lakes : Great Lakes ghost stories, superstitions and sea serpents / by Frederick Stonehouse.
        p. cm.
    Includes bibliographical references and index.
    ISBN 0-942235-30-4
    1. Ghosts – Great Lakes Region. 2. Sea monsters – Great Lakes. I. Title.
    BF1472.U6S76 1997
    133.1'0977 – dc21   97-36087
                                                                                    CIP

Printed in the United States of America

            Editor: Paul L. Hayden
    Managing Editor: Hugh E. Bishop
          Designer: Stacy L. Winter
        Cover Art: K.H. Courtland
            Printer: Cushing-Malloy Inc.
                    Ann Arbor, Michigan

To my mother,
Martina Mortensen Stonehouse

Preface

Frankly I've worried about doing this book. I have always tried to be a serious maritime historian, seeking to examine and interpret our Great Lakes maritime past. By no stretch could this book be considered "serious" history.

I even debated using a pen name to allow me to keep my reputation "pure," but then I reconsidered. *Haunted Lakes* may not be serious maritime history in itself, however, the superstitions and stories are certainly part of the great lore of the Great Lakes, and therefore have value and do relate to how our forefathers thought and acted. They are part of the thread of our past.

Previously, my efforts have always focused purely on Great Lakes maritime history, particularly shipwrecks and the U.S. Life-Saving Service. During that research I occasionally ran across various superstitions, traditions, stories of ghost ships, tales of sea serpents, haunted ships and lighthouses and all other manner of material I would previously classify under the pejorative term "folklore," nothing more than "intriguing" stories and tales. Some I saved, simply throwing them into the box labeled "weird stuff." Others I ignored. All I categorized as the mere creation of Great Lakes fiction writers instead of anything based even remotely on fact.

It wasn't until I started working with the Ivan Walton Collection in the Bentley Historical Library at the University of Michigan that I realized that much of the material did have a basis in "fact." Walton's interviews with retired sailing masters clearly established in my mind that these men, to a degree at least, actually believed in the old stories. In many instances they had lived them! The information in C.H.J. Snider's "Schooner Days" column based on old-time sailor interviews in the 1930s and '40s reaffirmed my conclusions. Whether one accepts such stories or not, they are part of the maritime tradition of the lakes.

With this consideration in mind, I resolved to try to pull together as much of the material as I could. No effort would be made to judge validity. How, for example, can you "prove" a ghost story? Most of the principals are unavailable for interviews. I would attempt, however, to establish them as having a basis in historical reference.

Although I neither believe nor disbelieve in ghosts and have no special sensitivity to the spirit world, I have had experiences that give me cause to be open-minded concerning those things we may not understand. A case in point is one particular encounter that left my hair "tingling." To this day I can give no rational explanation for it. I can only relate it as it happened.

In May 1993, I was making some copies of Life-Saving Service photographs in the Sturgeon Point Lighthouse Museum on the shore of Lake Huron. One of the older lights on the lakes, the stone structure was built in

1870. A Life-Saving Service station was established on the grounds in 1876, however the buildings are long gone. The day I visited was bright, sunny and completely the type to push thoughts of things that go "bump in the night" to the deepest recesses of the mind. The museum was not yet open for the season and was still shuttered against the icy blasts of winter. Inside it was damp, chilly and dark. The dim illumination available came from a few low wattage bulbs. The furniture and general decor were from the 1870 period.

Immediately upon entering the building, the hair on the back of my neck began to "tingle." Intuitively I felt uncomfortable, that I wasn't alone. After setting up my copy camera gear in the restored living room on the first floor, I climbed the stairs to the second floor and entered a room fitted out as a display area. Long glass cases filled with various small artifacts lined one wall. A single light switch on the wall near the door controlled the electric lights in the case. Turning it on, I quickly examined the contents. Finding nothing of interest for my task at hand, I turned the light off. From the adjacent wall I removed several Life-Saving Service photos for copying and took them down to my camera in the living room. When I returned with the photos several minutes later, the display case light was back on. After replacing the photos on the wall and selecting two more, I again turned the case light off and went back to my copy camera. All the while I felt an undefined apprehension. The hair on my neck continued to "tingle," and a penetrating shot of cold rolled up my back.

Again I returned to the display room. Again the case light was on! Enough was enough! Replacing the photos, I turned the case light off a third time and retreated downstairs. I hastily picked up my camera equipment and left the building. Outside the blue sky and warm temperatures instantly relieved my apprehension. Somewhat embarrassed by the experience, I said nothing about it.

All the while I was in the lighthouse I had seen nothing unusual, only felt it. Knowing nothing of the light in terms of ghost stories or the like, I had no reason to suspect anything unnatural. But I did experience something. It wasn't just a reaction to an old dark building.

A year later when I spoke with one of the museum personnel regarding whether there was any reason for my strange feelings, she stated there weren't any ghost stories connected to the light that she was aware of. Coincidentally though, she related that on occasion she did have a difficult time turning lights out. After closing down at the end of the day, she sometimes opened the next morning to find lights burning that she was certain she had turned off. She simply put it down to her error. But I wonder! I wonder if it was really the playful spirit of the first keeper, Percy Silverthorn, still keeping his light!

Contents

CHAPTER ONE

Haunted Lighthouses

TIME: Today

PLACE: Lighthouse Point Museum, Lake (unknown)

The pale figure quickly materialized out of thin air. Shadowy and indistinct, he was still clearly visible. He wore a thick black beard, peaked blue cap and blue uniform with shiny brass buttons. Although he moved silently down the hallway, the old wooden floor creaked loudly as he stepped over it.

Passing through the locked steel door, the spectre slowly climbed the spiral staircase. Footfalls echoed throughout the light tower. When he reached the lamp room he just vanished.

Below in the museum store, two volunteer guides looked at each other and smiled. They had heard it all before. Every time they looked, trying to see what made the sounds, they never found anything. They didn't even look any more. They just knew that it was the old keeper, still making his rounds. Still running "his" light!

Ghosts and old lighthouses seem to go hand in hand. Many lighthouses appear to have some degree of supernatural activity connected with them, real or imagined, in fact or lore. Stories often revolve around hearing footsteps on the tower stairs. When checked, invariably no one or nothing is there.

For those who believe in ghosts, this activity can easily be explained. After all, if there is one activity, one action deeply imprinted in a lightkeeper's daily routine, it is the simple physical work of climbing up and down the spiral stairs leading to the lantern room high atop the tower, one measured step at a time. The climb was done at

1

least twice a day, at sunset to light the beacon and sunrise to extinguish it, as well as other times to do such maintenance as required. Twice a day, seven days a week, 52 weeks a year or as long as the season ran on the lakes and for as long as the keeper kept the light, he made the long and laborious trek. Could it be that the importance of this daily routine was ingrained so strongly on the keeper's very soul that even in death his spirit continued it? From the number of lighthouses with "tower" ghosts, this would seem to be the case.

In other instances, the lighthouses still seem to be inhabited by old residents. Chicago's Grosse Point Light, where unusual sounds of walking are sometimes heard as well as doors opening and closing, is an example of this type of activity. Is an old keeper or a member of his family still "at home?"

In some lighthouses it's less what is seen or heard than what is felt. It's the "presence" of a wandering spirit that is disconcerting. Many people are more sensitive to this than others. A light that to one person may feel perfectly "normal," may feel to another "alive" with "energy."

A popular theory holds that ghosts have a powerful connection with the places they haunt. They could have lived there or experienced terrible tragedy or death. Perhaps they have returned in an effort to complete unfinished business. In some instances their living experiences may have been so pleasant that they want to stay, even after death, and not "pass on." However they manifest themselves – as an apparition, as the opening and closing of doors, sounds, a cold spot, the overwhelming feeling of being watched or some other activity – they are real in terms of the number of people who have experienced them. It is often said, "perception is reality."

Mugged for a Mug
Gibraltar Point Light

One of the oldest lights on the Great Lakes and the first one erected on Lake Ontario at Toronto is at Gibraltar Point. Located in the southwest corner of the island that forms the southern flank of Toronto Harbour, its steady beam has guided mariners since 1808. The tower stands 82 feet high. Its massive stone walls are extremely thick, four feet at the base and two to three feet at the top. A small story-and-a-half keeper's house stands to the west of the tower.

Some islanders believe that the spirit of the first keeper, J.P. Rademuller (1808-16), still haunts the lighthouse. Visitors report resounding footsteps echoing through the old structure. Others claim to hear his unearthly moans. Moving shadows that can't be explained and bizarre glowing clouds all add to the concept of a phantom keeper.

Legend holds that Rademuller was murdered during a drunken argument with soldiers from nearby Fort York. Rademuller, a dedicated and meticulous recent German immigrant, was in all respects the perfect keeper. The lighthouse was always clean and well ordered, with everything in its place. He carefully cleaned the lens every morning and properly trimmed the wicks. By all accounts, Rademuller was a keeper to be relied on.

But he did like his beer and, coming so recently from Germany, his brewing skills were sharp. It was well known that he made the best pilsner on the lake. He was also a generous man, always ready to share a mug or two with a friend or stranger. Nothing made life easier than a cool glass of foaming suds. He always kept a ready supply in the house.

A small fort or blockhouse was also located on Gibraltar Point and soldiers often visited the keeper for good conversation and better beer. On January 2, 1816, three soldiers, already drunk, arrived at the lighthouse and demanded beer. Seeing their inebriated condition, the good lightkeeper refused to give them any.

Rademuller tried to calm the men down, to convince them it was best to go back to the fort, or even bunk down in the lighthouse until they sobered up. But it was beer they demanded!

"Damn it, Rademuller, give us some of your best beer," growled a big brute of a soldier with a scar slicing down his cheek. He raised a wicked piece of firewood like a club and shouted, "Give it to us or suffer the consequences."

When the keeper again protested, the soldier's arm swung down in an arc and the makeshift club struck the keeper sharply on the side of the head, knocking him to the floor with a loud thump. Still enraged, the men dragged his unconscious body to the top of the tower and threw him to his death. To hide the evidence of their dastardly crime the perpetrators cut the keeper into pieces and buried them all over the grounds. Another version says they beat him to death with their belts and a club.

The soldiers fled and the mystery of the keeper's whereabouts went unsolved. With Rademuller's disappearance, authorities appointed a Mr. Halloway in his place. The whereabouts of the missing man was often a topic of local conversation, but no one had answers. They may have suspected foul play, but had no proof.

Sometime after 1832, keeper James Durnam discovered some bones while digging near the light. Authorities believed they were those of the missing keeper, and that certainly he had been murdered. Durham later claimed that on dark and foggy nights he not only heard the old keeper's howls, but also saw his ghost, vainly looking for his murderers.

There is one instance where the ghost provided some physical evidence of his presence. The inside of the antiquated tower was coated with plaster or whitewash. A newspaper reporter, staying the night in the light to "debunk" the ghost myth, carefully examined the structure early in the evening and found nothing unusual. During another inspection sometime later, he noticed a rubbing on the plaster wall at shoulder height and shuddered at his next thought. Had a ghostly shoulder made the marks? He also observed that some plaster had "flaked" onto the steps, covering them with a fine white powder. Unable to sleep and having nothing better to do to pass the long night, the unnerved young man swept the steps clean.

Sometime later he rechecked the stairs. Once again, there was white powder again on the steps. Perhaps it was the result of spirit shoulder rubs? More incredible, though, were the faint foot prints clearly visible in the powder. Who or what had climbed them?

It is unknown whether the ghostly keeper is still stalking the light seeking vengeance against his murderers or is just trying to finish his interrupted duties. However, during the turn of the century, many old lake captains frequenting Toronto Harbour believed that the ghost was still in the light. While they always referred to him as "the old man" or "old man Muller," it was the murdered keeper they meant.

The tales of the spectral keeper and his nocturnal visits to his old quarters persist. Use of the light was discontinued in 1959.[1]

Mysterious Tower Lights
Oswego West Pierhead Light

As lighthouses go, the Oswego West Pierhead Light in New York isn't old. Built in 1930, the plain concrete structure represents a modern simplicity of form and purpose. And according to some people, it is also haunted.

Several years ago, during the early morning hours of a long night watch, a Coast Guardsman on shore saw lights in the old Lake Ontario light tower. In concept, it wasn't an unusual thing to see, except that he knew no one was there. At least nothing human.

The beacon had been automated years before and even the windows were sealed shut. Knowing that he would be disbelieved if he waited until morning to tell his tale, he woke several friends – all of whom also witnessed the same mysterious lights. The puzzled group could find no rational explanation for them. Whatever they thought of – reflections from car headlights or nearby street lights – didn't stand up to their examination. When the sighting was inevitably reported to higher headquarters, it was laughed off as either a joke or the men's imaginations. Seeing ghostly lights was not part of the Coast Guard mission. "There are no strange lights now! There never were any strange lights! There will be no strange lights!"

Oswego West Pierhead Light. U.S. COAST GUARD

Why the light should be haunted isn't certain, but records show that there had been a terrible accident that claimed the lives of six brave Coast Guardsmen at the facility. During a severe storm on December 1, 1942, while the lighthouse was still a fully manned station, the light-keeper on duty was stranded. He was rapidly running out of stores. In a desperate attempt to resupply him, eight Coast Guardsmen managed to fight their way out to the lighthouse in a 38-foot picket boat with a relief keeper and supplies. After making the very difficult transfer from the wildly heaving boat to the lighthouse, disaster struck. A large wave smashed the craft against the concrete crib, wrecking the wooden boat. In the resulting disaster, six of the eight men aboard perished. Were their spirits returning from beyond?

Some say that the haunting of the light dates from this accident. Strange voices were heard in empty rooms. Light bulbs left tightly screwed in were often found unscrewed. Furniture left in one position would later be discovered to have been moved. It was as if an entire separate set of keepers were still using the light, rearranging things to suit themselves.

These unexplained events continued on and off until the light was automated in 1968. Even when human keepers no longer ventured into the old building, the bizarre light phenomenon continued. In some reports, every window in the structure was illuminated, even those covered over with steel plates! What was in Oswego lighthouse?[2]

Return of the Beam
Cove Island Light

It was a storm-lashed November night. No one quite remembers the year, but the steady beacon on Cove Island at the entrance to Georgian Bay from Lake Huron winked out. Since October 1858, the massive stone tower at the northeast tip of Gig Point had faithfully kept the light for all to see. Without its steady beam to guide the ships past the treacherous rocks and shoals, disaster was certain to strike. When all looked the blackest, the light suddenly came back on, its steady glow reassuring mariners on the stormy lake.

When asked why the light went dark, the lightkeeper first explained that the lamp had indeed gone out, but that through his skill he was able to relight it. It was many years before he reluctantly revealed the shocking truth – he was not at his station that tempestuous night. He was, in fact, not on the island at all. The light had failed due to his inexcusable neglect. But he had an even more bizarre explanation for why the light came back. It was relit by the ghost of Captain Tripp!

Captain Amos Tripp's story goes back many years before, to October 22, 1881. He was the master of the small 75-foot, 118-ton schooner *Regina*, bound from Goderich with a cargo of salt. The schooner, built in 1866, was overtaken by a fierce gale and badly beaten about. The old hull soon spit her oakum caulking, allowing great quantities of water to flood into her hold. The *Regina* was headed for the bottom; the only question was how quickly.

Captain Tripp thought that he could nurse the craft to safety on a sandbar off Cove Island. His crew didn't give a plugged nickel for her chances. They voted with their feet and deserted her in the yawl, leaving Tripp standing alone on his quarterdeck. The crew's assessment of the *Regina*'s seaworthiness was correct and the schooner sank just short of the sandbar. Tripp paid for his overconfidence with his life. The old captain's body eventually washed ashore on the island and was buried without ceremony behind the dunes. Since no coffin was available, it was simply wrapped in a sail. Perhaps for an old sailor this was most appropriate anyway.

Regardless of the facts, the unfaithful Cove Island lightkeeper always believed that Tripp's presence was with him on the island. He constantly felt the presence of the old captain's energy. And he claimed that it was Tripp's noble spirit that relit the light and kept it burning throughout the storm. Captain Tripp's help was seen in other, less dramatic ways. Sometimes wicks were found trimmed, brass polished and lens and mirrors cleaned. It was as if there were an unseen assistant working about the lighthouse. Sightings of Tripp were rare, but at least twice a shadowy figure thought to be him was seen on the beach during especially bad, gale-lashed nights.

Other stories hold that when the cold north wind blows hard, the ghost of old Captain Tripp returns to the lighthouse to play a hand of cards with the keeper. None of the keepers ever objected to sharing their old home with the venerable captain.[3]

The Guardian Spirit of Point aux Barques

The *Coast Pilot* describes the reef at Lake Huron's Point aux Barques as ... "dangerous ... with rocks covered less than six feet near its outer edge, extends two miles E from Point aux Barques Light. A five-foot spot is 1.2 miles NE of the light and boulders covered 13 to 15 feet extend up to 2.5 miles N and NE ...." Under any circumstances, it is a dangerous place for a sailor to be.

To warn mariners away from the reef's deadly stone talons, in 1847 Congress provided $5,000 to build a lighthouse. It became operational the following year. In the mid-1850s it was rebuilt. An assistant keepers house was added in 1908. The present tower stands 89 feet high.

As the result of the large number of vessels wrecked in the area, regardless of the light's effort to warn them clear, in 1876 a first class lifesaving station was built several hundred yards to the south. Time and again, these brave men ventured forth into the teeth of a gale to rescue shipwrecked sailors.

In 1958, the U.S. Coast Guard turned the land and facility over to Huron County, which presently operates it as a park, campground and museum. The old stick style lifesaving station building was moved to Huron City – a unique museum complex several miles to the west.

Point aux Barques is fraught with maritime tragedy. Many sailors drowned in numerous wrecks – the latest being the 587-foot steel steamer *Daniel J. Morrell*, lost on November 29, 1966. Dennis Hale, the sole survivor from her 34-member crew, actually washed ashore on a life raft at the point.

An especially terrible loss for local families occurred in April 1879, when seven of eight members of the lifesaving crew perished when their surfboat overturned in heavy seas, while they were trying to run the reef to help a schooner in distress.

From a sailor's perspective, Point aux Barques is certainly a place of both pulse quickening danger and deep sadness. If, as the old sailors believed, the spirits of drowned sailors haunted those places where good vessels and crews died in screaming agony, then this dreadful point is a home to many a restless soul.

But it is also home to at least one very gentle and concerned guardian ghost.

Because the old lighthouse grounds are now a county park, a resident manager is employed during the summer to handle the multitude of tasks necessary to make it a successful enterprise. The manager lives in the old assistant keeper's quarters, a hundred yards or so distant from the lighthouse proper. The building is far more spacious and comfortable than the old 1857 keeper's house, which is now used as a museum.

Several years ago, the manager's adult daughter was staying with her parents in the old assistant's house when she woke suddenly in the middle of the night to a strange and unidentifiable noise. At the time, she was sleeping in an upstairs bedroom. Knowing that something was there, but not what, she slowly opened her door and nervously peered into the dark but empty hallway. Seeing nothing, she crept carefully to the head of the stairs and looked down.

What she saw should have scared the wits out of her, but it didn't. Instead she was overcome by a feeling of intense calm, of pervasive relaxation. Instinctively she knew everything was all right. Standing at the base of the stairs, shimmering slightly in the pale moonlight streaming through the windows, was the distinct, almost solid, apparition of a woman from a time long past.

She appeared average in height, perhaps a bit on the thin side and wore a long old-fashioned dress with an apron tied about her waist. Her hair was done up in a tight bun. The face was neither old nor young, but instead had an ethereal and ageless quality. Her left hand rested easily on the banister, as if in preparation for climbing. The woman had shape and substance, none of the half-formed shapes commonly accepted as spirit manifestations. The strange visitor spoke not a word nor made a motion, but the daughter clearly received the overwhelming impression that the woman had been the old lightkeeper's wife and had come over from the original keeper's quarters to see what was going on in the new house; to determine if the new residents posed any threat to the old light. For the longest time, it seemed minutes but probably was mere seconds, human and spirit stood silently staring at each other, their eyes locked in eerie understanding. Reassured by the bizarre visitor, the daughter returned to her bed for deep and restful sleep.

Before her encounter with the ghost, the daughter had always been uneasy when she visited the light, sensing a feeling of foreboding – that something didn't want her there. But after encountering the ghostly woman, she found the light to be relaxing and peaceful, looking forward to her visits. The wandering spectres of sailors drowned in the wrecks may haunt the offshore waters, but the woman owned the land and there she would welcome friends.[4]

A Tunnel to Hell
Presque Isle Station

Loneliness was always a problem for lightkeepers and their families, especially at the stations isolated from the rewards of civilization. The new Presque Isle light near Alpena, Michigan, was an especially lonely sentinel on the coast and the story of its haunting is based, in part, on this overwhelming isolation.

Although unverified by fact, the tale is told of the lightkeeper's wife who went stark raving mad from the terrible solitude. The lack of human contact and the drab repetition of the station's numbing routine drove the poor woman over the edge of sanity. For reasons best known only to himself, the lightkeeper felt it necessary to seal his crazy wife in

a tunnel beneath the station grounds. There she spent her last miserable days in shrieking agony until her inevitable death.

Is it her spirit that still haunts the station grounds? When the wind blows from the right quarter and speed, her bloodcurdling screams are said to echo through the night, the long, low shrieks tearing eerily through the darkness!

New Presque Isle Lighthouse.
AUTHOR'S COLLECTION

9

Efforts to learn the truth of the story of the wife sealed in a tunnel are inconclusive. No mention of the incident can be found in official records, although that in itself is not unusual. Every occurrence at isolated stations was not common knowledge or always recorded in government journals.

A search of the station grounds fails to reveal any major tunnels, although a small one can be found running from the lightkeeper's house to the base of the tower. In addition, a strange sealed chamber is located directly beneath the rear entrance to the house. The only entrance is through the floorboards above. Could either chamber have been the mad wife's cell, or is there yet an undiscovered tunnel?

A slightly different version of the story claims that the keeper had a woman friend in a nearby village. When he visited her, he locked his wife away in the tower for safe keeping, as well as to prevent her from intervening. From the lamp room, she could easily watch as her husband traipsed off for a night of debauchery. The wife, of course, complained bitterly to him about her ill-treatment. To end her whining, he finally killed her outright and explained her absence by claiming that she had gone home to visit her parents. Whether he hid her body in a tunnel or secret room or buried her in the nearby forest isn't known. But the tortured spirit of the wailing wife continues to haunt the tower, a constant reminder to her husband of his unfaithfulness. While the keeper has since "crossed the bar," as old sailors used to say, when the wind is right the wife's spirited screams still echo through the grounds.[5]

There is yet another variation of the haunting. As a little girl living at the light, Anna Hoge, the daughter of one of the lightkeepers, remembered hearing the tower cry. The sound was very soft, almost like a cat meowing or purring, but very discernable. When her father heard it, he would always place his hands on the bricks and repeat softly, "Don't worry. We love you and will care for you." The tower always continued to cry, however everyone felt better that somehow the tower was reassured.

The old keepers always referred to their lights in the female gender, as a she, and they did their best to take special care of them, to protect them from all harm. As Anna Hoge's father demonstrated, there was a special relationship at work. Such was not the case when the Coast Guard took over; they viewed it as just a duty station.

To properly maintain the tower, it was necessary to whitewash it annually, a difficult and time consuming job. It wasn't done by outside contractors. Rather, the keeper and his assistants rigged the old tackle-operated stage and did the job themselves. One year, to save both time and money, the Coast Guard painted the Presque Isle tower with

enamel-based paint. The old-timers railed against the painting, but to no avail. In theory, the paint would last many more years and eliminate the need for an annual whitewashing.

In practice, it was a disaster! The enamel didn't allow the bricks to breath and rapid deterioration set in. The

The numbing routine of lighthouse life involved many trips up the stairs to maintain and check the lamp.

outer course of bricks began pulling out, causing great cracks in the tower facade. The tower that had withstood gale and storm for a century was threatened with total destruction. Strong community action convinced the Coast Guard to rectify their grievous error by rebricking the tower. It was an expensive solution to a self-inflicted injury, but at least it saved the gracious lady for future generations.

During the rebricking, a remarkable thing happened. One of the workers replacing bricks near the very top of the tower discovered a small gold wedding band wedged into the bricks. Had it been lost by one of the men during original construction or perhaps, more tantalizing, could it have been a women's plain ring stuck into the bricks by the keeper's wife when faced finally with overwhelming evidence of her husband's infidelity? Could it have been, in some strange way, connected with the crying of the tower? The workman kept his unique discovery, but he did tell Anna Hoge about it. To replace the tower's lost keepsake, she had the man place a small locket into the new brick course. The old tower lost one treasure, but gained another.

The Presque Isle lightkeeper isn't the only one reputed to have "done in" his wife. In the mid-1880s, the keeper at Sequin Island lighthouse in Maine killed his better half in a fit of red rage with an axe. Legend says that she played the same tune on the piano again and again for hours on end. Finally, the long suffering keeper snapped and chopped both her and her piano into little, tiny pieces. He later committed suicide. Today, when the air is very still, some passing ships claim that they can hear the wife's monotonous melody eerily wafting over the sea.

In the early 1900s, the keeper at Block Island, Rhode Island, became so enraged with his spouse, he threw her head-over-heels to her death down the steep spiral tower stairs. Her ghost is said to haunt the lighthouse. Perhaps, understandably, the ghost never seems to bother women, but is said to take great joy in annoying men.[6]

The Light's On Again
Old Presque Isle Light

Old Presque Isle Light, completed in 1840, provided critical navigational aid for vessels seeking shelter in the small harbor at the south end of Lake Huron's Presque Isle. It was not only a popular anchorage to wait out gales, but also a fueling point for early wood-burning steamers. The diminutive white light tower stands 30 feet tall, a clear and welcome sight for vessels for more than a century and a half. A small stone house is attached at the tower base as keeper's quarters. The light was discontinued in 1871, when the new Presque Isle Lighthouse was completed a mile to the north.

The beacon at Old Presque Isle Lighthouse inexplicably began shining in recent years. AUTHOR'S COLLECTION

In the early 1900s, the property was sold to the Stebbins family, in whose ownership it remains today. The family restored the building, furnishing it with period antiques. It is presently operated as a museum. In 1977, George and Lorraine Parris, a retired couple, took over as caretakers.[7]

Nothing much happened at the old light until 1979, when the beacon inexplicably began to shine again! This was a serious problem. Once a light is decommissioned, it is removed from the official light list. The sudden reappearance of a light could confuse mariners and result in disastrous consequences.

Lorraine Parris, the museum manager, remembers when it suddenly came on, revolving as in the old days. It was immediately turned off. There was no rational explanation for this unusual event. To make certain that it stayed off, the Coast Guard came out and assisted George in disconnecting it, even to the extent of removing the rotating motor and gears. For good measure, all electrical power to the tower was cut off. For museum purposes, the old Fresnel lens was left in place.

For 13 years, the tower stayed dark, as it should be. But one day in the spring of 1992, as Lorraine was driving alone along the lake road toward the lighthouse, she noticed a glow in the tower. Afraid of ridicule, she didn't mention the incident to anyone. Finally, she told her son-in-law. He and her daughter said that it must have been a reflection of car headlights. After all, what else could it be?

Thinking that it might be something more, Lorraine took two friends to the point on the road where she first saw the strange light. One of the friends had grown up around lighthouses. Her father had been a lightkeeper and she was well familiar with every facet of their operation. They saw the light again! The three friends thought the curious glow just might be caused by a reflection from the flood lights that illuminate the tower at night. To test the theory, the lights were turned off. The unexplained incandescence remained. Moving about the area, they determined that the mysterious glow was best seen from the marina pier. The following night they repeated the test, with the same result. One of the group closely observed the tower with powerful binoculars. She thought she saw a shadowy figure faintly visible in the lantern room. Lorraine also believed she saw it. The tower was supposed to be locked and entry was impossible. Whatever it was, it wasn't human. When seen on other occasions, Lorraine thought the figure seemed to dance.

To preclude any possible chicanery, the old bulb in the tower was removed. The Coast Guard later also changed the direction of the lens to defeat any unusual reflection. Still the glow appeared. Lake freighters steaming far offshore also observed the phenomenon. Other local people besides Lorraine and her friends have seen the light and, although some may not accept it as real, they can't explain it. In at least one instance, people were in the tower when the glow was seen by watchers on the pier. Those in the tower saw nothing, however.

Several other methods to extinguish the light were tried. The lens was covered with a thick Army blanket. It still showed! The next night, black plastic garbage bags were taped over the lamp room windows. It continued to show. During the summer of 1995, a boy scout group covered the lens with a heavy tarp, without effect.

Others claimed to have had disturbing experiences there, feelings of foreboding and dread. Some visitors say they have heard footsteps echoing on the old stone steps.

During an interview, Lorraine related another incident.

"Little things happen that you don't know what to make of. On September 5, 1992, a bad storm struck. I was sitting (here) doing my book work and everything, and it was an awfully bad lightning storm. I decided to go out my back door to move my car up to the lighthouse, but I couldn't get out. Two white chairs were braced up (outside) against the door, just like there were two people sitting there talking. I couldn't open the door – it would not open! Well, I thought, I guess I am not supposed to go outside. So I came back, sat down and started

Does the spirit of George Parris inhabit Old Presque Isle's tower and power up the light? AUTHOR'S COLLECTION

to do my work. All of a sudden, a bolt of lightning hit just outside the building. It blew my night light and sensor right out of the wall! If I had been outside, I would have been hit!"

Lorraine does have an explanation for some of the strange events, however. For 14 years, she and George ran the light and museum. Their lives were deeply intertwined with it. George died of a heart attack at the lighthouse just a few months before she saw the light reappear in 1992. It is her conclusion that it's just her husband, come back to help. A master electrician, what could be simpler for him than to "power up" the old light? Others say that it's the spirit of the first keeper, old Patrick Garrity, still trying to do his duty. [8]

Something's In the Tower
Saginaw River Light

The tower of Michigan's old Saginaw River light is said to be haunted, but by whom or what isn't known. Suspicion is cast upon an old lightkeeper who died at the station. It is said that before succumbing, he admonished his family to continue in his place and to faithfully keep the light burning. They were to maintain a never ending vigil over "his" light. The guiding beam of the light was critical for the sailors. Keeping the light going was an awesome responsibility, not to be taken lightly.

By all accounts, the family took the old man's words to heart and loyally kept the lamp burning. When the Coast Guard took over from the Lighthouse Service, strange things started to be reported in the old tower. Maybe the old keeper's shade doesn't trust these newfangled keepers, for the loud echoes of steps on the old circular iron stairway leading up the 77-foot tower are still said to be heard. When checked the stairs are invariably empty.

A classic case occurred in the 1960s, when two Coast Guardsmen were standing a late watch in the building. As was typical, one stayed awake while the other napped on a nearby cot. In the early hours of the morning, the sleeping man was shaken awake by the watch stander.

"Something is in the tower, something is in the tower," was all the frightened sailor could stammer. Together both men approached the tower door. They could clearly hear the slow thumping of heavy boots climbing the stairs inside. Blankly, they stared at the heavy steel door and back at each other. What was happening was beyond their comprehension. An oversize padlock still secured the hasp. It was locked tight. Obviously no one had entered the tower. But what was making the sound? They never found out. As suddenly as it started, it stopped. Was it the old keeper? Or was his family still carrying out his last desperate instructions – still trying to loyally keep the light burning?[9]

Morgan's Ghost
Thunder Bay Island

During the 1930s and '40s, the lighthouse at Lake Huron's Thunder Bay Island east of Alpena, Michigan, was reputedly haunted by the ghost of an old lightkeeper known only as "Morgan." Thunder Bay Island lighthouse is one of the oldest on the lakes, established in 1832. The original stone tower stood 40 feet tall. In 1857 it was raised 10 feet, to reach the present height of 50 feet. The brick keeper's quarters was added in 1868.

How Morgan came to haunt the island isn't known. Whether he died at the station of natural causes or foul play is obscure but, regardless of how or why, his uneasy spirit is said to still walk the desolate shore of the island. Although no particular reason for his wanderings is known, his presence unnerved Coast Guardsmen from the island's lifeboat station during their lonely night patrols, especially on moonless nights when the wind howled with a wild abandon and endless waves crashed on the rocky shore. Young surfmen often claimed he followed them, just out of their sight. Although they couldn't see him, they knew he was there … watching … and waiting. Is he still there?[10]

Since the light was automated in 1980, the island has been deserted. No humans walk the lonely shores. But, of course, Morgan's ghost may yet be wandering this deserted scene.

The Spirit of Chambers Island
Chambers Island Light

Chambers Island, first settled in 1857 and 2,900 acres in size, hosted an early population of 250 people. Principal occupations in those days included shipbuilding, lumbering and fishing. The lighthouse was built in 1868. As an important aid for guiding vessels through Green Bay's west passage, the tower stands 68 feet above the waters of Lake Michigan and had a nominal range of 16 miles. In 1961, the Coast Guard relocated the light from the old stone tower to a new 60-foot steel tower, placing the beacon 97 feet above the water.[11]

Although it may date back many years, the ghost of Chambers Island lighthouse first came to note in the spring of 1976, when the present caretaker, Joel Blahnik, arrived to take up his duties. At the time, the old lighthouse was in tough shape, having been abandoned for more than 20 years. Tremendous effort would be needed to upgrade the facility to the standard envisioned for a planned 40-acre Gibraltar town park and museum.

The first night he spent in the lighthouse, Blahnik awoke to a loud, "BOOM, BOOM, BOOM" – heavy footfalls of someone coming down the spiral staircase from the lamp room. At the time, Blahnik was camped out in the old bedroom on the main floor. He tried to wake his nine-year-old son, so he also could hear the strange noise, but the youngster simply rolled over, telling his father not to bother him. "Go back to sleep, dad."

Listening closely, Blahnik plainly heard the heavy footsteps of the mysterious intruder. They went down the hallway, through the living room, down the steps into the kitchen and onto the outside grounds. The kitchen door closed behind with a distinctive "click."

For the next 10 years the spirit always appeared the first night that Blahnik arrived to open the light in the spring. Although it was never seen, it was clearly heard. The pattern was always the same – down the stairs, through the house and out the kitchen door.

The ghost seemed to have a sensitive soul. If others visiting the light expressed a disbelief in his existence, the ghost was sure to wake the doubters during the night. The unbelievers were startled into consciousness by the loud footsteps and an overwhelming sense of unearthly presence. Someone, or something, was with them. Something was there, in the room, although they couldn't distinguish what it was. Unbelievers became believers!

The spirit was always friendly and at times even playful. During the summer of 1979, it behaved much as a poltergeist. Various tools and other minor items disappeared, only to be discovered later in unlikely locations. For example, when Blahnik and his father were working on a window, a screw driver placed on the sill "went missing." Later it was found under a pillow in the bedroom. Nothing bad ever happened, however. It was just a series of jokes and gags.

The haunting unexpectedly ended in 1987. A group of nuns from a local Catholic retreat took a tour of the lighthouse and grounds. After the director related the tale of the supernatural activities at the light, one of the nuns became concerned. Walking briskly to the southwest side of the building, she placed her hands firmly against the old brick tower wall and prayed intensely for the spirit's release from its earthly bounds. After a minute or so she stopped and returned to the group. Whatever she said was apparently effective. The ghost has not been heard from since. Has it left forever, or will it someday return to the old lighthouse?

Although there was no real evidence of whom the spirit was, Blahnik thought it was likely that of the first lightkeeper, Lewis Williams. His 22-year tenure was the longest of any of the island's keepers, long enough to sire 11 children while tending faithfully to the beacon in the tower.

Before the light was built, Lewis Williams operated a sawmill at the northwest point of the island. The water was deep close to shore and schooners were able to come right up the beach to load. When Congress decided in 1866 to construct a third class lighthouse on the island, it was Williams who, for the sum of $250, sold the property to the government. He also managed to have himself appointed keeper at a salary of $450 a year. He tried several times to have his wife appointed assistant keeper, but without success. The government must have reasoned that with 11 children, she was already an "assistant" in fact, if not by title.[12]

For now, at least, the playful and heavy footed ghost of the Chambers Island lighthouse is quiet. Has he found final rest or is he just taking a breather?

Green Light on the Shore
St. Martin Island

St. Martin Island sits in Lake Michigan roughly halfway between Wisconsin's Door Peninsula and Michigan's Garden Peninsula, at the entrance to the body of water known as Green Bay. Slightly smaller than 200 acres, the island is mostly rock bound. The light tower proper is six-sided, composed of six steel posts latticed together. The height from base to lamp room is 57 feet. The original Fourth Order Fresnel lens had a range of 24 miles. A brick building for the lighthouse keeper is nearby.

The ghost on St. Martin Island is supposed to be that of the light-keeper, still searching for his lost children. As was the custom, the keeper's children attended school at nearby Washington Island, 10 miles to the southwest. The tale goes that every day they rowed to class in the morning and back again at dismissal, weather permitting. One terrible day when they were halfway across the straits, the children were caught in a vicious squall. They and their boat disappeared in the churning waves. Heartbroken, the old keeper desperately searched the shore for his missing offspring. His efforts were in vain. Their bodies were never recovered.

Today some say that when the nights are dark and stormy, and the north wind blows down from an arctic hell, the faint green glow of the keeper's lantern can still be seen as he wanders along the island's desolate shore, ever searching.[13]

There is an additional chapter to this ghost story. It seems that one storm-blown night, the keeper failed to properly trim his wicks and the beam winked out. Without the trusty light to guide her, a schooner struck hard on an outlying shoal. Waves soon began to batter the help-less ship to pieces. The crew counted their chances for survival as nil. Turned around in the night and plummeted by the wild seas, they lost all sense of direction. Missing the steady gleam from the light, they didn't even know which way the shore was. Surely their end was at hand.

Suddenly, a small thin beam of green light pierced the darkness. While it shimmered like an old hand-held kerosene lantern, wobbling and flickering in the cold wind, it burned true. Eagerly, the desperate men jumped into the lake and made for the dim, but welcomed light.

When they finally stumbled ashore, the mysterious light was not waiting on the beach for them, but instead bobbed off in the distance. Anxiously they walked toward it, past an old cemetery and up a twisting path through thick and forbidding forest. It always seemed to "float" somewhere just ahead of them. Blusters of wind tore at their frigid bodies. Driving rain pelted them. All the while the bedraggled crew followed the strange, flickering glow. Finally they stumbled into a small clearing. Ahead was the partially open door to the keeper's house. A warm and welcomed glow leaked out into the forbidding night. When they entered, they saw a green-lensed lantern sitting on the table, brightly burning. It was the beacon that had guided them to safety.

Exploring further, the crew discovered the keeper laying dead on his bed. His oilskins hung from a nearby peg. They were dry to the touch. No one else was on the island. If the keeper hadn't carried the lantern out into the storm to guide them, who did?

The official report only stated that the keeper died in the act of saving the crew. No mention was made of the strange, green light. The crew, though, knew the truth. There was no doubt in their minds that it was a dead man that saved them – a dead man and his light that led them to safety.

In the following years, others reported seeing the unearthly green light. The ghostly lantern continued to search for shipwrecked crews to lead to safety on a dangerous shore near the entrance to Green Bay.[14]

"The Light's on Fire"
Sand Point Light

Not all lighthouse ghost stories are natural. Some were simply created because it seemed that there should be one. After all, every old lighthouse ought to have a good ghost story! A case in point is Lake Michigan's Sand Point Light.

The one-and-one-half story light was built in 1867 at a cost of $11,000. Located at the tip of a sand spit, the light was intended to guide ships safely into the growing iron port of Escanaba, Michigan. The first keeper was John Terry, but before the light became operational, he died of consumption. His wife, Mary, was appointed keeper in his place.

Friday, March 4, 1886, the light was swept by a devastating fire.

When the alarm finally was sounded in town at 1 a.m., the fire had broken through the roof and the building was a roaring mass of flames. Ominously, when the local citizens arrived, nothing could be found of the lightkeeper, 69-year-old Mary Terry. An 18-year veteran of the light, she was highly regarded in the local community. Extremely methodical in her daily business, she was careful in the discharge of her duties. To have a fire occur while Mary was keeper was considered unthinkable.

When daylight broke and the embers cooled enough for a search of the building, their worst fears were realized. The remains of what was thought to be Mary were found in the southeast corner of the house, in a room called the "oil room." There was little enough left – a part of her skull, a few bones and only a small portion of her viscera survived the deadly flames.

After closely examining all of the evidence, a coroner's jury reluctantly concluded that she came to her death from "causes and means unknown." They suspected foul play was involved, but had no proof. Could it have been a botched robbery attempt? By rights, if the fire were accidental, Mary should have died in her bedroom, not in the oil room at the opposite end of the building. What if robbers broke in, were discovered by Mary, killed her and dragged the body to the oil room, where they set a blaze to cover up the crime? Panicked, the burglers fled without their loot.

It was known that Mary Terry was frugal and had saved enough from her small salary to purchase some property in the city. But in searching the charred structure, they found her money in the form of gold coins, exactly where they would have fallen from her cupboard. The searchers also thought that the door to the light may have been forced open, based on the location of the bolt. Since the money was still present as well as a packet of charred legal papers, they couldn't find a motive. None of this agreed with Mary Terry's well known cool-headedness. The jury found it hard to accept that her death was accidental. Regardless of their suspicions, life went on. A new keeper was appointed, repairs made and the light continued to guide ships into Escanaba.

In the 1930s, due to various harbor improvements, including extensive dredging, the light ended up a quarter of a mile from the lake – too far to be effective. A crib light was built offshore to take its place and the old light was remodeled into living quarters for Coast Guard personnel. When the Coast Guard vacated the building in 1985, it was leased to the Delta County Historical Society for inclusion into their museum. After a tremendous amount of effort and money, the light was restored as a museum and dedicated in 1990. Visitors can still see Mary's bedroom and the smoke-darkened bricks in the oil room.

The only thing wrong with the new lighthouse museum was that it didn't have a ghost. So one was conjured up. Luther Barrett, a longtime society member and chairman of the lighthouse restoration project, created the ghost of Mary Terry to go along with the restored facility. The tale has since become

Sand Point Lighthouse.
AUTHOR'S COLLECTION

very well known locally – to the point where fact and fiction have merged. So is there a ghost or isn't there? Now, when unexplained lights are seen and strange noises heard, there is a ready explanation. It's just Mary making her rounds![15]

"Good Riddance"
Waugoshance Lighthouse

Waugoshance Shoal, 16 miles west of the Straits of Mackinac, is an especially dangerous series of reefs and islands ranging about seven miles out into Lake Michigan. In common conversation, lake mariners often refer to it as "wobbleshanks." The area is a graveyard of wrecks, the result of trying to navigate the treacherous run down the east side of Lake Michigan, between the Beavers and mainland. Waugoshance Shoal was first marked by a lightship in 1832. 1851 saw the first lighthouse on the site with additional construction in 1870, 1883 and 1896. The tower stands 76 feet tall, with a 20-foot base diameter. The walls are five and a half feet thick at the bottom, tapering to two feet at the top. Some early records suggest that Waugoshance may have had the first Fresnel lens used on the Great Lakes. After White Shoal light was erected in 1910, Waugoshance became expendable and was abandoned two years later.

According to legend, there are two ghosts at the lighthouse. During the construction of the crib, apparently a worker was killed. His spirit is said to still haunt the lighthouse. When conditions are just right, the wind blowing hard and cold, his hideous cries are said to echo across the lonely shore.

The second ghost is thought to be that of John Herman, the keeper from 1885 to 1894. He was known as a man who thoroughly enjoyed a good practical joke, as well as the spirits of this world, especially the 100 proof bottled kind. Normally, he did most of his hard drinking ashore when he was on leave, but on occasion he returned to the light still "potted." Apparently, he came back from leave, as sailors say, "three sheets to the wind" and, finding his assistant diligently working in the lamp room, locked him in as a prank. The assistant keeper called down for John to let him out, but John, of course, refused. The assistant could only watch helplessly as the drunken keeper reeled wildly back and forth as he tried to navigate down the narrow pier, eventually moving out of his view. He was never seen again. It is presumed he fell off the pier and drowned.

It was after Herman's disappearance that strange and unexplained things started happening at the light. Doors mysteriously opened and closed by themselves. There was no breeze or draft – the heavy steel doors just moved as if by unseen hand. Napping keepers were rudely jolted awake when chairs were knocked out from under them, sending them crashing to the floor. Climbing back to their shaky feet, they would roundly curse that "damned Herman." Coal was also clandestinely shoveled into the firebox for the steam boiler by an unseen fireman. This was dirty work that no keeper really liked, so having someone else do it – dead or otherwise – was a blessing, even if it was uncomfortable knowing that it was by ghostly hands.

Bizarre things just kept popping up. Dinner plates would rattle, lights flickered on and off. Personal items left in one place would vanish, then reappear elsewhere. Keepers blamed such a plague of interference on their missing companion, who had apparently come back from wherever he went just to make their lives miserable.

All these problems eventually filtered up to the Lighthouse Service inspectors. While they laughed at the fanciful stories, they also couldn't explain what was happening. Waugoshance was just trouble.

When Waugoshance Light was finally abandoned in 1912, many felt it was less that the new White Shoal light had made it redundant than the Lighthouse Service had tired of dealing with the ghost! Perhaps they just said, "Good riddance!"[16]

"I Am Not Going To Leave the Light"
White River Light Station

Karen McDonnell is the director/curator of the White River Light Station Museum in Whitehall, Michigan, a position she has held for a dozen years. She is straight forward and level-headed. While a bit of a romantic, she has the curiosity of a scientist and questions what she sees and hears. She also cares deeply about the old light and cheerfully does the many small jobs around the building to help make it a good home, not only for her family, but also for two friendly spirits.

When Karen McDonnell first moved into the lighthouse, she had no inkling that actual otherworld spirits also occupied the building. The previous curator had only said that he had sensed "good spirits" in the old place.

White River Light Station. AUTHOR'S COLLECTION

As part of her curatorial duties, she researched the life of the first keeper, Captain William Robinson. An English immigrant, he arrived at White River in the 1860s and immediately realized the need for a functioning light to serve lake mariners. Until one was eventually built, he took it as his personal responsibility to keep a welcoming beacon burning at the end of the old pier.

Congress recognized the need for a lighthouse in 1866 and authorized $10,000 for the project. However, it wasn't until 1870, when the White River Channel was cut from White Lake to Lake Michigan, that part of the money was spent for a small pierhead light that was finished in 1871. The lighthouse itself was completed in 1875-76.

Robinson duly became the first keeper and served faithfully for 47 years. He and his wife, Sarah, raised 11 children in its friendly confines, although two apparently died in childhood. According to local accounts, Sarah was a wonderful mother and well respected in the community. When she died at a relatively young age, it was a hard blow for Captain Robinson. He clung even closer to "his" light.

The circumstances of Captain Robinson's retirement were related by Loretta Bush Pearson, daughter of the second keeper Captain William Bush, the eldest grandson of Captain Robinson, in an oral history conducted by Mrs. McDonnell. In 1915, at age 87, Robinson was finally forced by the government to retire due to age, but was able to arrange to have his eldest grandson, Captain William Bush, named keeper in his stead. William Bush served 26 years, until the light was inactivated in 1941. Old Captain Robinson continued, however, to do much of the work of tending to the light, claiming that his grandson, even though he was the keeper, wasn't yet ready. Slowed by age, he needed a cane to get around, but he still performed the duties much as he always had. Against government rules, he continued to live for a time in the building with his grandson. But regulations were clear. Only the keeper and his immediate family could live in the building. Captain Robinson would have to leave.

As the day came closer for his departure, Robinson frequently became depressed. For nearly half a century the whole of his life had been wrapped up in

Captain William Robinson was first keeper at White River Lighthouse.
AUTHOR'S COLLECTION

24

the light, especially after his wife's death. He had known nothing else. Finally, he told his grandson with great conviction, "I am not going to leave this building." He kept his word, at least with the living. The morning that he was to vacate, he died. In compliance with his wishes, he was buried in the small cemetery just across the river so he could be as close to "his" light as possible.

About a month after McDonnell finished her research on Captain Robinson, she heard the clear sound of someone walking upstairs on the second floor. Slow and a little hesitant, the halting steps were accompanied by an intermittent thud. Intuitively, McDonnell thought it was, perhaps, the old keeper. Although she had never really subscribed to and was skeptical about the idea of ghosts, she still had this "sense."

Today, the strange upstairs pacing occurs on a frequent but irregular basis. In McDonnell's words, "The walking I hear is as if someone were checking. I have never felt fear, but I have never gone to the upper stairs when I have heard it. I feel it is a ritual and that I shouldn't disturb it. It's calming."

Strange pacing can frequently be heard coming from the second floor of White River Lighthouse.

McDonnell is not the only person to experience Captain Robinson's prowling. During a trip away from the lighthouse, she left it in the care of a couple who agreed to house sit. Not wishing to scare them away before they even started, she mentioned nothing about the captain's walks. When she returned, however, her friend greeted her with the question, "Do you have some kind of ghost walking around upstairs?"

Although a chill danced up McDonnell's spine, she kept a straight face and asked, "Why?" Her friend described identical experiences

25

with the strange walking upstairs. While the spooky sounds didn't frighten the house sitter, they did make her uneasy and uncomfortable.

McDonnell believes that Captain Robinson appreciates the extra work she does at the light. When she finishes a project, she has a sense of being silently applauded, of being rewarded by the old keeper. The next time she hears the captain's walk, to her ear the step seems lighter and quicker, less heavy and elderly. It is as if the old keeper were brought back to a happier time so long ago.

The meaning of the captain's eerie walk isn't known. McDonnell questions if it isn't him just checking on the children, walking down the hall looking into each room and then slowly climbing the iron spiral stairs up to the lamp room for a final check of the light. It's a ritual his spirit continues beyond life.

Just below the lamp room, at the top of the spiral staircase, there is a window

Sarah Robinson, wife of the first keeper at White River Light.
AUTHOR'S COLLECTION

set deep into the octagonal tower wall. The wooden resting board for the weight pulley system is inset even with the window. McDonnell claims that people have experienced a strong "pull" or attraction at the window, that it is a most romantic place. From the author's experience, it is also an extremely pleasant spot to just sit and think. It is indeed a perfect place for two people very much in love, as Captain Robinson and Sarah were, to sit and talk. Perhaps one on the window sill and the other on the tower stairs opposite. Even for a man alone it's a wonderful place to sit and rest after climbing the tower and just enjoy a pipe while thinking of the day's events. Perhaps it was Captain Robinson's habit to stop at the window after checking on his sleeping children.

The more McDonnell learned about Captain Robinson, the more

she wanted to know about Sarah. After all, behind every good man is a better woman. Being a lightkeeper's wife was especially arduous. Not only was she mother to the 11 children, but she had to help with the lighthouse duties. When the keeper was sick, she also tended the light in his place, while continuing all of her "normal" responsibilities.

After much work, McDonnell was able to locate several pictures of Sarah. She is particularly fond of a charcoal drawing that seems to have an unusual endearing presence about it. When she placed Sarah's photos on display, McDonnell felt she had honored a very special lady, but wondered how Captain Robinson would feel about it. She didn't have long to wait to find out.

Upstairs, in what had been a children's room, is a large flat glass display case containing miscellaneous artifacts. The top of the case is a dust magnet and it is necessary to clean it every other day, but there is something decidedly unusual here. In McDonnell's words, "A week after I got Sarah's pictures up, the phone rang. I had the dust rag in my right hand. I put it on the corner of the glass and I ran downstairs think-ing, 'I am going to open in 10 minutes and I don't want to have it on the case.' So I had a quick telephone conversation and ran back upstairs to finish. The case was dust free! No windows were open and the rag was over on the other side of the case. That gave me a chill. I was a little shaky. I knew I didn't dust that case. I just stood there and thought

The "dusted case" at White River. AUTHOR'S COLLECTION

about it. How could the cloth move itself to the other side without any wind? I picked up the rag and said, 'I am going to try this again.'

"After opening the museum, I got a hunch that, since I've brought Sarah back into view, maybe she is helping me. I thought some more and concluded that I could make this a fearful experience or I could just thank her. So later, when no one was in the museum I said, 'Thanks Sarah.' I have continued to play the game with her. Five minutes before opening, I'll place the rag on the case and go back downstairs. When I come back up, the rag will be moved around and the dust will be gone. It's only on that one case that it works. I do not know why it's just that case in that spot. I know that the younger children stayed in that bedroom. Maybe there was a younger child positioned where the case is now."

McDonnell is not disturbed in the slightest that her light is haunted. Quite the contrary, "I like the notion of the comfort it gives me. It's like a watchman, just making sure that everything is okay before it's too late at night."[17]

St. Joseph's Reluctant Spirit

Some ghosts are less obvious than others, just more reluctant to take center stage. The shade at the old St. Joseph, Michigan, lighthouse depot seems to fall into this category.

The U.S. Lighthouse establishment dates from 1789 and the first Great Lakes lights were built in the 1810s. The first Lake Michigan lights, one of which marked the mouth of the St. Joseph River, were established in 1832. By 1852, there were 76 lights on the lakes – 27 on Lake Michigan alone. The number on the lakes in 1890 reached 244, with 81 on Lake Michigan. By the turn of the century, 114 lights and four light ships guided the booming lake trade. And it was booming! In 1888, Chicago recorded 20,000 vessel arrivals in the eight months of navigation. By contrast, the port of New York had only 23,000 in a full 12-month season.

The job of a depot was to serve the lights by providing timely repair, maintenance and resupply services. In addition, they received, stored and overhauled buoys and received, stored and packed supplies and various stores for the far-flung light stations for delivery by the lighthouse tenders.

Originally, the 9th district (Lake Michigan) shared the 11th district depot in Detroit, which was established in 1869. Over time this proved to be an unsatisfactory arrangement. In 1890, the lighthouse board complained, "… not only is the 9th district tender obliged to tie up in Detroit and await the full opening of navigation in the most northern waters, viz, at the Straits of Mackinac, where the ice remains for some weeks later than at the head of the lake, but all the lampist and repair work and the distribution of supplies have to be made from the same inconvenient distance and with corresponding loss of time."

After due consideration and an appropriation of $35,000, plans were made to build a new depot at St. Joseph exclusively for the 9th district. Work started in 1891 and the storehouse, keeper's house and carpenter-lampist shop were finished in January 1893. Located on the north bank of the river and adjacent to the lifesaving station, it provided ready access for supply boats and tenders.

Keeper's residence at St. Joseph Lighthouse Depot. AUTHOR'S COLLECTION

The effectiveness of the depot was short-lived. The Lighthouse Board annual reports for 1899-1903 criticized that it was too distant from Milwaukee, where the district engineer had his office and it was "one of the best markets for materials." There was also too little room on the dock to moor the large tenders for the winter. In April 1904, $75,000 was appropriated to start the construction on a new depot in Milwaukee. Since all these problems were well known before construction, it is obvious St. Joseph was the political choice, or on the flip side, Milwaukee was the new politically correct choice when politics changed.

Regardless of the new Milwaukee depot, St. Joseph remained active as a depot until 1917, when it finally closed. In 1919, the property was transferred to the Navy Department and was used by the naval reserve for many years. In 1952, it was used by the Army Reserve and was taken over in 1956 by the Michigan Army National Guard as an armory. In September 1993, the Guard vacated the site.

Ghostly goings on have been reported not in the large and forbidding three-story brick storehouse as one might expect, but in the smaller keeper's house. The two-story, cross-gabled-roof dwelling has a brick first story and a shingled second story. Although long abandoned, it is still considered structurally sound.

Inside, the house is a wreck – everything a haunted house should be. It obviously has not been occupied for a long period. Windows are boarded over, walls punched through by vandals, floors and stairs rotted, dirt and dust piled high and plentiful. A wind from the right direction can set up an eerie moaning sound that echoes weirdly throughout the empty rooms. Strange cold spots chill the spine. You sense that you are not alone.

For a time, the National Guard unit stored miscellaneous supplies in the first floor of the house, which meant that Guardsmen had to enter several times a year. Men never volunteered for that job and, on at least two occasions, an eerie voice was heard coming from upstairs. It sounded like, "Get out. Just leave me alone." It was also not uncommon to have equipment that was left in one room be found in another.

Some people have reported curious lights in the old house, mysterious glowing and glimmerings where only darkness should rule. Is it the spirit of an old keeper still occupying his old home?[18]

Spirits of the Light
Big Bay Point Light

Perhaps the most haunted light on the lakes is at Lake Superior's Big Bay Point. Located approximately 25 miles northwest of Marquette, Michigan, the light was built in 1896. It was intended to cover the dead area between Huron Island Light built in 1868 and Granite Island Light built a year later. Sitting at the edge of a sandstone cliff high above the lake, its Third Order Fresnel lens casts a beam visible for 13 miles. The building has a 60-foot light tower and a two-story duplex that originally served as a residence for the keeper, his assistant and their families. Each half had a parlor, dining room and kitchen on the ground floor and three bedrooms on the floor above. Separate outhouses were located just outside the kitchen doors. The tower itself has five levels. The first was a combination keeper's office and school room for the lighthouse's children. The second contained charts and maps and doubled as a chapel for Sunday services. The third floor was used for storage and the top two for the lens and related machinery. A total of 18 rooms were in the building.

Big Bay continued as a manned light until 1941, when the Coast Guard automated it, placing a beacon on a steel tower erected in the yard. In 1961, the building, by then abandoned and decrepit, and 33 acres of surrounding land, were sold to Dr. John Pick, a Chicago surgeon. He extensively remodeled the facility, knocking out interior walls and generally opening the original duplex into a large home. Utilities, including plumbing and electricity, were added, as was a modern kitchen and heating plant. Dr. Pick used the lighthouse as a summer residence.

Shortly before his death in the late 1970s, Dr. Pick sold the property to Dan Hitchens, a Traverse City businessman. He made additional improvements, including several bathrooms and a sauna. Hitchens used it as a retreat for overworked executives.

In 1985, the light was purchased by a corporation of three men headed by Norman "Buck" Gotschall. The

Big Bay Lighthouse, perhaps the most haunted light on the Great Lakes.
AUTHOR'S COLLECTION

following year the light was opened as a bed-and-breakfast inn. After much urging by Gotschall, in 1990 the beacon was returned to the lighthouse tower by the Coast Guard.

The Gotschall group sold the facility in 1991 to a Chicago trio consisting of John Gale and Jeff and Linda Gamble. The new owners continued to improve the property adding authentic period furnishings and a tower library. It continues to be operated as a bed-and-breakfast inn.

The initial report of a haunting apparently surfaced when Gotschall opened up the B&B. The first night he stayed in the lighthouse, the north wind howled an eerie welcome. Gotschall huddled deep in his bed, warm from the icy blasts when "the darnest banging I've ever heard" erupted outside. He immediately went outdoors to see what had broken loose. As soon as he stepped through the entrance door, both the

31

wind and banging stopped. Carefully checking the exterior of the building, he found nothing loose. All shutters and doors were secure. There was nothing to bang. After he went back inside, the unearthly banging and wind started again. When he went back outside all was quiet. The strange process repeated itself several times.

In the days following, a cleaning woman "came screaming up the stairs from the basement" asking, "Who is in the shower down there?" At first Gotschall thought it was his son-in-law, but he soon realized that he was elsewhere. When Gotschall investigated, the shower was off and empty. What had scared the woman so badly?

Two guests were later startled to see the faint image of a man dressed in the full uniform of a Light-House Service keeper walking restlessly around the grounds. The grim guardian spirit stared right through them and simply faded into nothing. The ghost was on the prowl.

The only one of five keepers who met an untimely end at the light was William Prior. He apparently had a difficult time as keeper. In his logbook, he constantly complained about the quality of his assistants and their respective work habits. He went through several assistants before his son finally gained the position. By all accounts William Prior was a driven man who continuously sought perfection in himself and others. That his assistants didn't measure up to his standards must have been especially galling.

In April 1901, his son was working on the dock when he accidently cut himself. The wound was a bad one and was soon seriously infected. By June, gangrene had set in and he was taken to the hospital in Marquette for treatment. It was too late. He died a short time later.

Prior was grief stricken over his terrible loss. Perhaps he blamed himself for pushing the son too hard or for delaying medical help. Following the funeral, Prior returned to the light after traveling back with a party bound for the nearby Huron Mountain Club. Later they remembered him as showing signs of an unbalanced mind.

The next day, Prior disappeared. He reportedly left the light with some strychnine and a gun, marching directly into the forest. Suicide was feared. A long search proved fruitless. The local Odd Fellows lodge offered a reward of $50 for news of his whereabouts. After several weeks without clues, the offer was withdrawn.

On September 24, 1901, the mystery was solved. A landlooker reportedly discovered the keeper's body hanging from a maple tree, a noose still tight around its neck. Prior was more than a mile from the light and deep in the woods. It was a gruesome find. Other accounts say all that was hanging was his head, still dangling in the frayed rope. The body was in a clump on the ground. Identification was only made by the clothes still clinging to the skeleton. Why had Prior come so far? Why didn't he just jump from the cliffs or hang himself from the tower instead? Why commit suicide at all?

Gotschall assumed that it was Prior's restless spirit that haunted the light. As is common with suicides, the spirit of the dead keeper apparently didn't rest easy. This was confirmed when a woman guest with clairvoyant powers claimed that the apparition of a man in a beard and hat appeared to her at the foot of her bed. The description the woman provided closely matched that of the enigmatic old light keeper. The ghost reportedly told her that he wasn't going to rest until the light was restored to a proper condition and order.

When John Gale and the Gambles bought the light, the strange happenings continued, but with a new twist. A guest who professed to be a psychic claimed that there wasn't one ghost but five! While four were friendly, one was very angry – not violent, but angry. Prior's spirit could be explained, kind of, but who were the others?

Another psychic, an acquaintance of the Gambles, confirmed the presence of more than one ghost. About a year later, a reporter from Chicago, also a psychic, toured the second floor alone. Excitedly she came downstairs, stating that there was an angry young lady living in the suite upstairs. This startled Linda Gamble since, at the time, there were no guests staying at the light. The psychic further said that the young lady wasn't a guest, but a ghost and she was angry because no one knew she was there. The psychic also said she spoke to the spirit and calmed her down a bit, but that she was still very angry and frustrated. From what the psychic was able to glean from the ghost, the woman had died at the light during the late 1950s, when it was abandoned. The spirit knew nothing more and couldn't explain her presence. Speculation is that she could have been murdered at the light with her body taken elsewhere. Locally though, there are no "unsolved crimes" that would neatly fit this hypothesis. Her identity remains a mystery.

No explanation is offered for the other three ghosts. Perhaps they are wandering spirits of the crews of the steamer *Iosco* and the schooner-barge *Olive Jeanette* – both lost with all hands in a ferocious September 1905 storm somewhere near the Huron Islands just to the west. Their bloated and battered bodies drifted ashore for weeks afterward. Only the remains of 16 of the 26 souls aboard were found.

Prior's ghost seems to haunt only the original keeper's half of the building and the grounds. Both areas were well known to him in life. The woman's ghost in the suite, which was part of the old assistant keeper's duplex, would explain many strange experiences reported by guests in that side of the house.

Linda Gamble explains that she is a rational person. She can explain away such things as lights going on and off, closing and opening doors and strange sounds in a hundred different ways. But two things happened that defy logical explanation.

The first incident happened in the spring of 1994. "We had three couples staying with us; two couples were staying on the first floor and one was upstairs with the wife's mother. One couple downstairs went into town for dinner. They were a younger couple and a little rowdy, playing the radio loudly and drinking before they went out. The other downstairs couple went to bed early. The couple upstairs went out for a walk at 10 p.m. The mother-in-law stayed in the room reading. I decided to go to bed, but closed all the windows first. You never know if it is going to rain or not, but I didn't lock the windows. I never do. I also left the doors open knowing that two couples were still out. About 2 a.m., the phone rings. It's the couple that went into town. They were locked out. So I came and unlocked the doors. All three were locked!

"The next morning, the couple upstairs came down and said, 'The funniest thing happened last night. You locked us out.' When they came back from their walk, the doors were locked. They had to call to the mother to come down and open one. The third couple remained fast asleep and was not disturbed.

"None of the couples admitted locking the doors. All I can think is that the room the loud couple was staying in is the old keeper's office and they were in there laughing and drinking. Maybe he didn't like it! When I went to open the windows in the morning, all had been locked. None of the guests admitted locking the windows either.

"The second experience I have no explanation for at all. A couple checked in about 9:30 p.m. They were really tired from a long trip. After climbing to the lantern room for a quick look, they went directly to bed. They had no time to read the history and had no prior knowledge of the ghost. But before the woman went to bed, she read for a bit in the upstairs library. She took her flashlight and went to the library to read after everyone had gone to bed.

"After a while, she went back to her room and stopped in the bathroom, placing her flashlight on the sink. As she did that she looked up in the mirror and saw that there was a man standing behind her with a hat and a beard. Her husband was plainly visible, snoring in bed. When she turned around, no one was there! I can't explain it. This woman had no knowledge of the ghost."

Another husband and wife also had a close encounter with Prior's ghost. The honeymooning couple was playing a radio while taking a shower together. Suddenly the music went off. There was no power failure. The radio was turned on but just stopped playing! In any case, the couple left the shower and got ready for bed. Once they were both tucked in beneath the covers, the wife turned to her husband and asked him to turn off the light. Before the husband could react, the light went out by itself! A conclusion could be drawn that the old keeper didn't like rock and roll music and is thrifty about lights.

Other guests have had the experience of doors opening and closing and lights turning on and off. The light tower is an especially sensitive area for these occurrences, as is the suite occupied by the angry woman ghost. Actual sightings of the keeper have been on the grounds, at the end of the bed and at the head of the stairs going to the second floor. Perhaps more sensitive than other creatures, Linda Gamble's cat often sits at the bottom of the stairs and stares intently up at the top. Does it "see" something that escapes the rest of us?[19]

"Gunfire Erupted"
Crisp's Point Light

Today all that stands on Lake Superior's Crisp's Point is a forlorn brick light tower. Everything else is gone, bulldozed into oblivion by the Coast Guard after it was abandoned. Just after the turn of the century, though, it was a busy little community. The light station itself was extensive – a big duplex for the keeper and his assistant, fog signal house, oil house, out houses and all the other requirements for a well-equipped base. Also located at the point was the lifesaving station, which included another half dozen structures. The coast, then as now, is desolate and remote, far from any civilization. Sailors needed the light to keep them safely offshore and the lifesavers to rescue them if they didn't.

The lifesaving station was established in 1877 and the light with its Fourth Order Fresnel lens in 1904. In 1947, the light was abandoned, as the lifesaving operation had been earlier. Both had served their purpose. Their time had passed.

In the mid-1960s, the deserted lighthouse keeper's quarters were still standing, although long deserted. Young boys by nature are adventurous souls and one summer night three of them decided to spend the night in the old building. About dusk the trio tramped up the creaky dilapidated stairs to the attic and rolled out their sleeping bags. All carried .22 caliber rifles. The beach was an ideal place to "plink" and demonstrate their marksmanship and they had so spent their early evening hours.

Shortly after dark, the boys had just settled into their bags when they heard the slow tread of heavy footfalls climbing the stairs. Step by step, whatever it was, came closer and closer. In an effort to scare the

35

Crisp's Point Lighthouse is one of the most endangered in the world. This photo from the 1960s shows it in somewhat its original configuration. TED RICHARDSON COLLECTION

Crisp's Point Light in 1997. Wave action and erosion have destroyed everything but the tower. AUTHOR'S COLLECTION

intruder away, one of the boys yelled out, "Who ever you are, you better go away. We are armed and will shoot!"

Undaunted by the challenge, the steps continued until they reached the landing at the head of the stairs. Good as their word, the boys leveled their trusty .22s and let fly. A fierce fusillade of slugs tore across the upper landing. Apprehensively the trio waited to see what would happen. Nothing did. There was no sound from the stairs. It was as quiet as a grave.

Guns poised for another volley, the boys waited and waited. Nothing happened. Eventually two of the boys fell asleep. One, however, was too keyed up and stared intently at the black landing all night long, his rifle resting across his shaking knees. Nothing moved. All remained quiet. Until just before dawn.

At the first sound, the boy excitedly shook the others awake. All of them heard the brisk movement of someone, or something, turning at the top landing and then retreating down the stairs.

Whoever, or whatever, it was had evidently been there all night. What was it that remained unseen in the dark shadows and unaffected by the riddling bullets?

Crisp's Point was named for Christopher Crisp, the legendary life-saving keeper of the point's first station, who led his crews on many a wild adventure. Was it his ghost investigating the trespassers at "his point?" Or was it the spirit of a former lightkeeper? Could it have been the shade of one of the many sailors that drowned along the desolate coast?[20]

The Little Girl and the Bear
Point Iroquois Light

One of the more remarkable "unusual" paranormal occurrences involved Point Iroquois Light in eastern Lake Superior. The original light, including a wooden keeper's building, was built in 1855. It was replaced in 1871 by the present structure. The keeper's house, made of brick, was added in 1902.[21]

After being abandoned by the Coast Guard in 1965, the light was taken over by the U.S. Forest Service. To help maintain the facility and also operate a small museum, the Forest Service, with cooperation from the Bay Mills-Brimley Historical Research Society, employs volunteer caretakers. The light has proven itself a popular tourist attraction. About 20,000 visitors annually tour the facility, averaging 100 to 200 a day during the May to October season.

From 1984 to '86, the caretaker was DeVerna Hubbard. During the summer of 1985, Hubbard had a most extraordinary experience. A

37

woman she had never seen before (or since) came to the grounds and announced that a little girl had previously been killed there. The visitor then asked if she could walk the grounds. Mystified, Hubbard agreed and accompanied her.

The woman walked down the path toward the location where the original light stood and stopped between the old doors and a grove of trees. At this point she turned to Hubbard and said, "A little girl was killed right here and a bear carried her up the hill." As a way of explanation for such an odd claim, she also announced she was a psychic and that she had never been to the light before.

The woman continued to walk to the west of the old light talking continuously. "This way, it's cold, colder, this way, we are getting close." After moving roughly 75 feet from the original spot, she stopped and emphatically stated, "A little girl was killed right here, killed by a bear."

Hubbard noticed that when the psychic said she was getting colder she literally was. Goose bumps were visible on her arms and she was shivering. It was also an unseasonably warm day, with temperatures close to 80 degrees F. Whatever was chilling the woman, it wasn't the weather.

Finally, the woman stopped and announced, "The bear killed her right here." Apparently satisfied with herself, the psychic quickly left, leaving Hubbard in confused wonder.

Later Hubbard learned that a little girl had indeed been killed by a bear near the light and that the creature had dragged her body up a nearby hill. When local men later hunted and killed a large bear on the hill, parts of the child were discovered still in the stomach.

DeVerna Hubbard is an unusually steadfast person not given to flights of imagination. There is no reason not to accept her story as true in every regard. If she heard strange noises at the light such as creaking boards on a staircase, she simply put it down to the sounds expected in an old dwelling. The wind whistling around the lighthouse never disturbed her, although on occasion visitors claimed that it had the unmistakable sound of a woman wailing.

DeVerna remembers another event that was decidedly "unusual." On a mid-November afternoon, her sister Zelma was walking her dog along the beach in the area where an Indian massacre occurred more than three centuries before. At the time, Hubbard was gone for the weekend and Zelma had taken her place as caretaker. Her sister later told her that while she was hiking the shore the low moaning wind sounded eerily like human voices, which was greatly unsettling. Leaning into the wind, both she and the dog were suddenly hit with a

Point Iroquois Light Station. AUTHOR'S COLLECTION

blast of frigid air. The effect was as startling as having a bucket of ice water thrown in your face. The hair on the dog's back stood straight up. Fear-stricken, the animal immediately fled back to the light leaving the shaken woman alone on the desolate beach. Discretion being the better part of valor, Zelma quickly followed. Once safe in the light, she would not venture outside again that night. Something was in the air and she wanted nothing more to do with it.[22]

Other people at the light reported more strange occurrences. Some claimed to have heard heavy foot falls on the spiral tower stairs. On investigation, however, no one was there. An entry in the lighthouse log by Zelma on October 19, 1985, also speaks to other "visitors."

"I'm sure we have a ghostly resident here at times – I slept very little."[23] Was it the spirit of an old wickie still tending the lens or just imagination?

If violent death is a cause for spirits still roaming the earth, Point Iroquois Light is well located. According to Indian legend, in 1662 a large war party of Iroquois was moving from the lower lakes with the intention of seizing the great Ojibway campground at Sault Ste. Marie. They stopped at the point that would later bear their name to prepare for the onslaught and to start a great war dance. But the Iroquois had lost the vital element of surprise. The Ojibway had seen them coming and had prepared an ambush. Ojibway scouts, who according to legend

39

took animal form, penetrated the Iroquois camp and learned that to prepare for the epic battle the invaders would dance continuously for four days and nights, until they all collapsed from exhaustion.

True to plan, on the fourth day the Iroquois fell into a deep sleep. In the blackest hours before dawn, the Ojibway crept silently into the camp, attacked and slaughtered them all. The victors spared only two braves, but at a terrible price. They cut off their noses, ears, fingers and toes, gave them some food and sent them crawling home to let the Iroquois nation know of the overwhelming Ojibway power.

The Ojibway butchery was not complete until they lopped the heads off the dead braves and set them on poles all along the Lake Superior beach. The gruesome pickets ran for half a mile. As legend tells the story, the blood from the fresh skulls dripped onto the rocks below, staining them red. Today red-colored rocks, supposedly the result of Iroquois blood, can still be found along the shore.

The spirituality of Point Iroquois is still strong. Three hundred years after the massacre, local Native American children still do not play on the beach. Their elders still call it Nadouenigoning, or "the place of Iroquois bones." There are no houses or trees along this haunted stretch of Lake Superior, only the restless spirits of the Iroquois.[24]

"Now, Who the Hell was That?"
Split Rock Light

Split Rock light near Beaver Bay on the Minnesota shore of Lake Superior is one of the most spectacular lighthouses on the Great Lakes. The 54-foot brick tower stands like a lonely sentinel at the very edge of a 124-foot cliff. Its 370,000 candlepower lamp was officially listed as visible for 22 miles. Built in 1909-1910, its purpose was to warn vessels off the very dangerous rock-bound coast. Deep water runs extremely close to shore and it was exceedingly difficult for sailors to keep safely off using soundings. They depended on the light. In addition, large iron ore deposits nearby cause wide and alarming variations in vessel compass readings. The light was decommissioned in 1969 and since 1976 has been operated by the Minnesota Historical Society as a historic site. It is a popular tourist attraction. By the middle of the 1980s, nearly 200,000 people were visiting annually.

There are two commonly reported haunting stories at Split Rock. The first happened in the mid-1980s and has two slightly different versions. In one version, after the site closed for the day a visitor discovered that he had misplaced his wallet. He quickly returned to the tower building, where he believed he lost it, and started knocking hard on the door. No one answered. Irritated, he stepped back and gazed up at the lamp room. Looking over the rail and staring right back down at him was an old man in a lightkeeper's uniform. He gave no response to the visitor's demand to be let in or to questions about his wallet. When he looked again at the locked door, the visitor noticed that it was padlocked from the outside. He wondered what the man at the railing was doing locked in the tower.

The visitor left in frustration. When he returned the next day, he was able to recover his wallet but got no answers as to whom the strange keeper was. The museum guides often dress in period costume, but none admitted to being in the tower at the time the visitor was there.

The second version is slightly different. After pounding on the museum door for a long while, it suddenly opened and a man in a keeper's uniform silently handed the visitor his missing wallet (or camera?). The keeper said nothing, quickly closed the door and disappeared. Again the following day none of the museum staff admitted knowing anything about the incident. The visitor was left to wonder, "Now, who the hell was that?"

A second incident is less dramatic but perhaps in its own way more intriguing. Located on the grounds are three two-story homes originally used by the keeper and his two assistants. The middle one is now used by the resident curator as a dwelling. About 10 years ago, while in her bedroom dressing for dinner, the curator's wife was struck by a very strong perfume smell, as well as a strong feeling of being watched. Of course no one was found and there was no rational explanation for the aroma of perfume.

Other than two assistant keepers lost on the lake when their sailboat capsized, no death incidents have been directly connected with the station. The unfortunate pair were lost in 1910, a mere two months after the station opened. The keeper sent them to nearby Beaver Bay in the station boat to get the mail. Neither of them was an experienced sailor and the keeper warned not to tie down the sail, but to hold the end by hand, ready to release it if a sudden gust of wind blew up. The men never returned. Later the boat was found washed ashore. The sail was securely tied down, contrary to the keeper's firm instructions. There is no explanation for either the unexplained smells in the residence or the old keeper on the platform. It's just become part of the lore of the light.[25]

The Fourth Man
Stannard Rock Light

The 1976 *Great Lakes Pilot*'s description of Stannard Rock north of Michigan in Lake Superior is cryptic in the manner typical of mariners, but also accurate in its stark appraisal of a danger that can make a sailor's heart run cold, "...32 miles NE of Big Bay Point, consists of two large detached ledges. The S ledge is covered about 3 feet and the N ledge about 2 feet. In 1956, a few scattered rocks awash were reported between the ledges. A 14-foot shoal is 1,000 feet SW of the light and

Stannard Rock Lighthouse with supply ship approaching.
MARQUETTE MARITIME MUSEUM

an 18-foot shoal, plainly visible to vessels passing over it in calm weather, is 0.6 mile W of the light."

Ominously, the area is also known for the strange and powerful magnetic disturbances that can throw a ship's compass wildly off its marks. Navigating the area in a fog with an unreliable compass is especially unnerving, as well as extremely dangerous.

The reef was discovered on August 26, 1835, by the legendary Captain Charles C. Stannard, master of the brig *John Jacob Astor*. It was instantly recognized as a major danger to navigation. In 1866, the Lighthouse Board stated that the shoal presented the "most serious danger to navigation on Lake Superior" and strongly advocated a lighthouse. Two years later, a 12-foot diameter stone crib was bolted to the shallowest part of the reef. In turn, a six-foot diameter, 20-foot-high wrought iron shaft was attached to the crib. The shaft was topped by a six-foot diameter iron cage as a day beacon. Only after the structure survived 10 years of Lake Superior's pounding was it finally decided that it was possible to build a light on the hazardous shoal.

Construction on Stannard Rock Light began in 1878, after Lake Huron's Spectacle Reef Lighthouse was completed and the special equipment and crew could be made available. The crib and entire stone tower were assembled on the shore at Skanee, 55 miles from the reef, using stone blocks quarried from Kelleys Island on Lake Erie. Only after the construction engineers were certain that all fitted together perfectly was the process of assembling the light on the reef begun.

The work was extremely difficult and fraught with delay. Some of the blocks weighed 30 tons and just moving them into position was a challenge. Finally on July 4, 1882, the light was finished and the first powerful beams from the $25,000 Second Order Fresnel lens cut deeply into the black night. The total construction cost was $305,000, very expensive for the time. The 62-foot diameter crib stands 22 feet above the water. With the 88-foot tower added, the entire structure stands 110 feet high. The tower walls are 10 feet thick at the base and three feet at the top. Space inside the tower is limited. The galley room at the base is only 14 feet in diameter and the watch room at the top, a bare seven feet. An engine room outside the tower housed the coal-fired boilers necessary for steam heat and the fog signal.

Inside, the tower is divided into eight levels. When manned by the Coast Guard, they were, from bottom to top: laundry room, galley, chief's quarters, engineman's quarters, seaman's quarters, battery room and watch room, lens motor room and lens room. On entering the structure, a circular stairway goes up to a second level galley and dining room. The west third of the tower above the crib deck is occupied by the 141-step two-foot-wide stairway.

Stannard Rock Light is known as one of the "loneliest places in America," and "one of the most desolate places on the Great Lakes." It is the farthest from land of any lighthouse in the United States. Fully exposed to the sweep of Lake Superior, especially from the northwest through northeast, the tower was sometimes physically shaken by the power of the crashing waves. The total weight of the cement, stone, iron and steel that went into the light is estimated at 240,000 tons. Despite the massive weight, the pile driver force of the lake rattled both the tower and keepers within. Cans toppled from cupboards and chairs overturned. Wave spray often flew over the lantern room, 110 feet above the lake!

Opening the light in the spring could be an ordeal. It wasn't unusual to have to chop through 10 feet of ice just to get into the tower. The ice is sometimes so severe that one year it was July before the light was ready for business. The light was originally manned by the civilian keepers of the Lighthouse Service. Reflecting the difficulty of manning the lonely tower, the civilian keepers received the highest pay of any light in the U.S. When the Lighthouse Service merged with the Coast Guard in 1939, military Coast Guardsmen began to pull duty at the rock, which they sometimes derisively called "Stranded Rock." Some of the civilian keepers, though, enjoyed duty at the rock. Several stayed for 20 seasons.

The Coast Guardsmen never had the same love of the light. Although never admitted, it was long suspected that duty at the Rock was often used as punishment by the Guard. "Screw up bad enough, sailor, and it's out to Stranded Rock for you!" In the old days, when lighthouses kept their own boats, it was three weeks at the rock and one off. Later the Coast Guard removed the boats and used buoy tenders to shuttle the men on and off. Unfortunately, rotation increased to six weeks on and two off. Regardless of the duration, many men couldn't handle the isolation. Other than routine duties, the only activities were card playing, reading and fishing. Badly rattled by the overwhelming isolation, one Coast Guardsman threatened to start swimming ashore if he wasn't taken off immediately. He claimed no one had talked to him for three weeks and he just couldn't stand it any more. Another was reported taken off in a strait jacket and bundled directly to a hospital.

In 1944, the light was electrified. To provide the power, the Coast Guard added four large generators in the coal-fired boiler house. Instead of installing diesel generators, highly volatile gasoline powered ones were used. Heavy batteries were also installed below the lantern room. Regardless of storms, ice and the ever-present loneliness, life on the rock continued much the same.

On June 18, 1961, it all changed. The light was in the process of being automated and 1961 would be the last year men would stand watch in the old stone tower. On the rock that fatal day were four Coast Guardsmen – three that were normally stationed there and a fourth, an electrician's mate from the Soo. He was there to repair one of the generators. The officer-in-charge was on shore leave.

Shortly before 9:30 p.m., one of the men was asleep in the fourth floor seaman's quarters. Two others were in the second floor galley. The fourth was supposed to be on duty in the watch room, but instead was in the engine room (old boiler house) beside the tower. Minutes later the lighthouse was shaken by a terrific explosion. The blast shot up from the engine room through the tower. The two men in the galley were blown across the room. One was badly burned. The third, asleep in his bunk, was thrown onto the floor. Smoke and fire were everywhere. The three men salvaged a couple of jackets, a tarp and two cans of beans and fled outside to the north side of the tower. It was as far away from the burning engine room as they could get. There, they huddled from the cold under the tarp and waited for rescue.

The 1,800 gallons of gasoline had blown sky high in a massive fireball, which in turn ignited the coal in the bunker. Huge amounts of smoke and heat flowed up the tower like a giant chimney, destroying everything in it.

An explosion rocked the lighthouse and killed a U.S. Coast Guard electrician's mate. MARQUETTE MARITIME MUSEUM

Rescue took an incredible two days. The survivors were certain a passing freighter would report the 156,000 candlepower light out or, when routine radio checks with Manitou Island or Marquette weren't made, that someone would be quickly sent to investigate. Weather reports were radioed to Manitou every six hours and Marquette was contacted twice daily. Meticulous logs were kept to verify that the requirements were met.

Yet nothing happened. Stannard Light just dropped off the earth and no one noticed! It wasn't until 11:30 p.m. on June 20 that the Coast Guard buoy tender *Woodrush* discovered the tragedy when it arrived on the regular two-week supply run. The *Woodrush* put out the fire still burning in the coal bunker and rescued the stunned survivors.

The fourth man, the watch stander who was in the engine room, was blown to kingdom come! Searchers never found anything but his key ring. Divers carefully swept the water around the light but came up empty-handed.

What caused the explosion was never determined. But there is a theory that the blame was the watch stander's. One generator was under repair and the watch stander, although a qualified engineman, should have been in the watchroom, not the engine room. He should not have done anything foolish enough to cause the explosion. But he was also a constant pipe smoker. Wherever he went, his pipe went too. Could he, lulled by the deadly monotony of his duties, have gone down to the

45

engine room to check on the progress of repairs, puffing all the while on his pipe. When he opened the door, gas fumes could have hung heavy in the air and, sparked by his smoldering tobacco, an explosion ripped through the air.

The Coast Guard rigged the 900 candlepower winter light for the rest of the 1961 season and in 1962 finished the process of automating the rock. Automation equipment, including fog horn and radio beacon, were installed. Everything inside was stripped out and the old lighthouse was left as a lonely, empty shell. In later years, solar powered weather monitoring equipment was added. Today the light is sealed tight and only visited by Coast Guard maintenance crews.

The light is always an eerie place. Thick Lake Superior pea soup fog is common. Standing alone at night outside with the powerful beams cutting into the gray blanket infused the men with an eerie, supernatural feeling. Land is never in sight and, with the shipping lanes a long 17 miles to the north, even freighters were a rarity.

Since the explosion, Coast Guard crews have been reluctant to service the light anytime near dark – or even at daybreak. They only want to do the job during full daylight. Even then, it has an unusual sense of foreboding. Going on the light at other times is simply too scary. Following the blast, workers in the lighthouse have reported an overwhelming sense that they are not alone. The presence of someone else, someone unseen, has been plainly felt. They knew they were not alone. Some Coast Guard crews believe the fourth man is still on the light and they want no part of him.

Is it the ghost of the watch stander whose body was never found still on the light hiding from visitors, not wanting to explain how his negligence caused the terrible explosion? Perhaps the spirit of one of the civilian keepers who so loved the light is holding the spirit of the careless watch stander prisoner on the light in retribution for destroying it? Or is the ghost of one of the old keepers still on watch and deeply resentful of the new fangled "automation?" Lightkeeping is a man's job, not one for a damned machine! Whatever or whoever it is, the desolate old light is not a place that the Coast Guard crews want to visit. As one of them said, "It's just too spooky!"[26]

CHAPTER TWO

Superstitions

The men who sailed the old "wind wagons" were remembered as a queer lot and superstition played a strong role in their lives. Sometimes entire crews deserted a vessel and nobody knew quite why. Apparently, a crewman saw or heard something that was interpreted as a bad sign and that was enough to cause the whole crew to quit.

The dictionary defines superstition as: "1 – a belief or practice resulting from ignorance, fear of the unknown or trust in magic or chance. 2 – an irrational, abject attitude of mind toward the super-natural, nature or God, resulting from superstitious beliefs or fears."

Superstitions are inexorably part of a sailor's life. It could be said that sailors are among the most superstitious people on earth. The tremendous number of customs, beliefs and superstitions are often so contradictory that making sense of them may defy comprehension. At first, there was obviously a reason for every one of them. As time passed, the original purpose may have been forgotten, until only the action is repeated without logic.

There is a veritable ocean of books written on superstition and the sea. Nearly all of them, however, focus on salt water. To my knowledge, no book has attempted to capture those of the Inland Seas. The superstitions that follow are the ones that can be documented as having been used by lake sailors. They may have started on salt water and been transferred to the lakes, but they are verifiable Great Lakes superstitions. This makes them unique. It is intellectually dishonest to accept blindly that salt-water superstitions and those on fresh water are synonymous. It just isn't so!

Blasphemy

It was thought that blasphemy would cause bad luck or even the wreck of the vessel. Prudent mariners always avoided insulting the Almighty.

It was reported that one becalmed captain "cursed God almighty" for not sending a wind. Later, a storm came up and the vessel sank with all hands. When the captain of the schooner *Maggie Hunter,* also becalmed, cursed for a wind, the crew was certain they would all perish. One of her crew later remarked, "It's a wonder we wasn't all lost."[1] The same sailor said he heard of another vessel which, after a crewman cursed the heavens, had a sudden squall strike, tearing her sails to tatters. The vessel survived, but only barely. One hopes the irreverent sailor had learned the error of his ways.[2]

Cats and Rats

The very word "cat" has a negative connotation on board a vessel. The cat-o-nine-tails was, of course, a notoriously violent whip used as punishment on salt-water vessels. Additionally, much of the gear involved in raising the anchor, a difficult and unpleasant task, used "cat" nomenclature. The cat head, cat fall, cat block, cat tackle, cat harping, cat back and cat davit all meant hard work. A cat hole was thought fit only to be used by passengers and too lubberly for real sailors. Even an unsatisfactory rest was called a cat nap.[3]

Little wonder then, that cats, black or otherwise, have always been considered bad luck on lake vessels and were thought to be "breeders" of bad weather. They were never a ship's mascot. If one was found aboard, it was always considered someone's, but never the ship's.

There are many examples of problems supposedly caused by cats.

The wife of the captain of the schooner *John B. Merrill* carried a black kitten aboard the schooner just as the vessel was leaving its pier in Buffalo. The cat suddenly bolted, jumping a gap of four to five feet to reach the dock. The crew thought bad luck would surely follow. If the cat left, Lord knows what evil luck would befall them. Later the schooner wrecked near Detour, Michigan. Again, the cat was blamed. When the schooner's superstitious owner finally heard the story, he told the captain he should have stopped the boat and notified him so more insurance could have been obtained.[4]

The cat superstition died hard. When the Owen Sound Transportation Company decided to retire the old steamer *Caribou* in 1946, it called from retirement Captain Batten, her previous master for 32 years, to bring her down. The first thing the 79-year-old veteran did was personally check the vessel thoroughly to make certain no cats were aboard. He also delayed his departure long enough to assure that he left on a Saturday instead of Friday.[5] (More about Friday departures later.)

Considering their aversion to cats, it is a bit surprising that sailors seemed to like having rats aboard – likely because sailors believed rats would flee an unseaworthy ship. If rats were seen to be fleeing, it was considered a certain warning of impending doom.[6] There were cases where entire crews deserted when word spread that the rats were leaving. Some skippers turned the superstition to their advantage, by casually mentioning to men they didn't want that the rats were running, thus inducing the troublemakers to also run.

Before the Detroit tug *Erie Belle* left the dock in 1883 to pull the schooner *Carter* off the beach at Kincardine, two firemen abandoned her after seeing rats go ashore on the lines. Their caution was well placed. While pulling at the schooner, the tug's boilers exploded, killing four of her crew. Another crewman quit when he dreamed his dead mother warned him of impending disaster.[7]

Another example of rats leaving a sinking ship involved the steamer *Ste. Marie* in November 1886. As the steamer was at her dock in the Soo, a witness watched in awe as not less than 27 rats scampered down the breast line to the safety of the shore. The crew also noticed the rats' desertion and half of them left, too! On November 9, heavily loaded with freight and supplies, the steamer left for Grand Marais, Michigan, 90 miles to the west. During the night, a storm blew up, knocking the steamer onto a reef outside Deer Park. Quick action of lightering her cargo saved the vessel, but again the rats knew best – as did the men who followed their inexplicable lead.[8]

An old lakes verse echoed the sailors' respect for rats as fortune tellers:

> The rats have left her one by one,
> They tight-roped to the shore,
> And if we stay long enough on this old tub,
> We'll see our friends no more.[9]

Coins

Old sailors believed that throwing several small coins over the stern as a vessel left harbor assured a good trip. Some sailors always did it standing backwards, facing the bow and tossing them over their right shoulder.

A coin, usually silver, was always placed under the step of each mast to guarantee a profitable career.[10] The coin had to be placed face up – face down would invite disaster. It is thought that the custom originated as a requirement to pay the crews' fare to cross the River Styx, in case the ship was lost at sea. In modern times, it has simply become a good luck omen.[11]

Archaeologists excavating the wreck of the unknown schooner near Naubinway, Michigan, in northern Lake Michigan, reaffirmed this old superstition when they discovered an 1833 coin under the heel of the foremast.[12]

Friday

Lakes sailors continued the Friday superstition. Many would go to great lengths to avoid starting a trip or, even worse, a season on a Friday. Also, no vessel should be launched on a Friday. It was common for vessels to delay sailing until after midnight to hold a full crew.

Sometimes, the superstition extended to vessel owners, who would prohibit any of their fleet from starting on a Friday. An old ditty summed up their feelings:

> ship on a Friday for unlucky days,
> and on Saturday for a short stay.[13]

The old lake captains often had personal experiences with the Friday jinx. At the turn of the century, Captain McNeil, an old-time skipper, was supposed to take a schooner from Chicago to Bay City, Michigan. This was to be her first trip of the season. Although he was scheduled to leave on a Friday, he found reason after reason to delay his departure until after midnight. The schooner he moored next to, however, departed Friday afternoon as scheduled. Two days later, Captain McNeil overtook the same schooner with her pendant flying at half-mast – a traditional distress signal. When he spoke with her, he discovered her captain had suffered a bad fall and had died as a result. The crew was convinced the accident was because they started the season on a Friday.[14]

In May 1885, when a propeller and four schooners left Chicago on a Friday, it was enough to cause comment in the *Buffalo Express*. Old sailors were warned to keep an eye on them to see what would happen.[15]

After the steam barge *John J. Hill* grounded off Lake Ontario's Salmon Point in April 1895, her captain was convinced that it was just part of the Friday curse. He later complained to a salvager that he had started his trip on a Friday, lost a man on a Friday and went ashore on a Friday.[16]

In the late 1870s, a dispatch from Chicago stated, "There were a dozen good reasons given why the vessels of the grain fleet could not start on their first voyage of the season today (Friday), but not a single captain or owner would admit that Murphy Friday had anything to do with remaining in port. A big bunch of boats were due to leave at midnight tonight...."[17]

When the schooner *John Duncan* left on an April Friday in 1895 for Port Huron, the *Chicago Tribune* claimed, "No sane vessel owner would order his ship out of port for the first trip of the season on a Friday."[18]

The best (or worst) example of the Friday curse was the great storm of November 1913. Often called a "fresh-water hurricane," it is largely remembered as striking in full intensity on a Friday. The results were devastating – 245 sailors drowned, 17 vessels were completely wrecked and 11 were lost with all hands.

A popular example of a vessel that thumbed her nose at the Friday curse and prospered was the steamer *Petoskey*. But there are two sides to that story. The conventional version is that to debunk the Friday myth, her owner, R.A. Seymour, had her keel laid on a Friday, launched on a Friday and started her first trip on a Friday. Marine men were quick to comment "Nothing good will ever come from tempting fate beyond unreasonable endurance."

Built in 1888 at the Burger shipyard in Manitowoc, Wisconsin, for the Chicago, Traverse City and Petoskey run, old-timers predicted that she was certain to have a short life. Against all odds, the 171-foot wooden steamer plied the lakes for 44 years (as of 1932), surviving storms that sent others to the bottom.[19] Yet there is a darker side. The Friday omen struck the vessel in another way. A *Detroit Free Press* story claimed that her master, Captain Seymour, "took sick" with typhoid on a Friday and died on a Friday. Another Seymour brother, who worked as a clerk, was also "struck down" with typhoid on a Friday.[20]

The Friday superstition also went beyond the ill omen of starting activity on that day. If a sailor took sick on Friday, the next Friday would determine his fate. If he was better, he would get well. If worse, he would certainly die and might as well call the undertaker in early and perhaps get a better price.[21]

Hoodoo Ships

Old sailors believed that some vessels were "bad luck boats," cursed to have misfortune dog their careers. If they could avoid it, they refused to sail on a "hoodoo ship." Sometimes these ships were called "black cats" and comments such as "I only stayed two weeks on that black cat" were common.[22]

A case in point was the propeller *Susan E. Peck*. She was remembered as always being in trouble – going aground, having frequent collisions, losing rigging and sails, fighting bad weather and her crew members being frequently injured. Even when her name

51

changed to *Lewiston*, bad luck continued to follow her.

An old sailor remembered that his father had purchased a wrecked schooner on which some crewmen had perished. After being salvaged and returned to service, the father always had great trouble getting a crew. Sailors considered her ill-omened and usually refused to ship on her.[23]

The schooner *Walter H. Oades* was considered an extremely unlucky vessel. During construction in 1869 in Detroit, a fire destroyed nearly half the hull. Before launching, the supporting ways partially collapsed, dropping her three feet and causing heavy damage. Later, she went ashore at Rondeau Point. Afterward, her builders, apparently having enough problems, sold her. Her tribulations continued. While anchored in the St. Clair River, a steamer collided with her, forcing her into shoal water on the west bank. During the subsequent salvage operations, she slipped off into deep water and sank. Eventually raised, she was hauled to the Detroit Dry Dock yard for repair. Waiting for the final insurance settlement, another vessel ran into her, knocking off her jibboom. In a later accident, she was thrown against the Buffalo breakwater by a heavy sea and damaged. Mishaps continued to dog her. Even coldly analytical insurance companies took notice of such hijinks and, when she tried to obtain coverage, the underwriters wisely refused it.[24] She finally sank on August 20, 1888, in Lake Erie, after a collision with the schooner *R. Holleran*. There was no loss of life.[25]

On reflection, the 1872 loss of the schooner *George F. Whitney* in Lake Michigan was seemingly preordained. First she wrecked on Sugar Island in 1871, while bound from Buffalo to Chicago. After being recovered the following spring, she was rebuilt but, on her next trip, went ashore at Vermilion, Ohio. Again she was hauled off and repaired. The next trip out, she disappeared with all eight hands on Lake Michigan. At the time, she was bound from Chicago for Buffalo with a cargo of corn. Before leaving the Windy City, Captain Wellington Carpenter inexplicably flew all of his flags upside down, including the national ensign. Although he told local marinemen it was merely an invitation for tugs to bring him down the river, they shook their heads in bewilderment over such strange antics.[26]

Sometimes bad luck went from ship to ship. The tugs *M.J. Cummings* and *Eliza J. Redford* were built in the same Oswego, New York, yard, launched the same day and alike in every way. In 1892, the *Cummings* wrecked just east of the Oswego breakwater trying to rescue the gale lashed schooner *Flora Emma*. The *Redford* was destroyed the same night by fire at Cape Vincent on the St. Lawrence. Mere coincidence or ... something else?

There was also a schooner *M.J. Cummings*. On May 18, 1894, she was driven ashore on Fox Point, Lake Michigan. Although the seven-man crew took to the rigging, all but one perished. Some of the bodies hung stiffly in the rigging for a full day, until the storm calmed and rescuers were able to cut them down. One of the crew was considered a notorious hoodoo. After she wrecked, grizzled old sailors repeated a long list of vessels wrecked or otherwise damaged that he had sailed on. The old timers just said "good riddance."[27]

Schooner **Rosa Bell** *in tow by the tug* **Peter Russ.** *K.E. THRO COLLECTION*

A lakes vessel infamous for killing two complete crews was the 100-foot, 132-ton, two-masted schooner *Rosa Belle*. Built in Milwaukee in 1863, she was found by a Lake Michigan carferry floating upside down in midlake in 1875. Her entire crew of 10 were missing. Towed into port and righted, she soon returned to service. On October 20, 1911, the *Rosa Belle* was found by a Grand Trunk carferry, again floating hull up. The stern was missing, which implied a collision, but the other vessel could not be identified. None had reported a collision or showed up with unexplained damage. As with the previous incident, her entire 10-man crew had again disappeared. They had just gone "through the door."[28]

The Canadian schooner *Explorer* is another vessel that killed two complete crews. A small, 100-ton windbag, she exterminated her first crew when she capsized off the Tubs at Tobermory, Lake Huron. Afterward, there was some suspicion that her captain may have scuttled her for the insurance. Since he was one of the dead, it was either a plan gone awry or an unfounded rumor.

Without too much effort, the schooner was righted and returned to service. In the fall of 1883, she wrecked on Greenock Shoals in Lake Huron at Stokes Bay, off the Bruce Peninsula. When found, the spars were still above water and her crew of five was grotesquely frozen to death in the rigging. Two years later, Harry Jex, a diver from Port Huron, Michigan, purchased the wreck, intending to salvage her supposed whisky cargo. All he found was railroad iron and what he thought might be auger holes in her hull. Had another scuttling plan gone awry? The true story of the *Explorer* will probably never be known. However, there isn't any doubt she killed two crews![29]

The big schooner *George E. Hartnell* earned her hoodoo status in November 1900. When she arrived outside Ashtabula, Ohio, she was already missing her starboard anchor, lost in an accident at the Soo. Trying to enter Ashtabula harbor, she grounded on a sand bar. Three tugs were needed to push her free. She then ran smack into the west pier, breaking her port anchor and damaging her bow considerably. Afterward, sailors always viewed her with a leery eye![30]

There are old tales of human twins being so close that, when one died, the other quickly followed. In the case of the barges *Algeria* and *Armenia*, the same was true. Built side-by-side at the Davidson yard in Bay City during the winter of 1895-96, a third sister, the *Abyssinia*, was also built during the winter in the same yard. For practical purposes, all were identical in build and purpose – to haul iron ore down from Lake Superior to lower lakes mills.

For 10 years, the *Algeria* and *Armenia* performed well in the trade, until May 9, 1906, when both sank in the same Lake Erie storm. The *Armenia* was downbound behind the steamer *Fred Pabst* when, after coming out of the Detroit River's Pelee Passage, she suddenly developed an unholy appetite for fresh water. Realizing that she was close to sinking, the captain of the steamer removed her crew just before she broke in half and sank near Colchester Shoal. It was her first trip of the season. During the same storm, the *Algeria* was anchored off Cleveland with her first cargo of the spring. The storm was pounding her mercilessly. When it became apparent the vessel was in danger, the captain sent five of his men ashore. He, the engineer and the cook, known as "One-Eyed Sullivan," waited for a tug to come help the beleaguered vessel. None came. The *Algeria* also broke in half, drowning those aboard.

Unusual similarities continued. Both wrecks were in shipping channels and loaded with full cargoes of iron ore. Both were considered hazards to navigation. Ironically, the hulks of both vessels were also inadvertently hit by steamers. The *Armenia* was struck by the steamer *Charles B. Packard,* which in turn became a total loss. The steamer *Henry Cort* was damaged when she hit the *Algeria* wreck. In a final irony, both wrecks were removed in September 1906.

Barge Armenia, *which sank with its sister ship, the* Algeria, *in the same May 9, 1906, Lake Erie storm. K.E. THRO COLLECTION*

The Algoma Central Railroad lost three of its ships, including the Leafield *on the islands off Thunder Bay, Ontario. RUNGE MARINE COLLECTION*

The barge *Abysinnia* survived the fate of her sisters for another 11 years. On October 18, 1917, she wrecked near Tecumseh Reef, Lake Erie.[31]

The loss of three of four vessels of the Algoma Central Railroad fleet in the same area of Lake Superior gave strong evidence to those

Believed to be hoodoo ships, Monkshaven *(top) and* Theano *(bottom), along with the* Leafield *(previous page), were lost by the Algoma Central Railroad in the early 1900s. K.E. Thro COLLECTION*

who believed in hoodoos. The four ships, *Theano, Paliki, Monkshaven* and *Leafield*, were strongly built in England for salt-water tramp or coastal service. On the lakes, they were known as "canallers," since their 249-foot length was the maximum size for the Welland Canal. They typically carried iron ore from Lake Superior's Michipicoten Harbour mines to either the Algoma Steel mill at the Canadian Sault or to a mill at Midland, Ontario. Return cargo was coal or steel rails up to Thunder Bay. Occasionally, grain was substituted for the ore. It was a good and productive trade.

Three of the four were all lost on the islands off Thunder Bay, Lake Superior. The *Monkshaven* wrecked at Pie Island on November 27, 1905. Hauled off the following year, she broke free of the salvagers, only to fetch up on nearby Angus Island, where she beat herself to pieces. The *Theano* went up on Trowbridge Island on November 17, 1906, where she also became a total loss. The *Leafield* disappeared with all hands near Angus Island on November 9, 1913. Only the *Paliki* survived Lake Superior, being sold off the lakes in 1916 and scrapped as the *Carmella* in 1930. She alone avoided the fate of her doomed sisters.[32]

Of four similar Algoma Central ships, only the Paliki *avoided the fate of its doomed sisters.* HAMILTON COLLECTION, RUTHERFORD B. HAYES LIBRARY, FREMONT, OHIO

Small craft could also be jinxed. The Bois Blanc Island Coast Guard motor lifeboat is a case in point. The boat was considered the hoodoo of the Tenth District when it set out from the island in January 1939 with a crew of five to rescue three Detour fishermen adrift on the

This motor life boat was considered by Coast Guardsmen throughout the Tenth District as a hoodoo. TED RICHARDSON COLLECTION

ice in northern Lake Huron. Turned back by the ice, the Coast Guard lifeboat crew attempted to return to the safety of the station, but the ever thickening ice blocked their way. Unable to make significant progress, the crew shut the boat down for the night, hoping for better weather in the morning.

During the night, temperatures plummeted to 20 degrees below zero and the men suffered terribly from the piercing cold. They were caught tight in a moving sheet of ice. The first rays of the gray dawn found them pushed far to the south. Even worse, the recalcitrant engine refused to start, leaving them totally at the mercy of the ice. Eventually they were driven against the shore ice pack 20 miles south of Cheboygan. Numbed with cold, the men left the lifeboat and scrambled over three miles of rough ice to reach the beach. There, they began their desperate trek to Cheboygan, finally staggering into the city the following day. All of the crew had second degree frostbite on their hands and feet. It had been a near-death thing for the Coast Guardsmen. Had they been out much longer, death would have been inevitable. Their valiant effort in a jinxed boat was all for naught. The fishermen were rescued earlier by some companions, who manhandled a small boat over the ice and brought them ashore.

Before its assignment to Bois Blanc, the lifeboat had been at Muskegon, where it was used in the ill-fated attempt to rescue the crew of the steamer *Henry Cort*. Reportedly, one of the Coast Guard crew was thrown from the boat in the wave action while responding to the call for help. It was as if the boat didn't want any of the men to stay aboard or that it was trying to throw them out. This was very odd behavior for a design that had proven itself over many years as the finest lifeboat in the world. During the attempted rescue, one of the Coast Guardsmen drowned.

The boat had a long history of problems and old-timers often called it the "boat that wouldn't go." Any station knew that it would be trouble if it was transferred to them. Regardless, it was government property and could not be abandoned, even though it lay forlornly on the shore of Lake Huron. Eventually, the Coast Guard used a bulldozer to haul the boat over the ice to the beach at Grace Harbor. Damaged beyond repair, but also perhaps with a touch of benign management, they declared it beyond salvage and stripped it of anything useful. In the spring of the year, they soaked the hull in gasoline and burned it. Doubtless, Coast Guardsmen throughout the district were relieved it wouldn't turn up in their boathouse.[33]

Warlocks and Wizards

Finns held a special place in Great Lakes superstitions. When they began to emigrate from the old country, they tended to take up their same occupations in the new. Those that were sailors often signed on to sail the inland seas. Because by their nature they were efficient and thrifty, especially as skippers and mates, they were popular with ship owners. But they were not at all popular with the crews. Many were drivers, who got everything possible out of both men and ships, pinching a nickel until it "squeaked." Sometimes the newcomers passed the local men by, due to their enterprise, gaining jobs others thought were rightly theirs.

Trip after trip, Finnish captains beat the competition. To disparage the newcomers, the locals sometimes spread stories from the Old World that the Finns were warlocks and wizards and that they bought and sold the winds in cooperation with the devil himself. They were said to especially hold power over wind and storm.

An old legend was told of a Finnish master who made phenomenal trips by means of a magic rope, in which many knots were tied. When the wind failed, in lieu of the time-honored method of whistling, throwing coins over the stern or striking a knife in the mast, he just untied a knot or two. To lessen the wind, he retied the knots, instead of reefing the sails. The Finn was finally lost with his crew, when his wife, a very tidy and organized woman, saw the knotted rope and untied all the knots when he wasn't watching. The devil was paid in full.[34]

Jonahs

As there were unlucky ships, so were there unlucky sailors. Known as Jonahs, they were believed to bring misfortune with them. It was common that, when a vessel experienced a spell of bad weather or if other things were not going well, a crew member would try to fasten blame on another crewman, " ... that SOB is a Jonah. We had nothing but bad luck since he got on...."[35]

Cross-eyed or "swivel-eyed" sailors were considered Jonahs. It was said that a wheelsman couldn't steer straight if a cross-eyed person, crew or passenger, was aboard.[36] Some also thought a cross-eyed wheelsman brought head winds and, at a minimum, tempted fate.[37]

Captain George McKay of the barge *Antelope* considered himself the luckiest man on the lakes. Others probably called him a classic Jonah. The *Antelope* was one of a string of five barges in tow of the propeller *S.C. Clarke* when she tried to pass down river at Tonawanda, New York, in a storm. The wind proved too powerful for the steamer and four of the five ended up ashore. Only the *Antelope* held fast and made port. McKay was the wheelsman on the *Lady Elgin* when she sank in 1860 with the loss of an estimated 300 lives. Although he couldn't swim a stroke, he made shore by holding onto a bale of hay. In 1883, he was master of the barge *William Trent* when she was overtaken and sunk by a vicious storm off Sand Beach. For six days, he and his crew drifted on Lake Huron before safely coming ashore at Goderich. He dodged disaster on Lake Erie when sailing on the barge *Joseph*, in tow of the tug *Moore* with the barges *Baltic* and *Adriatic*, when they were struck by a strong gale. The *Baltic* and *Adriatic* sank, but the *Joseph* safely rode out the storm. Did he bring good luck to his vessels or was he a Jonah, spreading the seeds of disaster wherever he went?[38]

Another Jonah, although he also considered himself a "lucky" sailor, was Captain Martin Daniels of Marquette. When his schooner *Tom Boy* sank off the city on August 1, 1880, it was his *ninth* shipwreck in 22 years of sailing. It was, however, his first fresh-water disaster. The previous eight happened during his salt-water days. Undaunted, Daniels continued his sailing career. Just to add spice to his sailing, he often carried cargoes of high explosives from the powder mills for the mines.[39]

There was no good reason for the June 7, 1902, collision between the wooden steamer *George G. Hadley* and the 308-foot whaleback steamer *Thomas Wilson*. The *Wilson* was leaving Duluth fully loaded with ore and the *Hadley* was inbound, when the wooden vessel inexplicably rammed the whaleback, cutting deeply into her side. Within minutes the *Wilson* went to the bottom of Lake Superior and nine of her crew perished. The only explanations were that of

The wooden steamer George C. Hadley *sank after slicing into and sinking the whaleback* Thomas Wilson *near Duluth, Minnesota.* K.E. THRO COLLECTION

unforgivably bad seamanship on the part of the *Hadley*'s master or that other "forces" were at play.

One of the men that escaped the *Wilson*'s death plunge was fireman E.H. Shoemaker. Prior to the *Wilson-Hadley* collision, he walked (or swam) away from four shipwrecks. He survived the *Wilson* too, making it five wrecks. Unfortunately for the *Hadley*, that vessel hauled him aboard from the cold lake to what was assumed to be safety. Although the captain thought the *Hadley* would easily make it to shallow water, his vessel sank with unnatural speed. Shoemaker walked away from that sinking too, giving him a record of six survived shipwrecks – an enviable one for any self-respecting Jonah!

It is worth noting that the *Wilson* did not have an auspicious launching. When she rushed down her ways in Superior, Wisconsin, in 1892, she hit the water and kept on going, smashing hard into the opposite slip and wrecking the standing scaffolding there. Despite the fact that she was undamaged by the accident, it was not a good beginning in many old sailors' eyes.[40]

Hunches and Dreams

Old lake sailors believed in hunches and dreams as omens of things yet to come. There are many examples on the Great Lakes of sailors' dreams influencing their actions.

Audie Behn, a crewman on the tug *Zinc Bell*, left her hurriedly when he dreamed his dead mother told him to get off. The tug's boilers exploded on a subsequent trip.[41]

Milton Smith, the assistant engineer of the steamer *Charles F. Price*, despite the strong protests of chief engineer John Groundwater, left the vessel "with an uneasy feeling." Barely 27 hours later, the *Price* went down with all hands in the great November 1913 storm.[42]

Before the steamer *Morning Star* sank in 1868 in Lake Erie with the loss of 23 lives, a Windsor ferry boat sailor reportedly dreamed about it. Other sailors claimed to have dreamed of the loss of the schooner *Mockingbird*, before its wrecking at Long Point in 1876, and of the foundering of the propeller *Lac La Belle* in Lake Michigan in 1872 with the loss of eight lives.[43]

The November 1869 gale that swept Lake Huron was a real hell-banger. Caught out in the lake that terrible night was Captain Dishrow and the schooner *Volunteer*. During the deep of the dark night, the captain's young granddaughter woke suddenly and excitedly in her bed at home and told her mother that she had seen her grandfather standing by the bed. The mother shrugged off the child's vision as only a nightmare. When the storm waters finally calmed and the damages totaled, the *Volunteer* and her captain/grandfather were among the lost. Did he pay one last visit to a favorite grandchild?[44]

In another instance, the mate of a Detroit schooner dreamed three nights running that he fell overboard. Each time, he experienced the vice-like pain of drowning. On the fourth day, while sailing in Lake Erie, he fell from the jibboom and drowned.[45]

John G. Parker, one of the early Lake Superior navigators, had a particularly revealing dream that accurately foretold the future.

On June 9, 1847, Parker was aboard the schooner *Swallow* at the Soo, waiting for the schooner *Fur Trader* to arrive. One night, he dreamed the *Fur Trader* sailed under reefed canvas in a northwest squall and came to anchor under the *Swallow*'s stern. Several men boarded a small yawl and, when he looked again, it had sunk out of sight. The following morning, Parker told Captain Brown about the dream. Brown only laughed.

Later, the wind blew up northwest and the *Fur Trader* arrived, just as Parker dreamed, and dropped her hook under the *Swallow*'s stern. To check if there was enough water to run the *Uncle Tom* down, Parker, Captain Brown of the *Swallow*, Captain John Stannard of the *Uncle Tom* and several other men attempted to run the rapids in a pulling boat. While making the "shoot," the boat capsized. Only with the greatest of effort were all aboard saved. One man, a Mr. Seymour, was pulled from the river bottom by a Native American chief who was fishing the area. Taken to shore, he was "rolled" to force the water out. While this crude resuscitation was under way, another man, Little Duncan, ran up yelling, "Roll him, roll him! He owes me 10 dollars." Seymour recovered, but whether he repaid the $10 loan is unknown.

It all happened just as Parker had dreamed.[46]

Men who spent enough time on the lakes sometimes developed a remarkable sense of premonition. After the 295-foot wooden steamer *Orinoco* sank in Lake Superior on May 18, 1924, the captain's wife claimed that he had a foreknowledge of the disaster. She stated in an interview that, in his last letter, he sounded as if he feared something, that something was going to go wrong. The captain and four of his men were killed in the sinking.

The captain of the ill-fated Orinoco *had foreknowledge of the ship's sinking.*
MARINE HISTORICAL COLLECTION, MILWAUKEE PUBLIC LIBRARY

A Coast Guardsman's particular hunch played a major role in the rescue of a steamer's crew. During a strong north gale accompanied by snow and subzero temperatures, the 286-foot steamer *Thomas Maytham* was driven hard on Point Isabelle Reef, 10 miles from Lake Superior's Keweenaw Point.

When the storm moderated two days later, the lightkeeper at Gay sighted the stranded steamer. He straightway telephoned the news to Anthony F. Glaza, the legendary officer in charge of the Coast Guard Lifeboat Station at Eagle Harbor. Glaza immediately launched his 36-foot motor-lifeboat and proceeded for the *Maytham*. A veteran of many difficult rescues, Glaza knew exactly what to do and just how difficult it would be. The lifeboat battled its way through rough seas and frigid northerly blasts. It was a brutal 35-mile run, with temperatures dropping to 10 below zero! The relief felt by the *Maytham*'s crew when the lifeboat reached them was evident, as cries of, "We're all right now! We're all right now! The Coast Guard is here," rang through the air.

Glaza planned to bring the 22-man crew to nearby Mendota Light, six miles to the southeast at Bete Gris but, in his own words, " ... took all in lifeboat and got under way. Suddenly, an irresistible urge came over me to head back to our station instead of the light station. Mentioned this to members of my crew, who said they had the same feeling. Unable to overcome this inclination.... " Glaza threw his wheel over and headed back for Eagle Harbor.

At 3 p.m., several miles from Copper Harbor, they discovered the deserted and ice encrusted hulk of the steamer *City of Bangor* resting fast on a reef just offshore. Carefully, they scanned the coast for the crew. About an hour later, just before the blackness of night fell, they saw the bedraggled men stumbling over the rough beach. Running close inshore, Glaza yelled that he had a full load, but would drop them in Copper Harbor and quickly return.

The City of Bangor *crew was fortunate that the life boat crew had a premonition.* EDWIN T. BROWN COLLECTION, MICHIGAN STATE ARCHIVES

The *City of Bangor* was bound from Detroit to Duluth with a cargo of 230 brand new 1926 Chryslers and a quantity of Whippets. The fierce norther' that put the *Maytham* on Point Isabelle also blew the *Bangor* ashore.

After assuring that the *Maytham* crew was cared for, Glaza and his men made it back to the *Bangor* that night. Because the lifeboat drew too much water to slip over the reefs and onto the beach, Glaza used a rowboat that he borrowed in Copper Harbor to bring the men, three at a time, to the lifeboat. Finally, all of the 29 crewmen were safe aboard. He later reported, ". . . found them all suffering from hunger and exposure, some hardly able to move and ready to give up. . . heard them say we came in answer to their prayers. It was then that we knew that some divine power had guided us in returning to find them that night."

Glaza's comments were not overblown. The survivors were in rough shape, having left the ship without heavy clothing or boots. Most were suffering from frostbite and many required hospitalization.[47]

Horseshoes

As is common in the general population, horseshoes were always good luck talismans to Great Lakes sailors. Practically every schooner had a horseshoe nailed to the davit post – prongs up so the good luck would not run out. Sometimes, they were nailed over cabin doors or to a mast. The practice was so widespread that Captain James McConnell, ex-master of the Canadian Pacific Railroad steamer *Assinaboia*, claimed that there were, "enough horseshoes on the bottom of the lakes to shoe the entire British cavalry."

Despite such cynicism, should a schooner not have a resident horseshoe, sailing was delayed until one was found.[48]

Launchings

Sailors all over the world considered the launching of a new vessel to be the most important action in determining her future luck. No matter how well built, named, crewed, fitted out or managed, it was how she was launched that really counted. Anything that went wrong during this defining ceremony was considered a bad omen. Consequently, yard crews made extremely careful preparations to ensure that everything went off without a hitch during a launch.

When the big steel steamer *John McGean* was lost in the great November 1913 storm, many old-timers remembered that when she launched in Lorain on February 22, 1908, she experienced problems. When she hit the water, the resulting wave washed into a crowd of spectators, sweeping many into the water. At least two were injured.[49]

A modern example of launching trouble occurred on May 29, 1969, with the 730-foot Canada Steamship Lines self-unloader *Tadoussac*. While the Collingwood shipyard workers were still preparing her for launching, she suddenly started on her own, killing two men and injuring more than 40 others. Deaths during a launching are an especially bad omen – however, as of this date, she is still sailing. Still, the fates have a way of being patient before claiming their due.[50]

Christening a new ship with water, instead of the traditional bottle of spirits, was always considered to be a bad omen by sailors. The 195-foot *Adella Shores* was built in Gibraltar, Michigan, in 1894 for the Shores Lumber Company. After a quick and unceremonious launch, the incomplete vessel was towed to Ashland, Wisconsin, where the Shores mills were located. There it was formally christened by Bessie Shores, daughter of the owner. It was named for Adella, another daughter and the apple of her father's eye. Instead of smashing a flagon of alcoholic libation on her bows, one filled with water was substituted, causing old-timers to cringe.

The Adella Shores *was dogged by bad luck, after being christened with a bottle of water, rather than spirits. K.E. THRO COLLECTION*

The steamer experienced several mishaps. In 1898 she sank at her Manistee, Michigan, dock, the result of stoving-in several bow planks in heavy ice. Three years later, she settled in shallow water in Duluth, after hitting a log and punching a hole in her bow.

Bad luck struck with a vengeance in April 1909. Upbound on Lake Superior for Duluth with a cargo of salt, she and her crew of 14 disappeared without a trace somewhere west of Whitefish Point. To this day, she remains one of the "went missing." Did water instead of alcohol make a difference? The old-timers think so.[51]

Name Changes

Changing a vessel's name was always considered bad luck by lake sailors.

The sailors felt that when a vessel was named and launched, it acquired a unique personality. Renaming it injured that personality and the vessel reacted accordingly. There are many examples of vessels that met disaster, as the old sailors believed, because of a name change.

Bad luck accompanying a name change was often the subject of talk, as the following item from the *Detroit Free Press* of August 25, 1889, shows.

They were talking of luck in a vessel office and one of the owners of the propeller Samoa *remarked that she had struck her share of lefthanded favors this year.*

"She is one of the vessels with a changed name," spoke up the owner of a tow. "It always turns out that way. If you want a vessel to hit everything she comes within a cable's length of, give her a new name."

"That accounts for the Caledonia'*s beautiful time at the bottom of the Sault River," remarked a newspaper man.*

The owner of the tow nodded and said, "Yes, and for the terrible knocking about that the John C. Pringle *had to stand for the first year or two after she got her new name. My boats are going to stick to their maiden names, if I know myself."*

The Samoa *was christened the* T.W. Palmer*, but the name wasn't sold with the boat when she last changed hands. The* Caledonia *was formerly the* W.B. Morely*, but took her new name on being sold. The* John C. Pringle *was the* W.H. Gratwick *until her first owners sold her to make way for a new* Gratwick*. Tinkerers of names beware!*[52]

The tug *Cornell*, lost with all hands on Lake Erie in 1922, was christened as the *Grace Danforth* in 1888. The tug *Admiral*, sunk with all hands in December 1942 on Lake Erie, was built in 1922 as the *W.G. Meyer*. Her tow, the barge *Clevco*, was also lost with all hands. Ominously, her name had just been changed. The tug *Sachem*, lost with all hands in December 1950 on Lake Erie, started her career in 1907 as the *John Kelderhouse*. [53]

Early sailors were also always nervous about shipping on a vessel named for a dead person.[54] They considered all such boats cursed.

They were equally leery of vessels with "unlucky" names. It was said that "give a schooner a good, but an unlucky, name and you might as well notify the coroner."[55]

Some sailors believed too many As in a name also was unlucky, thus explaining the loss of the *Mataafa* at Duluth in 1905. Ships with 13 letters in their names were certainly thought to be unlucky. The

James Pickands, wrecked in 1894 on Sawtooth Reef, is a case in point. The *Mesquite* (WB305), lost on Keweenaw Point in December 1989, is another.

Another name superstition involved the destruction of vessels with similar names. When one was destroyed, the others were sure to follow. This superstition was strong enough that men often deserted their ships in fear of the premonition. When skeptics pointed out the absurdity of

Changing the name of a vessel can be bad luck, as the sinking of the tugs Admiral *(above)* and Sachem *indicated. K.E. THRO COLLECTION*

such beliefs, the old-timers presented telling evidence of it

A sloop, *Lady Washington*, wrecked on the North Riv Ontario, in 1803. Other *Lady Washington* wrecks included wrecked near Portsmouth on the Ohio Canal, a schooner th west of Buffalo in 1828, a brig of the same name that sank i. .u. Guf of Mexico and a steamer that went down off Manistique, Michigan.

The destruction of the steamer *Washington* on Long Point, Lake Erie, in 1833 was quickly followed by the loss of other ships of the same name on the Upper Lakes, in the Erie Canal and on the Ohio River. Five years later, the sidewheeler *George Washington* burned at Silver Creek near Dunkirk, New York, on Lake Erie, with the loss of an estimated 50 lives.[56] (A broader treatment of this "same name" superstition is contained in Appendix A of this book.)

A brave Oswego captain provided the ultimate temptation to the fates when he named his schooner *Friday*. She reportedly sank with all hands on her first trip.[57]

Of course, all of the episodes "proving" these superstitions are coincidences but, nonetheless, they greatly contributed to the sailors' belief in "unlucky" names.

Sea Gulls

With their wild and plaintive cries, sea gulls were also supposed to contain the souls of drowned sailors, holding a special place in the hearts of lake sailors. A gull landing on a vessel under way was always a good omen.

Captain Harry Ingraham, an old lakes veteran, reported an extraordinary occurrence on Lake Superior. A larger than normal gull landed on the bow and, according to his lookout, called out to the man by name. He recognized the voice of a friend lost on the lake years before. It warned him of an unknown danger.[58]

Birds also foretold the future. In one instance, when a bird flew through an open doorway and into the Oswego home of a lake captain, he regarded it to be an ill omen. Sometime later, the captain and all crew were lost on the schooner *Mollison*. About the same time the schooner would have foundered, another bird flew against a window pane at the captain's home, alerting his wife that something was amiss. Several days later she received word of the loss.[59]

In another bird superstition story, the carferry *Pere Marquette No. 18* was christened in August 1902, but instead of the traditional bottle of champagne smashing across her steel bow, a flock of doves was released. The doves must have jinxed her for, on September 8, 1910, she sank in Lake Michigan, with the loss of 28 lives.[60]

₎sed Gear

Great Lakes sailors were always against using any gear or equipment salvaged from wrecked vessels. They believed that bad luck would follow it.[61]

The schooner *William Crosthwaite* is a perfect example of the used gear jinx. The vessel was ravaged and finally sunk by fire while storm-bound behind Whitefish Point on November 13, 1904. The fire apparently started in the forecastle from an overheated pot bellied stove used to heat water for the crew's laundry. The captain, Frank Patterson, said he wasn't at all surprised by his loss. The lifeboat the crew escaped in was salvaged from the steamer *Sitka*, wrecked the month before at Au Sable Point. The oars were from the steamer *Waverly*, lost in a Lake Huron collision with the steamer *Turret Court* the prior year. The *Crosthwaite* was the *Waverly*'s consort.Worse yet, one of the crew was a survivor of the schooner *F.B. Gardner*, burned and sunk off Port Sanilac, Michigan, in September. The towing vessel, the steamer *D. Leuty*, later wrecked at Marquette on Halloween night 1911. What equipment she may have carried from the *Crosthwaite* isn't known.

Although the *Crosthwaite* was raised the following year and returned to service, she had less than two years to live. In September 1906, she was run down in Lake Erie and sunk by the steamer *Homer Warren*.[62]

When two Lake Michigan fishermen accidentally brought part of a uniform from the *Chicora* wreck up in their nets, they quickly deep-sixed it. The men were "seized with fear at beholding this symbol of those who had drowned. They hastily threw it back," wanting no part of its bad luck.[63]

Whistling

Whistling was treated seriously on a sailing vessel, since sailors believed that it would bring on a gale. If a wind was blowing, whistling was forbidden. If becalmed, the whole crew whistled softly for a moderate breeze. Shrill whistling was especially thought to bring on a gale. On some vessels, whistling for a wind was restricted to the captain and mates.[64] Another trick some masters used was to change wheelsmen, hoping the new man would "bring a wind."[65]

Sailors summarized their thoughts on the importance of wind in the old saying:

Head winds bring money in over the bow.
Following winds bring money in over the stern.

The sense of the saying is that head winds caused a slow trip and

increased crew wages, while following winds sped the vessel on her
way and made more money for the owners and officers.[66]

Women and Priests

Women aboard were always considered bad luck and were sure to
bring foul weather. On one trip to Marquette aboard a schooner-barge,
Captain Patrick McManus remembered having two women passengers
with him. The mate was certain something would go wrong. Sure
enough, when going through the rapids at Port Huron, the tow line
broke and the barge drifted down river, scattering other traffic before it.
It finally came to rest against some piles on the Canadian shore. The
mate was firm that the accident was all the fault of the women.[67]

In the early days, women cooks were not welcomed by the crews.
The sailors believed the women were not able to "lend a hand" during
emergencies.

There were also more traditional problems with women aboard. In
one instance, a captain shipped a woman cook from Buffalo's infamous
Canal Street and she proved "too much for the entire crew." He put her
ashore at Detroit.[68] In later days, when the need for good food overcame
superstition, women cooks became common, often being the wives of
captains or mates.

Some mariners carried the female prejudice further, believing a
female name brought bad luck. Ships should simply not be named after
women. After all, women always got honest sailors into trouble.[69]

Unlike women, preachers were never redeemed from their status of
being a bad luck omen. Old sailors always thought preachers to be
dangerous company when aboard ship.[70] One reason may be their
habitual black clothing, coupled with their job of comforting the dying
and burying the dead. Another reason may have been the belief that the
devil was their everlasting enemy and would send storms to destroy
them, imperiling the vessel and crew.

After a vessel carrying an early Lake Superior Methodist
missionary, Reverend J.H. Pitzel, experienced a series of gales, one
captain attributed it to having preachers and women aboard. He claimed
that he "never knew it to fail, with women and preachers aboard, sailors
were sure to have storms." It also seems that every time Catholic
Bishop Baraga traveled by water, storms plagued him.

Miscellaneous Superstitions

A slight list to port when towing out of a harbor meant a lucky trip.
A starboard list foretold an unlucky one.[71]

Some sailors, including one mate on the big CPR steamer

71

Assinaboia, refused to pass anyone on a companionway, believing it was certain to cause bad luck.[72]

Others would leave a vessel if a hatch cover or strong back fell into a hold when battening down. Also, spitting in the hold was a sure sign of certain bad luck.[73]

Shipping with an odd number in the crew was sometimes held to be bad luck. One old-timer remembered sailing with a crew of 23 for an entire season and said that they seemed to lose a man on every trip. When they sailed the following season with a man short, giving them an even number, they never lost a man.[74]

Other superstitions included a broken mirror foretelling a broken mast and a broken glass warning of a broken compass. A sneeze meant bad luck unless directed to the right.[75]

Appendix A at the end of this volume continues a description of other superstitions practiced by some Great Lakes sailors.

CHAPTER THREE

Ghost Ships

TIME: Late 19th Century
PLACE: Sans Souci Saloon, Chicago

"I tell you, I seen it. I seen the damned thing as clear as day, well almost. It kind of came and went a bit but that was because of the fog banks she was sliding in and out of and such." Putting down his empty beer mug, the sailor reached around and took another mug from the bartender, "Olaf the Swede." Several of the crew continued to look at him questioningly. Other sailors looked at him intently, nodding with understanding. Wiping fresh foam from his mouth, the sailor turned back to the men and said, *"Old Pete saw it too, didn't you Pete?"* The second man looked up quickly and said, *"Jim, I hate to admit it, but I sure as hell did. Maybe for only a minute, but I saw her. It was the old* Alpena *steam'n along just as proud as the day she came out and here she has been gone these 10 years."* Another man chimed in. *"And good men she took with her. I knew most of them, old Red, Mickey, Squash Nose Kelly, each was a damn good man in a pinch. I wonder about them. You know, we seen the ship, but what about the men – do you think, do you think they ... ?"* The first man looked hard into his beer and said, *"Aw, shut up and drink."*

Before I began the research process for this book, I believed that stories of ghost ships on the Great Lakes were simply the result of 20th century writers' overzealous imaginations. Surely there was no historical basis for such wild claims as phantom schooners sailing effortlessly through a storm-tossed lake. It was not until reviewing the Ivan Walton material that it became clear there was a factual basis for

73

ghost ship stories. In interviews with old-time sailors, many claimed to have either seen ghost ships or had known others who had. To these men, ghost ships were very real.

As with other Great Lakes maritime legends and superstitions, the ghost ship idea may have been transferred from the ocean, as in the example of the famous *Flying Dutchman* of classic fame. There are several versions of the *Flying Dutchman* legend. One story relates that a Dutch captain named Falkenberg of the *VanderDecker* was involved in a desperate attempt to beat his way past Cape Horn, but was unable to make progress. In a fit of raging frustration, he swore he would keep trying until he was successful, despite how long it took. He would be "damned" if he would give up! This affront to the Almighty resulted in his being cursed to continue trying to beat around Cape Horn for all eternity.

Sighting the phantom of the *Flying Dutchman* was always considered bad luck. Such vessels cannot be boarded. If mail is taken from them, the receiving vessel will surely perish. Some accounts placed ghostly crews on their decks and swarming over their yards. The crew, made up of shirkers, rogues and cowards, was as cursed as the captain. The figurehead was a skeleton whose bones glistened yellow with an unearthly shimmer. Such ships usually appeared before storms and frequently were sighted in fog, rain or snow. In some versions, the ship changed its appearance, mimicking many doomed vessels.[1]

Coincidentally, there were two vessels named *Flying Dutchman* on the Great Lakes. The first was a 74-ton schooner built in Madison, Ohio, in 1845 and wrecked on Long Point, Lake Erie, in 1851. The second, also a schooner, was built in 1862 in the small Lake Ontario port of Jordan. As far as is known, she enjoyed a profitable career in the grain trade.[2]

Vessels that lived out a useful life and were just abandoned on a muddy river bank were not candidates for ghostly reincarnation. Ships that wrecked or sank with loss of life, usually those gone missing with all hands, often became spectre ships and sighting such vessels was considered a warning of storm or other danger.

Bertha Endress Rolla, the granddaughter of one of the Whitefish Point lightkeepers, remembered standing with her grandfather on the beach in front of the light when a ghost ship of a schooner came into view. The vessel was plainly seen, its side lights burning brightly through the fog and the voices of the crew clearly heard.

The old grandfather, still holding the child's small hand, looked hard at the phantom and exclaimed, "Some poor sailors will soon lose their lives."

Although there was no wind, the strange ship moved eerily through the water, heading northeast, her sails filled with an unearthly breeze. She soon faded from sight into the fog.

The lifesaving station at Vermilion Point, eight miles to the west, also sighted the apparition. Two days later, the steamer *C.F. Curtis*, with the schooner-barges *Selden E. Marvin* and *Annie M. Peterson*, were lost with all hands off Grand Marais in a terrific gale.

Anna Hoge, the daughter of the Passage Island lightkeeper, recalled hearing stories of such ghost ships from other keepers. The spectral ships always appeared briefly and warned of impending ill-fortune.

The idea of a ghost ship is not just a relic of the past – a figment of the imagination of the old lake masters. In July 1966, a school teacher from Ontonagon, Michigan, was startled by a most incredible sight. Standing alone on the lakeshore at approximately 8 a.m. on a wonderfully bright and clear day, he saw a 19th century two-masted schooner inbound for the harbor. The schooner was about three-quarters of a mile offshore, close enough that the voices of the crew were plainly heard.

Driving to the marina, the teacher asked local boaters where the tall ship was, believing she was a replica vessel. They looked at him like he was crazy. There wasn't any schooner in the harbor, nor had anyone seen one. Returning quickly to the lakeshore, he searched the horizon. Nothing was in sight, although visibility was virtually unlimited! It was gone. The visitor from a bygone age disappeared back into history.[3]

Griffon

The oldest ghost ship on the lakes is the *Griffon*. More than one old "salt" reported her phantom shape gliding through a storm-whipped lake. The fact that the vessel disappeared with all hands and has yet to be found only adds fuel to this earliest of the Great Lakes' "Flying Dutchmen."

The small, single sailed, 45-ton barque, *Griffon* was built in 1679 near Cayuga Creek in Lake Erie at the direction of the famous explorer Rene Cavalier Sieur de La Salle. It was named for a mythical creature with an eagle's head, wings and a lion's body. He intended to use her for combined fur trading and voyages of discovery. On August 7, 1679, on her first trip, she left with 32 men aboard bound for Lake Michigan's Green Bay. There she loaded a rich cargo of furs and, with a crew of six, sailed back for Niagara on September 18. She never reached Niagara nor any other place yet known to man. She and her crew just "went missing."

Various stories have surfaced explaining her disappearance, but none can be proven. Reportedly a party of Native Americans saw her sheltering from a storm in northern Lake Michigan. Warned by the natives to wait out the blow, her impatient and quarrelsome pilot, "Luke the Dane," was said to have laughed at their heathen fears. Without a second thought he sailed off into a still rough lake, never to be seen again.

Over the intervening centuries, many stories regarding her fate have surfaced. One said that the crew mutinied and tried to make off with her valuable fur cargo. Others said that Native Americans boarded her and massacred the crew or that the vessel perished in the storm. The wreck has been reportedly discovered at locations as varied as Russell Island on the tip of Lake Huron's Bruce Peninsula, Meldrum Bay on the northern end of Manitoulin Island and Lake Michigan's Door Peninsula and Beaver Island.

Perhaps the most intriguing claim was that of Manitoulin Island, Lake Huron, in which the lightkeeper declared to have found five or six skeletons in a cave shortly before the turn of the century. One was especially large. The Danish pilot was known to have been a very big man. Old French coins and brass buttons added authenticity to the find. At the time, the importance and relationship to the *Griffon* wasn't realized. When it finally was, all the important artifacts had been lost.

For sometime, however, the keeper kept some of the bones in a burlap sack, including ribs, arm bones, shin bones and pieces of vertebrae. He eagerly displayed them all for interested tourists and it was common for him to even give bones away as souvenirs. The assistant keeper carried one of the skulls on his fishing boat for years until a storm finally rocked it off.

An old fashioned gold watch chain found hanging from a tree led to the discovery of the cave. A matching watch was found alongside one of the skeletons.

Regardless of how she met her end, generations of old sailors periodically reported seeing the *Griffon* "coasting along the north end of Lake Michigan, with all sails set." When they tried to approach the strange apparition, it just disappeared.[4]

Ghost Fleet of Lake Ontario

Seeing a single ghost ship is eerie enough, but seeing an entire fleet is beyond reason. At least as far as reason can be taken in such events.

The facts are comparatively simple. During the War of 1812, the British and Americans struggled for control of the Great Lakes. In early August 1813, Commodore Isaac Chauncey attacked the British at York on Lake Ontario, then successfully withdrew with his fleet to Niagara.

On the morning of August 7, a British fleet under the command of Sir James Yeo arrived off Niagara to challenge the upstart Americans.

Chauncey and his men bravely sallied forth for battle, but the lack of wind kept the combatants from joining for a general action. When dark arrived, both fleets were floating peacefully on a calm lake, well within sight of one another but too far away for any fighting. Canvas hung limp from their yards. Not a breath of wind moved across the silver waters of Lake Ontario. The bloodletting would wait for tomorrow.

During the predawn hours of August 8, while the fleets lay becalmed, a violent squall unexpectedly roared down on them. Two of the American vessels, the 75-foot *Hamilton* and the 60-foot *Scourge*, were knocked over by the blast and sank, with large loss of life. Some estimate that 53 sailors were drowned in the disaster, but the true number will never be known.

Both vessels, drifting barely a quarter-mile apart, were converted merchantmen. The heavy cannon on the topdecks made them very tender and they were no match for the sudden squall. Aboard the ships, the unsuspecting sailors slept uneasily, knowing the horror of the coming battle. Gunners lay between their guns, boxes of shot, canister and grape all within close reach. Cutlasses were at the bulwarks, ready for the order "boarders away" or to repel British ones if necessary.

The terror of the moment when the two vessels sank is best described by a survivor from the *Scourge*, who remembered being asleep on deck when heavy raindrops falling on his face woke him. "I awoke ... in consequence of large drops of rain falling on my face. . . it was so dark I could not see the length of the deck. I ... heard a strange rushing noise to windward as I went towards the forward hatch ... a flash of lightning almost blinded me. The thunder came at the next instant and with it a rushing of winds that fairly smothered the clap."

The man ran for the jibsheet forward but, by the time he reached it, "The water was up to my chest and I knew the schooner must soon go over. All this occupied less than a minute ... The schooner was filled with the shrieks and cries of the men to leeward, who were lying jammed under the guns, shot-boxes, shot and other heavy things that had gone down as the vessel fell over. ... It rained as if the flood-gates of heaven were opened and it lightninged awfully."[5]

The wrecks of the two warships remained essentially forgotten until 1975, when a Canadian dive team discovered them. Both are wonderfully intact, resting quietly 290 feet below the surface. Their physical rest may be undisturbed, but there are stories of other ... things.

The tale is told that occasionally, when the fog was thick and cold, old sailors saw the two lost vessels again. Described as square rigged and under full sail, their gun ports yawned open and a dull glow radiating from deep within the hulls, the dim yellowish light from lanterns hung in the rigging showed small groups of men standing quietly about the decks. Without warning the phantom ships were seen to shake furiously, as if struck again by the violent squall of so long ago. Quickly they dipped their sides under and dove for the bottom, leaving only the babble and shrieks of drowning sailors. As suddenly as they came, they were gone. The sailing spectres had disappeared.

Sighting the ghost ships was given different interpretations. All were taken as an ill-omen, but one version held that if they crossed your wake, one of your crew would die. As late as 1942, several crewmen on the steamer *Cayuga* claimed to have seen them cut the wake of their ship just before sunset. An old steward repeated the old superstition to the surprised men. By morning he was dead![6]

The name *Hamilton* was not an especially lucky one on the lakes. Four other vessels with the same name became wrecks. Perhaps it was the first that set the fates in motion.[7]

South America

A less well-known ghost ship is that of the 100-ton, two-masted schooner *South America*. On October 15, 1843, she disappeared on Lake Erie while bound from Buffalo to Toledo with salt. She simply "went missing," sailing away without explanation. Reportedly, during a foggy night the schooner, still under sail and with her crew of six, was sighted by another schooner four years later. The sailors who saw the reincarnated *South America* had no doubt of what passed in front of their eyes. She had become one of the spiritual rovers of the lakes, doomed to sail the sweetwater seas for all time.[8]

Alpena

Some people believe that ghosts can be the result of actions unfinished, that the spirit is trying to complete the job interrupted by death. If so, the strange sightings of the old side-wheeler *Alpena* can be, to a fashion at least, explained.

The 197-foot, 653-ton *Alpena* was built in 1867 at Marine City, Michigan, by Thomas Arnold. Owned at the time of loss by the Goodrich Steamship Company, she had recently been rebuilt and was considered in prime condition. Her 24-foot diameter paddlewheels were driven by a massive single-cylinder vertical-beam engine with a long 11-foot stroke. The huge walking beam was visible amidships just aft of the stack. Although she served a variety of ports, she usually ran the Muskegon-Grand Haven-Chicago route. Her captain was Nelson W. Napier, an experienced and well-respected mariner. He was considered the best captain in the fleet and was highly popular with passengers and

With a massive "walking beam" just aft of the stack, the Alpena *was a classic side-wheel steamer and has gone on to become a spectre ship.*
K.E. THRO COLLECTION

shippers. The lakes ran deep in his blood. Two of his uncles were also masters on the sweetwater seas.

At 10 p.m., October 15, 1880, the *Alpena* steamed proudly out onto a calm Lake Michigan. Behind her the lights of Grand Haven winked in the dark. Ahead was Chicago. Indian summer weather, including temperatures in the 60 to 70 degree range, promised a quick and comfortable passage. Three hours later, the *Alpena* passed close enough to her fleet-mate, the *Muskegon,* to exchange whistle signals. The excellent weather continued and both vessels continued on their way; the *Muskegon* to the east shore and the *Alpena* to another world.

At 3 a.m., all hell broke loose! The temperatures had plummeted to 33 degrees. The wind screamed down from the north with the fury of a thousand shrieking banshees. Mountainous seas smashed into the staunch vessel, each wave sending a shudder through the wooden hull. It is assumed that Captain Napier kept trying to fight his way through to Chicago. He didn't make it. What really happened to the *Alpena* isn't known. The wreck has never been located. It is conjectured that she was knocked over on her beam ends, floated for a while and then sank to the bottom of the lake. The fierceness of the storm, which later became known as the "*Alpena* Storm," was devastating. Approximately 94 vessels were damaged or wrecked and at least 118 people perished. An estimated 70 to 80 souls went down with the *Alpena*. Passenger lists were unreliable and the true number will never be known.

Although the hull and machinery rests somewhere on the floor of the lake, old-time sailors claim that the *Alpena* is still trying to finish her trip. In sailor hangouts on both sides of the lake, in engine rooms, forecastles and pilothouses, men tell tales of still seeing the *Alpena*. On foggy days, her dim outline has been seen plowing through the waves in a hopeless effort to reach the windy city. Dead men manned her pilothouse and fed her boiler fires. Ghostly passengers played cards in the salon and looked mournfully for the glimmer of lights of Chicago. If the men listened carefully, the noise of her rocking beam engine could just be heard above the waves.[9]

Jamestown

A Great Lakes "Flying Dutchman" story involved the lumber schooner *Jamestown*. Whether true or false is, of course, open to question, but it is nonetheless a great story. Those that might doubt the truth of the tale should realize that there was a schooner *Three Brothers*, a 349-tonner built in Black River, Ohio, in 1873, and there were also several vessels sailing under the name *Flying Cloud*. The following is from the April 17, 1886, issue of the Ishpeming (Michigan) *Iron Agitator*.

"I'm telling you that the Great Lakes have their mysteries as well as the seas," said the captain of the schooner *Three Brothers*, as he laid down the paper he had been perusing for the last half hour. "Boy and man, I've sailed the lakes for the last 25 years and I've met with some things that have staggered me. Perhaps the strangest of all was the loss of the crew of the *Jamestown*.

"This affair took place in 1862, during the excitement and hurly burly of war, and the circumstance was speedily forgotten under the press of other matters. At that time, I was in a wheat carrier called the *Flying Cloud* hailing from Chicago. The *Jamestown* belonged somewhere on the Ohio shore of Lake Erie – at Painesville, I think. She was in the lumber trade, making her runs between Saginaw and Toledo and Saginaw and Sandusky. On the night of the 21st of August in the year named, as we were abreast of Alpena on Lake Michigan, the wind died but we scarcely had steerage way and the lake was almost as smooth as a mill pond. It was a warm, starlit night and the only sail in sight when night shut down was a propeller far to the east of us, evidently bound for Georgian Bay. What little wind there was, and what we had for several hours, was directly aft or from the north, and any vessel beating up against it could not have made a mile an hour. Remember, now, I have told you that at dusk no vessel was in sight to the south of us.

"About 10 o'clock, with the wind so light that our booms were swinging inboard when the schooner lifted now and then on a long swell and when everybody aboard except the mate, lookout and a man at the wheel had turned in, the voice of the lookout was heard shouting, 'Port! Port! There's a schooner dead ahead of us! Over with her, heave!'

"The man at the wheel pulled her over and her head went around slowly and next moment we rubbed alongside of a craft so close that any of us could have jumped aboard of her. I was on deck as she came abreast of us and I ran to the port side, followed there by three or four of the crew and called out to know what she was doing without a light in the rigging. She hadn't even a light in her binnacle and all aboard was dark and silent, with never a man showing his face. She had all sail set and as true as I sit here she was sailing dead in the wind's eye! She passed us slowly and majestically and though we hailed again and again not a human being showed himself. She hadn't passed us more than two lengths before her head fell off to the northeast and she seemed to lose her way. I know we weren't making a mile an hour and so you may reason that what sailing was done was performed by the strange craft and that dead to windward.

"Well sir, as she lay to after passing us, the mate comes running up and sings out that everybody aboard of her must be asleep or dead and it seemed the proper thing to drop the yawl into the water and board her. Before doing so, however, we hailed her several times at the top of our voices without getting an answer. I took the boat and two men and pulled over to her. She was in ballast, with nary a rope trailing overboard and I had to get up by the chains. I took a lantern with me and one of the sailors climbed over the bows with me while the other held the yawl fast. We found everything as shipshape as you please, every rope coiled down and every halyard made fast in sailor fashion. There wasn't a sign of a struggle on deck and no more could you discover any evidence that the crew had left in a hurry. The yawl was missing, but the curious thing about it was the tackles had been hauled up as if by somebody on board. This wouldn't have been the case, you know, if the boat had been lowered in a hurry and brought alongside.

"We made a dive into the forecastle but found no one. The men's bags were there and nothing had been taken. We visited the cabin, but with the same result. Clothing hung on the hooks and everything looked as if captain and mate had just stepped on deck. We examined the pantry, but there were no signs that food had been taken away. Here was a vessel on a calm sea with every sail set and nobody aboard and I found myself growing chicken-hearted as we looked her over. Had she sprung a leak? I don't believe it, because she had the buoyancy of a dry vessel, but we pulled off a hatch and descended. She was as dry as a bone.

"I had recognized the craft long before as the *Jamestown* and knew her captain to be a man named Charles Day. She carried six men before the mast and there was captain, mate and cook to make the supplement nine. When we had hunted from top to bottom without finding a soul aboard, I just felt my hair trying to stand up and a cold chill climbing up my spine. The man with me was completely unnerved and I had to cuss good and stout to keep him from running away.

Here was a big chance for salvage, as you can see, and I called the other man aboard and we took in all sail. We then got her hawser over the bows, pulled her head around and took it aboard of the *Flying Cloud*. With any sort of decent weather, we had a good show of getting her into Tawas or Port Austin. When it came to putting a man at her wheel, not any of my crew would go, no matter what promised. I had therefore decided to go myself in case a breeze sprang up, when what should come booming down upon us but a white squall. It caught us in a box and we escaped by the skin of our teeth. When we got time to draw breath and look around the *Jamestown* had disappeared, the hawser having snapped, and she was not seen again by mortal eyes.

"I reported the case, of course, and it was unknown all around the lakes, but I'm telling you, sir, that the schooner not only passed out of sight forever, but neither her nor a man of her crew has been heard from to this day. They were looked for by tugs and other craft and the shores were watched for months, but all in vain."[10]

Chicora

Occasionally, crew members on the Lake Michigan car ferries reportedly sighted the ghostly image of the long lost steamer *Chicora*. Each time the ghost ship was picked up a few miles off the bow, only to quickly disappear – although the image lasted long enough for the men to point it out to each other. Afterwards, the crews were always ready for a "hell of a blow."[11]

The *Chicora* was built in 1892 for the Graham and Morton Transportation Company. The wooden steamer was 217-feet long and 1,122 gross tons. Her 1,300-horsepower engine powered her along at a fast 17 mph. Designed especially to run passengers and freight between Milwaukee, Wisconsin, and St. Joseph, Michigan, she was well fitted out with excellent accommodations and public rooms. Ornately decorated with heavy drapes and rich wood paneling, she was very popular with the traveling public. Commercial shippers also found her dependable and fast and she was consequently given considerable business. By any measure, she was a well found vessel, with many years of life built in her.

A famous *Chicora* sighting occurred in 1926. A ship was sailing across northern Lake Michigan in a gale and snowstorm when the crew in the pilothouse observed a wooden steamer blowing distress blasts dead ahead.

The captain first swung clear of the derelict, then turned back to render aid. In the thick snow, he lost sight of the mystery ship and failed to relocate it. When he reported the details of the incident to the Coast Guard at the Straits of Mackinac, the men in the station looked at him queerly. The description matched no vessel that regularly sailed the straits route. None of the men had ever seen a boat like the captain described.

Finally, one old veteran chief said, "Maybe boys, just maybe. I don't see how, but what the hell? Follow me, Captain, please."

He led the way down a hallway and into another room, where he pointed at a faded picture on the wall. "Is this the ship you saw, Captain?"

The captain looked closely at the old picture and said, "Yep, that's the boat. No doubt about that."

The chief said, "Captain, I don't know how to say this so it doesn't make both of us out to be damned fools, but this here is the *Chicora*, lost in 1895 in the same area you saw your ship. You're the first man I've ever met who has seen her, but I've heard of others. Are you sure you want to make this official or do you want to just drop it?"

The captain looked hard at the chief, then said, "Chief, I know what I saw."

Reportedly, the captain came close to losing his sailing ticket – thought to be crazy or a drunk.

In the fall of 1894, the *Chicora* was laid up for the winter in St. Joseph. Typically, traffic lessened during the winter and the big steamer wasn't needed. But the harvest that year was abundant and a surplus of flour in Milwaukee needed transportation to the railhead at St. Joseph. To meet this demand, the steamer came out of lay-up and, with a 23-man scratch crew, ran over to Milwaukee. She was commanded by 42-year-old Edward G. Stines, her regular master and a 25-year veteran of the lakes. William J. Russell of Benton Harbor, the normal second mate, was too ill to make the trip. His place was taken by Bennie Stines, the captain's son.[12] Captain Stines was sick the morning they sailed from Milwaukee. Earlier he had consulted a physician who advised him not to make the journey. Captain Stines was inclined to agree with him, but inexplicably at the last moment he changed his mind. He decided he had to take his boat and crew on the final trip of the season.

Insurance was unavailable because of the lateness of the season, so the *Chicora* ran without it. The high freight rates would cover the risk. The *Chicora* was especially built for running in the ice. Although sailing during midwinter was always risky, little real apprehension was felt.[13]

In the predawn darkness of Monday, January 21, 1895, the *Chicora* steamed out of Milwaukee bound for St. Joseph. Deep in her hold were 40 carloads of barreled flour. Shortly after leaving, a powerful storm swept down, whipping the lake into a frothing sea of demented fury. Torrents of rain lashed the *Chicora*, followed by thick snow squalls. The wind shrieked 60 to 70 mph, piling the lake into 20-foot-plus waves. Between morning and night the temperature fell 40 degrees! For two full days the storm blew unabated.

When the *Chicora* didn't reach St. Joseph as expected, little concern was initially felt. Local marine men thought that she probably just returned to Milwaukee or sheltered in another port. But the *Chicora* wasn't anywhere, at least not in any port on Lake Michigan.

People refused to believe that the *Chicora* was gone. She was reported to be in different locations, sheltering behind a nameless island, disabled and adrift north of somewhere else. Was it all wishful thinking or did people really see the ship?

The most spectacular sighting was off Chicago on Sunday, February 3. The Graham and Morton Company received a telegram stating that the hull of the *Chicora* was floating in the ice seven miles out in the lake and that a signal from the ship indicated nine people were still alive. The name could clearly be read with field glasses.

Tugs promptly went out to the rescue, forcing their way through ice floes. When they got to where they thought the wreck was, it was gone. Yet others on shore claimed they could still see it. Some reported that people were aboard waving their hats. The observers counted between 15 and 19 survivors.

One tug, the *Protection*, sighted a dark form off Hyde Park. The captain thought it could be the hull, with men moving on it. When he reached it, he saw it was only an iceberg covered with sea gulls and ducks. The mystery of what the Chicagoans were seeing was never solved. Some said the *Protection*'s captain was right – nothing but ice and birds. Others were just as adamant in claiming it was, indeed, the missing steamer.

Wreckage was first discovered on the beach near Grand Haven, 35 miles north of St. Joseph. Consisting of hull sections and part of the upper bulwarks, it was jammed in the ice about a mile offshore. Later searches in the same area found furniture, deck railing, curtains, hull planking, barreled flour and both spars. The beaches were carefully swept by 200 searchers, while the steamers *City of Ludington*, *Petoskey*, *Nyack* and tug *Crosby* cruised the offshore waters. Despite their diligence, the searchers didn't locate a single body. There was a story, however, that years later a cloth cap with a G&M on it was found on the beach, with a skeleton hand still grasping it.[14]

It is worth repeating the story of the *Chicora* and the duck. Joseph F. Pearl, a local St. Joseph druggist and a friend of James R. Clark, the temporary clerk, was mentioned in a *Milwaukee Journal* story of January 24, 1895. "Joseph Pearl took with him on the trip to Milwaukee a gun, with which he shot a duck that was in the act of alighting on the boat in midlake. The appearance of the duck in such a place and the fact that it had been shot awakened a superstitious dread that spread among the crew. The incident preyed upon the captain's mind and he constantly referred to it as an evil omen while the *Chicora* was loading for the return trip."[15]

There were also two reported "bottle" messages from the *Chicora*, both discovered in the spring of 1895. The first stated, "All is lost. Could see land if not snowed and blowed. Engine give out, drifting to shore in ice. Captain and clerk are swept off. We have a hard time of it. 10:15 o'clock." The second note was found sealed in a glass preserving jar. "*Chicora* engines broke. Drifted into trough of sea. We have lost all hope. She has gone to pieces. Good-bye, McClure, Engineer."

What actually happened to the *Chicora* is unknown. The wreck remains one of Lake Michigan's fleet of the missing, only to reappear as a "ghost ship" of the lakes; at least according to the old time carferry sailors.

Hudson

The following is less a tale than a recollection of an old fisherman. Ghost stories, especially those that purport to be real, are best told to those who believe in such things, not to skeptics. "Solid" citizens don't go around telling such stories, especially if they want to retain their reputation as sober, upright members of the community. But sometimes there are things that people just have to "get off their chest." This is such a case.

As with similar stories, some of the facts, at least to those points that would identify the person who experienced the incident, are missing. That doesn't necessarily mean the tale is false – rather it only speaks to the unwillingness to be laughed at. In many ways, the story rings true with other, more verifiable stories.

During midmorning on September 16, in the late 1940s, a lone fish tug was rounding Michigan's Keweenaw Point in Lake Superior, bound

The spectre of the steamer Hudson, *lost September 16, 1901, was reportedly boarded in the late 1940s by a Keweenaw fisherman.*
MARINE HISTORICAL COLLECTION, MILWAUKEE PUBLIC LIBRARY

westerly. The tug was running a couple of miles offshore and moving along well in a big dead swell from the southwest. Visibility was extremely poor, patchy pea soup fog interspersed with just plain miserable mist. Running on time and bearing through the gray vapor, the tug would soon be at her nets. The two men aboard were taking a chance, trying to get to the nets and back before an expected northwester struck. Money was at stake, both in fish and damage to the gear. Under those circumstances, taking a chance was well worth it.

Ahead, the fog unexpectedly became thicker and blacker. Without warning it wasn't fog anymore, but the tall sides of a vessel directly off the bow. Throwing the wheel hard over, the captain barely swung the tug clear of the stranger. The other vessel wasn't moving, but drifting dead with the swell. The tug's skipper could also see that she sat low in the water, down a bit by the stern and listing well to port. A strange brown patina covered the steel hull and large brown rust rivulets ran everywhere. She looked a total wreck.

Chopping his throttle back, the tug's captain slowly circled the big vessel. There wasn't any doubt that she was an old one. He made her to be about 300 feet long and she had the smallest pilothouse he had ever seen on a freighter. The twin stacks were unusual, too. One of them was also knocked over and the other looked none too steady. A boat that old had no business still sailing in this day and age, regardless of how good the freights were. No wonder she was adrift off the Keweenaw. Probably broke a cylinder or maybe even a propeller shaft. She must be leaking like a sieve with all the rusted-out plates he could see on her high side bilge. With her engine dead she couldn't even pump herself out. How was she even staying afloat?

He hailed the steamer several times, but got no response. Utterly perplexed by the lack of a reply, the tug's captain decided to go aboard the strange steamer. Something was very wrong. After carefully working his way alongside the rust-streaked hull, he jumped from the tug's roof and hauled himself over the rail. The tug, with the mate at the wheel, lay about 20 yards off, just at the edge of visibility. The gray fog held both vessels in their own surreal world.

The tug's skipper noticed the steamer's decks, like her sides, were covered with a slimy brown coating. Great rust bubbles were everywhere. The steamer's mate certainly wasn't doing his job to let her get this bad. It almost looked as if the boat had recently been on the bottom. The hatches were also different – all wood, just like in the old days when his dad sailed the boats for a few years. Several were broken and others were even missing. This old bucket was really a disaster. Looking toward the stern, the tug man saw a shadowy figure in dripping oilskins looking directly at him. When the tug man yelled, "What the hell's going on? Why didn't you answer my hail?" the sailor responded by silently pointing to the bow.

As he walked forward, a shudder of cold apprehension chilled him. He again had the unshakable feeling that something was wrong here, very wrong. When he glanced back at his tug for reassurance, he saw it wasn't there. The drifting fog had swallowed it.

After two dozen steps he saw the rear of the pilothouse crystallize out of the grayness. The white paint was peeling off the wood and several windows were broken out. A tattered canvas dodger hung loosely from the railing. He thought, "Well, at least I'll get some answers here."

Climbing the companionway, he paused for a second at the closed pilothouse door. While he was afraid of what he would discover, he was also a fisherman and didn't earn a living by being scared of his shadow.

Opening the door, he found two men, or what once were men, staring straight at him. One, the farthest away, held the wheel fast in his bony hands. The other, evidently the captain judging from his short peaked cap, stood closest to him. To the tug man, both looked like death warmed over. Thin and gaunt in stature, their ragged clothes hung loose over emaciated limbs. Their faces were white and chalky with leathery skin drawn tight against their skulls. The eyes were the worst of all. They were lifeless, black as coal and without even a single spark of animation.

Thinking, "What the hell, I've gone this far," he asked the captain, "What's going on? You are drifting bang in the middle of the shipping lane in a fog thicker than my mother's bean soup, without even a whistle blowing! You look in bad shape, all wrecked up and all. Is there anything I can do?"

Speaking slowly and with a voice resonating deep and cold, the steamer's captain replied, "We are beyond help – have been for many a year. And indeed we are a wreck. Don't you know what ship this is?"

Backing away slightly, the tug man said, "Your name was covered by rust. I couldn't make it out when I circled you."

In the same tired voice the master replied, "Why this is the *Hudson*, lost September 16, 1901, in this very spot. Twenty-four men went to the bottom with her. It's cursed we are, damned by the devil himself. Every year we must come up, only to be dragged back down again. We relive our terror for all eternity. Haven't you heard the tales – of ghost ships and spirit sailors and haunted spots on the lakes? Well it's true. We are the proof. If you know what's good for you, you will get off this damned ship now, this very instant. Our time is almost done."

The tug man never looked back. He bolted out the door and ran as fast as his legs could carry him – flying down the companionway to the weather deck and on to the place where he first climbed aboard. His tug was just yards away, its old Kahlenberg diesel engine rumbling roughly in the thick air. Not waiting for it to pull alongside, he dove off the deck and, after a few strong strokes, was alongside. With a heave, he went up through the stern barn doors and, safe aboard, yelled, "Get her out of here, now."

The mate quickly pulled the throttle back and the tug surged off into the fog. Looking at the captain, the mate asked, "Now what was that all about?"

Through clattering teeth, the captain just muttered, "You wouldn't believe me and I ain't going to tell you anyway. Steady her up north northeast. I've got a feeling this isn't a healthy place to be."

The mate asked, "What about our nets?"

"To hell with them," the captain said. Looking back where the steamer had been he saw nothing, not even a darker patch in the fog. It was gone.

Within minutes, the lake was churned into a savage gale. Waves assaulted the tug from every side in a confused melee of water. The glass in the portside pilothouse window blew out when a vicious wave smashed into it. Another wave struck the forward door, ripping out the center lock and flooding into the well. Hammer and nails closed the hole and saved the tug from a watery grave. Desperately the tug struggled on, rolling and plunging in the steep seas until she finally slid safely between the rock piers at Eagle Harbor. It had been a very near thing and it was a story that wouldn't be told for a very long time. Many vessels simply went missing on the big lake. Some losses were explained, but others defied logic. Which category would the tug have fit into?[16]

Hunter Savidge

One of the strangest of the Great Lakes ghost ships was the *Hunter Savidge*. The 117-foot, gaff-rigged, two-masted schooner was typical of the hundreds of small vessels that plied the lakes when sail was king. It was part of a small fleet of three schooners owned by lumberman John Muellerweiss Jr. When not used in the trade, it paid its keep by carrying whatever freight it could, wherever it could.

The captain of the schooner Hunter Savidge *believed his wife, the owner's wife and daughter were alive in the sunken vessel.* INSTITUTE OF GREAT LAKES RESEARCH, BOWLING GREEN STATE UNIVERSITY

On August 20, 1899, the *Hunter Savidge* was off Point aux Barques, Lake Huron, bound up the lake for Alpena. Aboard with Captain Fred Sharpsteen and his six-man crew was the captain's wife, Rose, the owner's wife, Mary Muellerweiss, and her six-year-old

Captain Fred Sharpsteen and his wife, Rose. AUTHOR'S COLLECTION

daughter, Etta. Mrs. Muellerweiss was not feeling well and it was
hoped that a lake trip would help her regain her health. The captain's
wife went along to provide her company. Having just delivered a cargo
of coal to Sarnia, Ontario, the *Hunter Savidge* was running light. The
little wind that earlier wafted the schooner over Lake Huron's calm
waters had died out completely and she lay becalmed. Her limp canvas
hung lifeless from the yards.

Without warning the schooner was struck squarely by a powerful
white squall. Blasted by the screaming wind, she dug her bow in and
rolled completely over, finally ending up with her bow underwater and
the transom projecting above the waves. Within what seemed like only
seconds, the deadly squall passed, leaving the devastated vessel dying
in its wake. The broken schooner dangled at a 45 degree angle, seemingly ready to plunge for the bottom at any second.

Captain Sharpsteen and four of his startled crew, all on deck when
the squall hit, were tossed into the lake. Finding various pieces of
floating wreckage, they hung on until the steamer *Alex McVittie*, which
witnessed the tragedy from several miles away, rushed to their rescue.
One of the missing men was the captain's 16-year-old son, thought
drowned when he was unable to shed his heavy sea boots.

Also gone were both women and the child. Captain Sharpsteen
believed that they were still below decks, trapped in the stern cabin.
He knew that they could still be alive, breathing desperately in a caught
air bubble.

It had happened at least three times before. Years earlier, the schooner *Experiment* capsized during a squall on a sand bar at St. Joseph, Michigan. Resting hull up, she was firmly anchored in the sand bottom by the stubs of her shattered masts. The following day, curious townspeople climbing over the broken vessel were startled by frantic pounding coming from within the dead hull. Quickly chopping through the bottom planking, they discovered the captain's wife and two children still alive. Their remarkable survival was attributed to an air bubble trapped inside when the schooner went over.

On June 1, 1853, the schooner *G.R. Roberts* was sailing in Lake Michigan about eight miles northwest of Grand Haven, when her crew was surprised to find a schooner floating nearly bottom up. When they climbed aboard to assess the chances of salvage, they were startled to hear desperate cries coming from inside the hull. Cutting through the thick planking, they soon released the captain, Andrew Bergh, and a passenger and part owner, Lukas A. Farnsworth. Both told their sad tale to the *Robert*'s crew of how the schooner departed Michigan City, Lake Michigan, on Sunday, May 29, bound for Grand Haven. At midnight, Captain Bergh left the deck in the charge of two sailors and went below. About two hours later, he woke to a loud noise on deck. He flew out of his berth, running for topside. Just then the schooner went over, topside becoming bottomside! Working his way into the cabin, he found Farnsworth and two crewmen. To keep their heads above black water, the four had to wedge into one of the narrow berths. By Monday, the two sailors could no longer keep their grip and slipped into the water and drowned. Bergh and Farnsworth hung grimly on until rescue two days later.[17]

A third example was the schooner *New Connaut*. When a white squall knocked her over in Lake Erie in the fall of 1883, all of the crew, except an elderly woman passenger, were able to escape in the yawl. The survivors believed that the old woman had been drowned. But five days later, when the schooner was righted and partially pumped out, she walked unharmed out of the cabin. She had survived in an air pocket.

Captain Sharpsteen believed his wife, Mrs. Muellerweiss and Etta were also trapped in his schooner. If he could just get through to them, he could save their lives. Try as he may, however, he was unable to convince the captain of the *McVittie* to stay by the wreck and explore it. The *McVittie*'s master callously told him that all were dead and it was foolish to waste time there. The best he would do was transfer the survivors to the steamer *H.E. Runnels*, which would in turn drop them at Sand Beach on Lake Huron, where the U.S. Life-Saving Service crew could assist. The *McVittie* captain was utterly unwilling to do anything more. After all, he had a schedule to keep.

At Sand Beach, Captain Sharpsteen urgently tried to hire a diver to explore the still floating wreck but, by the time he located one, it was night and the diver refused to make such a dangerous attempt in the dark. He did charter the fish tug *Angler* to take him on a fruitless search for the missing schooner.

Although the lifesaving crews from both Sand Beach and Point aux Barques looked hard for the schooner, they never found her. Local tugs also combed the lake, with equally empty results. All the while, the desperate Captain Sharpsteen continued to hope for a miracle. It wasn't to be. The distraught captain patrolled the shore for months following the disaster, but in vain. The *Hunter Savidge* was gone forever – or was it?

In later years, sailors plowing through the cold, clammy tendrils of a Lake Huron fog claimed to have sighted the ghostly stern of the lost schooner. It was still floating, waiting forlornly for the rescue that never came. One minute it was there, then it was gone, swallowed again by the hungry lake. In about 1987, David Trotter and other members of Undersea Research Associates discovered the wreck of the schooner in deep water. Its location has never been revealed.[18]

Ella Ellenwood

During the dark and brooding nights when the mists roll heavy over Lake Michigan, the ghostly image of the lumber schooner *Ella (or Ellen) Ellenwood* is said to periodically return to the waters just offshore of White Lake, Michigan. The 157-ton, 106-foot schooner was built in East Saginaw in 1870 and home-ported out of White Lake for many years. On October 1, 1901, she ran hard up on Fox Point, just north of Milwaukee, during a roaring gale. The crew safely made shore in the yawl, but savage fall storms battered the schooner to kindling. However, the schooner would not end her association with White Lake quite so easily. In a strange effort to finish her trip, her name board was discovered the following spring, floating in the White Lake Channel, nearly 100 miles away across Lake Michigan. She had come home at last!

The old schooner is remembered locally to this day. A giant replica of her is mounted on top of the "world's largest weather vane" at the White Lake causeway.[19]

Bannockburn

The classic Lake Superior ghost ship story is that of the 245-foot, 1,620-ton Canadian steel steamer *Bannockburn*. Built in 1893 in Middlesborough, Scotland, she was of a class known as canallers, designed to work within the size limitations of the Welland Canal. Rated A-1 by Lloyd's of London Insurance, she was owned by the Montreal

Transportation Company of Quebec. Her captain was George Woods. His brother, John, commanded *Rosemount*, *Bannockburn*'s sister ship.

On November 20, 1902, the *Bannockburn* departed Port Arthur, Ontario, bound for Midland, Ontario, on Lake Huron, with a cargo of 85,000 bushels of wheat. The following afternoon, she was sighted on Lake Superior by the upbound steamer *Algonquin* southeast of Passage Island and northeast of Keweenaw Point. The weather was hazy and the

The steamer Bannockburn *sailed from Port Arthur, Ontario, into myth on November 20, 1902. MARINE HISTORICAL COLLECTION, MILWAUKEE PUBLIC LIBRARY*

Bannockburn was bucking a good headwind but, to the crew of the *Algonquin*, all appeared normal. Later, when the *Bannockburn* disappeared, Captain James McMaugh of the *Algonquin* reported that his sighting was a short one. One minute, she was in plain view. After turning away for several minutes, he looked back again, but she was gone, vanished from sight. Did she sink while the captain glanced away, or just fade into the gray mist? The captain later thought that a boiler explosion could have caused such a rapid sinking, but he had heard nothing. Surely a blast potent enough to sink the strong steel steamer in minutes would have been heard by the *Algonquin*. Later that night, a storm rolled across Lake Superior. It wasn't the worst of storms, but it certainly was a "banger." Unlikely as it seemed, could it have sunk the *Bannockburn*?

When the steamer failed to reach Sault Ste. Marie, a massive search was launched. Three tugs combed the lake, looking for any sign of the missing vessel. Was she aground on a desolate coast or disabled but still adrift on the lake? Stories circulated that she was sighted ashore near Michipicoten Island and other north shore locations. Investigations proved them all false. By this time, she was long on the bottom. When the steamer *John D. Rockefeller* reported a small wreckage field off Stannard Rock, the mystery was at least partially solved. A single battered life jacket was later found on the beach at Grand Marais, Michigan, by a patrolling surfman. A full search by the lifesavers, including the inshore waters, revealed nothing more.

No acceptable explanation for her loss has ever been offered. Some thought it was the result of storm stress, others that she suffered a boiler explosion during McMaugh's gap in observation. Another mariner suggested that she might have been dropping hull plates all season and that during the storm her bottom simply fell out. There was also the chance that she gutted herself on the then uncharted Superior Shoal and plunged to the bottom in deep water. Regardless of the true cause, precious little wreckage was ever found.[20]

One especially intriguing wreckage story was the legendary "*Bannockburn* oar." The tale goes that 18 months after the loss, a single oar, carefully wrapped in a worn tarpaulin, was found by a grizzled old trapper on the desolate Michigan shore. The word *Bannockburn* was scraped crudely into the wooden shaft. Some writers embellished the tale further by claiming that, to be sure the words were visible, each letter was filled with a dying sailor's blood.[21]

As soon as a year afterward, Lake Superior sailors reported seeing this Flying Dutchman of Lake Superior steaming past Caribou Island, plowing on for the Soo to complete her unfinished voyage. Others said that she appeared as a "ghostly apparition of ice, scudding through the gloom."[22] Another writer stated that "sometimes at night when the chill north wind sweeps across the swollen bosom of Lake Superior and the stinging ice devils fill the air, the lookout on some lonely point calls loudly to his companions and points to where he imagines the *Bannockburn*, all white with ice and ghostly in the darkness, slipping through the black mystery of the lake."[23]

The *Bannockburn*'s legend doubtless grew when James Oliver Curwood, a popular writer from the turn of the century, used the vessel in several of his fictional stories. This further served to confuse fact and fiction.[24]

Regardless of the legend, the fact remains that *Bannockburn* and her crew of 22 went missing on Lake Superior. To this day, she has never been found nor has the cause of loss been determined. The *Bannockburn* has truly joined the fleet of the lost.

The French Yawl

One summer night in 1913, Canadian artist and historian Rowley W. Murphy was sailing a small boat into Toronto Harbour, when he chanced on a most remarkable sight. He was slicing along on a port tack in his sailboat in the misty moonlight and saw a small sail craft up ahead. As he gained on it, he noticed that the sail looked very much out of date. It used a sprit-sail – not the more popular gaff-rig or marconi. The boat itself was also very old, with a transom stern higher than typical, even for a Great Lakes schooner yawl. Propelled by a steady breeze, he continued to gain on the strange old boat.

From a distance of 50 feet, he saw three men in the boat. One, near the mast, looked "rather shapeless" and wore clothing appearing too large for him. The man seated midships had high-cut dark trousers, a torn white shirt with large sleeves and a dirty bandage around his head. The man standing in the stern had a battered tri-cornered hat and an old coat much in the style of a navy jacket. All looked grim. None said a word. They just continued to stare ahead.

Looking closer at the unusual craft, Murphy noticed that the transom was missing and water was "fully running in and out of her hold." He was so close, the feeble shine from his port running light reflected from the blank faces of the three occupants. Mouth agape, he passed the bizarre boat, never saying a word. When he looked again, it was gone. After due consideration, Murphy could only conclude that he had seen the ghost of a small French boat from an era long past.

Toronto Harbour is rich in history. Explorers, voyagers, French and British crossed paths there. Pitched battles were also fought for king and country. Battle cries had echoed loudly over the water. Many vessels met their death in the depths offshore and shoals closer in. Whatever Murphy saw that misty moonlit night can never be proven, but there are things we do not understand. This was one.[25]

Reliance

A strange "ghost ship" sighting provided Captain John McPherson with warning of his own demise. In August 1922, Captain McPherson, the superintendent of the Booth Fisheries, was a passenger on the 124-foot tug *Reliance* steaming through the fog off Cape Gargantua in eastern Lake Superior. Suddenly he and part of the crew sighted the indistinct image of a ghost ship dead ahead. Although unable to definitely identify her, they thought initially that it was the tug *Lambton*, lost with all hands the previous April. The *Lambton* had disappeared with 22 men during a fierce blow, while delivering Canadian lightkeepers to their posts.

The ghost ship was also sighted from shore. Mrs. Charles Miron, the wife of the Gargantua Harbour lightkeeper, observed the vessel through powerful binoculars and identified it as the tug *Lambton*. Mr.

Although lost the previous April, the Lambton *(left above) was sighted by Captain John McPherson in August 1922, warning him of impending death.*
AUTHOR'S COLLECTION

and Mrs. Charles Graham, also ashore, confirmed Mrs. Miron's sighting. McPherson reportedly sighted yet another ghost ship in October. Since there were no other witnesses, he was reluctant to discuss any details. With both bad omens on his mind, he expressed great concern to his wife about the future.

On December 15, 1922, the *Reliance* was heading down to the Sault, after picking up 20 lumberjacks from camps along the Canadian north shore. Also on board was the tug's captain and a crew of 13, a company forester and Captain McPherson. Before leaving on the trip, McPherson told Mrs. Miron, "I hate to make this trip, but something is pulling me and I must go." Overtaken by a roaring north storm, the tug blew onto Lizard Island, 70 miles northwest of the Soo. Subzero temperatures placed the survivors in dire circumstances. Without food or shelter, it seemed certain that they would freeze to death. After a great effort, the tug's captain and six crewmen managed to get a lifeboat safely through the breakers to the mainland beach. Following a wretched hike, the bedraggled survivors eventually reached a railroad station where they telegraphed for help. The tugs *Favorite* and *Gray* responded to the plea and rescued the men left at the wreck, except Captain McPherson and two others. Believing that the tug's captain had perished before being able to get help, McPherson and two men launched the remaining boat hoping to succeed in their stead. They didn't make it. The boat was later found wrecked on the shore without a sign of any of the three men. Whether McPherson and his men drowned in the lake or reached shore only to perish in the piercing cold was never known. Captain McPherson's premonition of disaster had come true.[26]

| The tug Reliance *with a log raft in happier circumstances.*

Rum Runners

During the prohibition era, a vessel popularly known as the "gray ghost" was sighted in several areas – notably the Detroit River, off the Colchester Light, Monroe, Michigan, Port Stanley, Ontario, and Ashtabula, Ohio. The ghost vessel was supposed to be that of a fast Cleveland rum runner lost in a storm. Legend claims that it had put out from Canada with a full load of illicit booze and never made safe port. In later years, it was asserted that during stormy weather the cruiser was seen to leap from wave crest to wave crest in a hopeless effort to complete the unfinished trip. Among other periodic sightings, in May 1932 the crew of the freighter *Fellowcraft* bound from Cleveland to Detroit reported seeing her off the Colchester Light.[27]

To protect America from such interlopers as the "gray ghost," a ragtag navy made up of the U.S. Coast Guard, U.S. Customs, U.S. Immigration, U.S. Border Patrol and other agencies actively patrolled the Great Lakes and connecting waters. Because of their proximity to Canada, where booze was legal, the Great Lakes were the scene of an especially heavy trade. Cities like Port Huron, Sault Ste. Marie and Detroit were major crossing points. The Detroit River, Lake St. Clair and the St. Clair River became an ineffectual barrier.

In the beginning, the rum runners relied on the greater speed of their boats to outrun the forces of the law. As the U.S. blockade tightened, the bootleggers placed greater stress on subterfuge, as well as running under cover of storm and night. One little known technique for smuggling booze involved ore freighters. As a freighter loaded ore at an upper lakes dock, truck loads of local moonshine or Canadian booze were taken aboard, hidden below decks and transported to the lower lakes. There it was unloaded and distributed to the gin mills for sale. Enforcement efforts were directed at what was coming across the border, not domestic trade, thus the ore carriers came in the "back door."

Old schooners were also used for bootlegging, especially on lakes Erie and Ontario. A case in point is the small, black-hulled schooner nabbed in an out-of-the-way part of Oswego Harbor. When an old-timer saw a gang of men hurriedly unloading sacks of beer from the schooner's hold into three trucks, he ran for the cops. After the bootleggers saw the local constabulary bearing down on them in a rush, they ran for the hills, disappearing quickly into the countryside. The trucks dashed off in a scatter of flying gravel. In the confusion of "arresting" the vessel, the police were distracted and a crowd of spectators made off with much of the loose contraband. Men, women and children all helped "clean up" the site. Good police work, however, resulted in locating the beer-laden trucks hidden in an old barn at the end of a quiet country lane. Later that night the thirsty local citizens managed to liberate two-thirds of the truck's cargo, leaving enough for the police to make an arrest, but not so much as to waste evidence!

The rum runners often risked their lives to slake America's thirst. In at least one instance, that of the "gray ghost" of Lake Erie, one of them is still trying to complete its trip.[28]

Edmund Fitzgerald

"Look cap, there it is again! What the hell is it?"

The master stared hard through the pilothouse window into the patchy gray fog. "Damn it, Bill, I don't know – I just don't know. I damn well don't believe it, but just for a second … Anything on the scope?"

"Cap, I thought I saw a weak return, but it's gone now."

"Well, Bill, I guess we just put it down to another one of those things on the lakes we can't explain. I do know this, though. I ain't saying anything to anybody. I didn't see nothin'!"

With that final comment, both master and mate returned to their duties. The big freighter, now 15 miles or so northwest of Lake Superior's Whitefish Point, plowed on for the Soo.

What the unidentified master and mate saw, or perhaps more

The Edmund Fitzgerald *sank on November 10, 1975, but sailed on into history and the legends of the lakes.* AUTHOR'S COLLECTION

properly thought they saw, was the ghost of the *Edmund Fitzgerald*. Although for obvious reasons unwilling to come forward officially, men on several vessels have had the unnerving experience of seeing the most dramatic of modern day shipwrecks return from the grave.

Several years ago, I was atop the Point Iroquois light tower overlooking Lake Superior's lower Whitefish Bay. The weather was calm and a thin mist covered the lake. I could just make out a Columbia boat working its way down, appearing and disappearing as it slid silently through the wispy gray. If my imagination were more active, I also could believe that it was another ship – one that never made it past the point. It's easy to understand how men can see things – that maybe are not there.

While not to be considered a hoodoo ship, a chain of events can be built around the *Fitzgerald* that can be considered "strange."

When launched on June 7, 1958, it took three solid strikes on her bow by Mrs. Edmund Fitzgerald, wife of the ship's namesake, before the traditional bottle of champagne finally broke. More than one hit is considered unlucky. It was as if the vessel didn't want to begin her career or accept her name.

The launching crew spent much time and effort knocking loose her keel blocks before she could begin her slide into the water. One block was especially difficult. Overall, the reluctant blocks delayed the launch by 36 minutes.

After striking the water in the distinctive Great Lakes sideways launch, the hull didn't stop as intended, but continued across the slip, hitting the far side.

During the ceremonies, one of the bystanders died of an apparent heart attack.

Each of these launching incidents was a bad omen. In the old days, sailors would have labeled her a hoodoo, but in the modern age such beliefs are brushed aside.

The reason the Cousteau research team did such a short dive on the *Fitzgerald* in 1980 was reported in some circles as a result of their being badly shaken by seeing strange lights in the steamer's pilothouse. Common sense told them it was obviously just a reflection of their own lights, but at 530 feet in a dark and foreboding lake, common sense is sparse.

When the ROV in the 1989 expedition reached the *Fitzgerald* stern for the first time, it suffered an inexplicable total power failure. Rapidly hauled back aboard the *Grayling*, technicians examined it with a fine-toothed comb. During an active exploration, such a power failure could result in the loss of the ROV. It was extremely serious. Despite their best efforts, they found no problems. When the crew lowered the now fully functioning unit a second time, it again lost all power as it approached the stern. Again no reason was found. One participant later said it was "almost like the wreck just didn't want us there!"

At least one of the *Fitzgerald*'s crew had a premonition of disaster. He was soon going to celebrate his 25th wedding anniversary and had purchased two new wedding bands as a special gift for his wife. He planned to present them to her at the end of the sailing season, when the *Fitz* went into lay up and he was home every day. But he had a bad feeling about this trip and gave the rings to a friend to hold for him. If anything happened, he didn't want to lose the rings. He just had this terrible feeling!

The U.S. Coast Guard Cutter *Woodrush* had an unusual relationship with *Fitzgerald*. *Woodrush* was one of 38 180-foot buoy tenders

The Coast Guard cutter Woodrush had an enduring series of mysterious
events associated with the sinking of the Edmund Fitzgerald.

built at Duluth as World War II construction. A long veteran of the
lakes, *Woodrush* and *Fitzgerald* doubtless passed often, but it was not
until November 10, 1975, that a direct relationship developed.

When the Coast Guard Rescue and Coordination Center in Cleveland realized that *Fitzgerald* was missing, they dispatched *Woodrush*
from Duluth to the scene of loss. After fighting her way through terrible
seas, *Woodrush* reached *Fitzgerald*'s last position the following day.
The cold, gray Lake Superior waves had already swallowed the big
freighter and crew. Nothing was left for *Woodrush* to do, except
recover what little floating debris they could find.

The following May, *Woodrush* served as the support vessel for the
CURV III survey of the wreck. The lake didn't make the job easy.
After the cutter laid in her three-point moor, a vicious 60-knot storm
swept over the lake. Seas rushed at *Woodrush* from every quarter. The
Woodrush strained so hard at her mooring lines that two of the steel
buoys were pulled far enough under water that they were crushed,
imploding as the result of the extreme pressure. Captain Jimmie
Hobaugh, master of *Woodrush* at the time, thought that the buoys could
have been dragged as deep as 200 feet below. With the *Woodrush*
rocking and rolling violently on the *Fitzgerald* moor, the captain spent
a long night on the cutter's bridge. The next morning, Lake Superior
was flat calm and remained so for the next 11 days. At night the surface
shimmered like glass. Superior is an inexplicable lake.

The video signal from the CURV III fed into the *Woodrush*'s on-
board television. Every man not otherwise employed had the opportunity
to watch through the CURV's unblinking electronic eye. Hobaugh

remembered that when they started, "The ship (*Woodrush*) got silent, even the generators sounded muted. Once we found the ship (*Fitzgerald*), it got very silent." The field of vision was very narrow and "it was as if you were looking through a dark house with a flashlight.

"We were looking for people. We would swim CURV right up to a porthole and as you looked in … you were looking for a face with a body. It was scary. It was like being in a graveyard."

In a terrible coincidence, "Goliath Awaits," a film about a sunken ocean liner with its crew and passengers still aboard and alive after many years on the bottom, had just played on the ship's TV. This added to everyone's nervousness.

The survey work performed by CURV and *Woodrush* provided the critical evidence for the Coast Guard investigation. The hours of videotape and hundreds of still photos provided mute testimony to the strange loss of a good ship and crew.

Fitzgerald's hold on *Woodrush* wasn't over. The next winter, *Woodrush* was assigned to break ice from Duluth to the Soo while escorting several commercial vessels. The small fleet reached the Whitefish Point area before a large pressure ridge of ice finally stopped it. At the time, *Woodrush* was three to four miles from the final *Fitzgerald* position. Since the big Coast Guard ice breaker *Mackinaw* was going to come out the next morning and break them out, they hove to for the night. Then the wind kicked up and the ice began to move, taking the trapped *Woodrush* with it. When the shifting ice stopped the following morning, *Woodrush* had been set nearly directly on top of *Fitzgerald*. *Woodrush* had returned to *Fitzgerald*![29]

Another mysterious event happened just minutes before the Canadian Navy submarine tender *Cormorant* arrived at the *Fitzgerald* site to participate in the 1995 bell recovery. The *Cormorant*'s wardroom bell inexplicably fell off the bulkhead, crashing heavily to the deck. John Creber, the captain of the vessel, said, "It's never fallen before and we've been through 30-foot seas with it!" Was there an omen here, the vessel coming to take the *Fitzgerald*'s bell loses her own? In some strange way, was the *Fitzgerald* reaching out to the *Cormorant*?[30]

The *Fitzgerald* was the second vessel of the name lost on the lakes. On November 14, 1883, the 135-foot, 297-ton schooner *Edmond Fitzgerald* stranded on Lake Erie's Long Point in a storm. Instead of waiting for the local lifesaving crew, the sailors launched their yawl in a desperate attempt to reach shore. The boat overturned in the surf, drowning all seven aboard. The schooner later went to pieces in the heavy seas.[31]

The sailors of today are not like the superstitious "old salts" of

yesteryear. They don't see a ghost ship in every fog bank. But the *Fitzgerald* is different. The *Fitzgerald* has made the remarkable transition from the world of man to being part of the legend of the

The bell in the ward room of the Canadian submarine tender Cormorant *fell from its mount when the ship was recovering the Fitzgerald's bell.*

Great Lakes. So is the idea of her being a ghost ship quite so wild? Is she really any different from the *Bannockburn, Chicora* or *Jamestown*?

Mary Celestes of the Lakes

Like the famous *Mary Celeste* of salt-water fame, whose discovery sailing along between the Azores and Portugal in 1872 without a soul aboard led to the wildest of stories, the lakes also had instances of strangely disappearing crews.

When the schooner *William Sanderson* drifted ashore at Empire, Michigan, Lake Michigan, on November 26, 1874, there wasn't a soul aboard. All the crew had vanished – somewhere! The schooner had left Chicago the week before, bound for Oswego with 19,500 bushels of wheat. Whether the crew was driven off by storm – perhaps the schooner was thrown on her beam ends, forcing the men to leave her – or just panicked taking to the boats, was the hot topic in maritime circles. The answer was unknown, but what is known is that the *William Sanderson* was on the beach without her crew.[32]

The tale is told that around the turn of the century on an early winter day a three-masted schooner left Duluth, only to disappear in the frigid vastness of Lake Superior. Arriving vessels were questioned, but answers were not forthcoming. No one had seen or heard from her. In the middle of the winter, a lone fisherman trekking along the desolate north shore stumbled onto a remarkable sight. High on the beach was a schooner, coated heavily in shimmering, translucent ice. Climbing aboard, he found three of the crew, their lifeless bodies entombed in ice. The rest were gone, their whereabouts unknown.[33]

The 518-ton schooner *Ellen Spry* was another vessel with a disappearing crew. The schooner was found after a November 1886 blow in mid-Lake Michigan without a soul aboard. Several vessels sighted her in this condition before she finally drifted ashore at Point Betsie, Michigan. But where was the crew?[34]

The story of the 361-ton three-masted Canadian schooner *Bavaria* could qualify as another Great Lakes *Mary Celeste*. On May 29, 1889, it was discovered ashore at Great Galloo Island, New York, Lake Ontario, by the steamer *Armenia*. Except for a missing yawl, all seemed to be in order. When the *Armenia* blew her big steam whistle, there was strangely no response from the schooner. Surely someone was aboard. As they slowly approached her, the *Armenia*'s crew concluded that she was anchored and all the crew had gone ashore in the boat. When they boarded her and found an empty boat, they were unable to make sense of the puzzle. Every rope was in place and all sails properly stowed. In the cabin, a canary chirped merrily away in a cage. Loaves of freshly baked bread filled the galley oven. In the master's cabin, the ship's papers were in order and the freight money was still in his desk. It was obvious from the wood shavings in the scuppers that the crew had been working on a new spar on a trestle on the deck. Some water was in the hold, but not enough to be concerned about. There wasn't a sign of the eight-man crew. Neither the Galloo Island lightkeeper or local farmers had seen anything of the missing men. When the dawn broke, the schooner was simply on the beach. How she got there was anyone's guess. The schooner's men were gone as surely as if swallowed by the lake.

The question of the fate of the schooner's crew didn't immediately concern the *Armenia*'s crew. After quickly pumping her out, the steamer returned *Bavaria* to Garden Island, its home port on Lake Ontario.

What is known is that the *Bavaria* had been one of three vessels under tow of the steamer *D.D.Calvin* when a strong gale struck. The other vessels were the tow barge *Valencia* and the schooner *Norway*. All were heavily loaded with lumber. About 15 miles off Point Petre, Ontario, the towline to the *Calvin* broke and the three were cast loose to their fates. In the tempestuous weather the steamer made no attempt to pick up the tow again. This was normal procedure. The vessels were expected to ride it out on their own. When eventually the storm blew itself out, the *Calvin* intended to recover them and continue the trip. The strength of the sudden storm was such that it was later thought that the *Bavaria* was unable to even set a staysail. Driven by the fierce blasts, she was lost to view by her companions. The *Valencia* eventually managed to anchor and ride out the blow, although the crew spent a miserable 24 hours perched on her cabin roof as grasping seas swept over her decks. All the deck load went over the side. She was later picked up by the *Calvin*.

The *Norway* was able to make sail and reached Kingston with the first news of the trouble. She had a tough time of it, battered by the mountainous waves and terrorized by the screaming wind. She also lost her deckload.

Later the lightkeeper at Point Petre claimed to have seen a yawl capsize with several men in it. The master of the schooner *Nicaragua* said he sighted a yawl with two men in it. They waved in distress, but the violence of the storm prevented him from trying to rescue them. He had two barges in tow and tried to come around for them, but couldn't bring his head into the wind. Reluctantly he left them to their fate. The captain of the schooner *Cavalier* stated that he saw Captain Marshall of the *Bavaria* clinging to the bottom of the yawl and another man holding onto a piece of lumber. As with the *Nicaragua*, the storm prevented him from trying to save them. The next day, when the weather calmed, a fish tug sighted the yawl, but it was then empty.

The question remains, however. What happened to the crew of the *Bavaria*? Why did they abandon her in midlake? After all, the schooner eventually fetched up on Great Galloo Island safe and sound and in good order.[35] The mystery remains unsolved.

The schooner *Orphan Boy* was also reported as a *Mary Celeste*. The 365-ton, 144-foot vessel was built at Black River, Ohio, in 1862. She enjoyed a profitable career until December 17,1885, when she was caught by a vicious gale in Lake Michigan. Heavily loaded with lumber, she was no match for the riled lake. The wrecked vessel was eventually driven ashore at Point au Sable, near Lundington, Michigan. None of the bodies of the 12 men aboard was found. It was just another riddle of the lake – a ship without a crew![36]

Manabozo Island

An old story tells of the ghost ship of Lake Superior's Michipicoten Island, or as Native Americans called it Manabozo Island. The spectre ship was reputedly a notorious harbinger of disaster. According to the tale, Jack McPherson, a trader who was also the keeper at Gargantua Light, believed ancient Indian legends claiming that there was a mysterious power coming from the island and that it was a special sanctuary of the Indians – guarded by the spirit of the Great Manitou and unfriendly to settlement by whites. After McPherson sighted the infamous ghost ship, he knew that he was inescapably doomed. Regardless of whatever he did, he knew that he could not elude his fate. His life was ruled by the awful knowledge of his imminent death. A short time later he was caught offshore in a storm with four other men and drowned.[37]

"What Other Boat?"

Not all ghost ship stories involve great schooners or wooden steamers cutting through the centuries. There are some very strange and unexplained things that happen on the lakes today, especially when an impenetrable fog clouds both vision and mind.

A modern tale goes that, several years ago, the Coast Guard station at St. Joseph, Michigan, heard a radio call from a small sailboat lost somewhere in the fog, asking desperately for assistance. The boat's navigational instruments had failed, the engine refused to run and the crew was panicked.

The Coast Guard's replies to the boat went unanswered as, evidently, the boat's radio could transmit but not receive. Eventually, the Coast Guard was able to get enough of a fix on the boat's position to allow them to send out a patrol boat.

After a time, the Coast Guard reached the sailboat, determined that all aboard were safe and, subsequently, towed it to safety at St. Joseph. Aboard were two couples. To the Coast Guardsmen's observation, the sailboat crew had not been drinking, was not on drugs or was otherwise anything but weekend sailors out for a cruise. Bound out of Chicago, the unearthly fog overtook them and then everything went wrong.

It was only later, when the sailboat crew stopped at the station to fill out the inevitable report, that they inquired, "What about the other sailboat?"

The Coast Guardsmen replied that they had seen no other boat. Their radar had shown only the single boat within the entire 24-mile search range. The screen had otherwise been empty of targets.

This simple statement rattled the sailboaters. They knew different! According to their story, shortly after they realized the seriousness of their situation – lost in blinding fog without instruments, a broken radio and engine – another sailboat suddenly loomed out of the gray mist, stopping close alongside. The crew aboard that vessel calmed them down, told them all would be fine and took them in tow for St. Joseph.

On the way in, the crews discussed fogs and storms long past and adventures yet to come – typical summer sailor talk. Just before the Coast Guard arrived, the second boat inexplicably dropped the towline and silently disappeared into the gray wall of fog. But from where had they come? And why didn't they show on radar?[38]

The *Selvick*'s Light

Another modern story involves the 72-foot tug *Stephen M. Selvick*. Built in 1915 in Lorain, Ohio, this tug is well representative of the many small tugs that were so common to the Great Lakes. After many years of service, it was laid up with every expectation of being scrapped out. After due consideration, it was then donated to the local committee of Michigan's Alger Underwater Preserve near Munising on Lake Superior. After being cleaned to environmentally acceptable standards, the tug was sunk just offshore from Munising on June 1, 1996, to serve as an underwater interpretative site for divers.

The *Selvick* was towed to Munising two years earlier from Sturgeon Bay, Wisconsin, by the 42-foot *Rec Diver*, a vessel well-known to area divers. Although a long tow, the tug behaved well until June 7, 1994, when the pair was off Whitefish Point. At about dusk, the *Rec Diver* hove to in order to allow her crew to rig the proper night navigational lights on the *Selvick*. As they shortened up the towline and started to swing around to board the tug, the men were startled to see that the tug's pilothouse searchlight was on, sending a bright, sharp beam into the gathering gloom.

This was most remarkable, since all battery power was disconnected and it should have been impossible that the light could shine.

Once the crew boarded her, the light vanished. Look as they might, the crew found no mechanical reason for the impossible behavior. Was

The mystery of the lighting of a spotlight on the depowered Stephen M. Selvick has not yet been explained. CAPTAIN PETE LINQUIST

it only an incredible reflection of the setting sun? Or was the tug trying in some small way to signal that she was ready to cast off her old life and start a new one?

Several days earlier, the *Selvick* had an unusual brush with ... something. While running on Lake Huron at night between St. Ignace and the Detour Passage, about abreast of the Les Cheneaux Islands, the helmsman on the *Rec Diver* saw a strong radar return from a large west-bound vessel. The radar screen indicated that it was close and coming fast. The *Rec Diver* and *Selvick* were running nearer inshore than normal, thus were well clear of the regular shipping lane. The night was black as sin – not a star lit the sky and the moon was covered by thick clouds.

Rec Diver attempted to contact the stranger on the radio, but received no reply, just the dull emptiness of the airwaves. No lights could be seen on this unknown vessel. Inexorably, the silent return bore down on the tow. Finally, judging from the radar, it passed close to starboard. Despite the nearness of the stranger, the helmsman on *Rec Diver* never heard a sound, felt no wake, saw no light and heard no radio call. A more excitable man might have panicked, but the helmsman was nothing, if not calm. He only wondered a minute or two later, "Now what the hell was that?"[39]

A White Rowing Boat

Over the years, I have given a number of public programs on shipwrecks and Great Lakes maritime history in general. Invariably, people will come up to me afterward and volunteer various information and old stories. For me this is especially enjoyable, a real highlight of the presentation.

Quite sometime ago, I don't remember when or where, I finished a program and was approached by a man about 60-years-old who related a story that, while interesting at the time, I frankly blew off. The gentlemen intended it to illustrate how easily even modern sailboats can get into trouble on the lakes, but since this wasn't directly applicable to my program, I paid little attention.

When I began to assemble material for this book, I realized he had recounted a most remarkable tale. I just had no particular interest in the Great Lakes supernatural when he told the story and had not yet been deeply enough involved in researching the Life-Saving Service to fully put two and two together. In any case, this is the story as I remember it being told to me.

"This happened about 1965, although it could have been a year later or earlier. It was April and I was sailing north with my family

108

along the Michigan coast of Lake Huron. We had a good breeze, nothing great but we were going along very well. It was late in the day, just a little before dusk.

"Visibility was really terrible, one of those gray days of fog and mist. We kept waiting for it to blow off, but it never did.

"I wasn't real certain where we were. (Remember, this was prior to LORAN and GPS) Our depth gauge was showing good water, several hundred feet or so and I figured we were well out in the lake, probably approaching the mouth of Saginaw Bay. Once we cleared Point aux Barques, I thought I'd be clear up to Alpena.

"I was at the helm and my son was up forward. We were getting ready to fly the jenny when this white rowing boat just suddenly appeared dead ahead. I don't think it was 50 yards away! It was full of men – at least eight of them. All were rowing, except for one standing in the stern who had his left arm and shoulder cradled over a long steering oar. He looked right at me and waved slowly with his right arm. I was in the Navy during the war and I remember the chiefs had us do lifeboat drill, but this boat was different. The sides were a lot lower. There was some lettering on the bow but I couldn't see it clearly enough to read. It was definitely a wooden boat though.

"I thought for sure we would hit them. I yelled to my son to hold on and threw the helm over, heading more northeast. It was pretty frantic for a minute. This unknown boat in front of me, my son hanging on, me trying to steer and trim up on the new course. My wife was below making supper and my quick turn over turned her stew, so I had her yells ringing in my ears too!

"When I looked again to be certain we would clear the boat, it was gone. Visibility was bad, but I still should have seen it. I always wondered what happened to it.

"A shout from my son brought me back with a start. He said he could see bottom! A glance at the depth gauge showed a bare five foot under the keel. I thought, 'What the hell? Have we blundered into Point aux Barques Reef?'

"In any case, the depth increased within a minute or so and we were in back good water. Whatever that reef was, we just cut the edge of it.

"After an hour or so, the fog finally blew off and I could make out Point aux Barques Light. Handing the helm to my son, I went below and pulled out my chart. Using the bearing from the light, I tried to figure out what happened.

"As best I can guess, we almost hit Point aux Barques Reef. If we hadn't run across that strange rowing boat and turned when we did, I'm certain we would have run right up on it and wrecked. I don't know where that little white boat came from, but it saved us from a very dangerous situation. It shows how easy it is to get into trouble on the lakes."

The story was meant to illustrate how quickly a sailor can run up on even a well-known reef, even in a modern yacht. As I mentioned, I didn't really think much of it at the time.

Four years ago, while I was researching the old U.S. Life-Saving Service for *Wreck Ashore*, I came across the terrible account of the loss of the entire Point aux Barques Life-Saving Station crew, except for the keeper, during a rescue attempt.

While obviously it can't be proved, a little imagination would provide the answer to the strange encounter the yachtsmen had. The Point aux Barques crew perished in April 1879 and it was an April day when the sailor saw the strange rowing boat. The location for his sighting and the surfboat disaster are nearly identical.

Did that long vanished lifesaving crew return to save him from disaster?

The Lester River Phantom

Another unexplained sighting occurred on a bright sunny day in 1977. A man and his wife were driving north on Minnesota's North Shore Scenic Drive. A winding and picturesque road, it largely follows the northwest shore of Lake Superior, angling northeast from Duluth to Two Harbors, where it joins Minnesota Highway 61. Wide sweeping vistas of Lake Superior are common.

Near the mouth of the Lester River, the pair spotted a freighter running close in and parallel to the shore. Black smoke curled up from the stack and a white mustache hung off her bow as it plowed majestically toward Duluth. Having grown up on the lakes, both noticed two things. First, it was far closer to shore than normal and, second, it was an old style vessel. Wanting to get a closer look at the unusual ship, the husband drove several more miles until he came to a place he could safely turn off the narrow road and still see the lake. Since the initial sighting, the road cut inland and trees blocked the lake view. But when they looked again for the ship, it was gone. The lake was absolutely clear, without even a hint of fog, smoke or mist. From horizon to the rocky shore, nothing but water could be seen. What had happened to the stranger? Did a window briefly open ... and close?[40]

Others

Old sailors swore that they saw images of other ghost ships. The steamboat *Water Witch*, lost on Lake Huron in November 1868 with 28 passengers and crew, was reported sighted months after she disappeared. The side-wheeler *Keystone State*, sunk with all hands on November 10, 1861, off Port Austin, Lake Huron, was also a later apparition. The freighter *City of Detroit*, lost in Saginaw Bay December 1873, was another. The schooner *Eclipse*, sailing away on Lake Huron in November 1874, schooner-barge *Celtic* vanishing in a 1902 gale and the schooner *Kate L. Bruce* coming up missing in 1877 were also claimed to have been observed after their loss, gliding along on misty nights. The schooner *Wells Burt* was glimpsed on a foggy night well after she went down.[41]

"Phantom ships under full sail" were also seen near the village of Huron on Lake Erie. Other sailors spoke of the side-wheeler *Lady Elgin*, lost with perhaps 300 souls, still plowing over Lake Michigan, either heading for her fateful meeting with the schooner *Augusta* or trying to finish her interrupted trip. Were all these cases only an overworked sailor's imagination – or were ghost ships something else?

Sounds

Many old sailors believed ghost ships manifested themselves in ways other than just sailing through the waves on storm-tossed nights. When passing Keweenaw Point or Whitefish Point on Lake Superior, Point aux Barques on Lake Huron or Long Point on Lake Erie – all areas where many ships were lost and sailors drowned – some sailors claimed that they could hear wretched cries for help from drowning sailors and see ghostly images of wrecks. The terrible disasters replayed themselves again and again. In effect, these areas were forever "cursed" by the vessels that were lost there. Bad weather was always expected after having such an experience. In addition, if a ship sank at her slip, that batch of water was often also considered haunted.[42]

As previously stated, many ships were discovered without their crews, but otherwise in good condition. Could the ghosts of lost sailors have come back aboard in the dark of a moonless night to claim the living crews?

CHAPTER FOUR

Shipboard and Underwater Ghosts

TIME: Mid-19th Century
PLACE: Topsail Schooner, Lake Erie

The man at the wheel nervously pointed forward. The blackness of the moonless night was almost total. "Frank look, there it is. See it right next to the foremast." His companion said, "Yeah, yeah, I do." The wheelsman, now increasingly agitated, muttered, "There's another one. Why it looks like five or six of them. They're just stare'n at us!" The second man said, "Are you going to tell anyone about this?" Holding the wheel tight but visibly shaking, the sailor said, "No, not a soul, but when we make Buffalo I'm off this black cat! I knew shippin' on her was a bad deal. They're the guys that drowned when she went over in that white squall off Milwaukee."

Some vessels had the reputation of being haunted. Sailors claimed that sinister spirits walked their decks or made things "go bump in the night." Based on the history of particular ships, overactive imagination could provide an explanation. In other examples, the reason for the haunting is unclear. The schooner *Augusta* of *Lady Elgin* infamy, later renamed the *Colonel Cook* in an unsuccessful effort to escape her past, was reportedly haunted.

During the stormy evening of September 8, 1860, on Lake Michigan, the *Augusta* smashed into the big side-wheeler, *Lady Elgin*, with devastating results. The schooner, however, was little damaged and continued on its way, her captain thinking he had done little harm to the steamer. For the *Elgin*, it was a death blow and she dove for the bottom with the loss of an estimated 300 lives. Old sailors believed the

Augusta was forever cursed in retribution for the terrible deed.

One old-timer who signed on the vessel before realizing who she was claimed that every trip she lost a man overboard or injured one in some other way.[1] Others remembered that she always had trouble getting crews. Sailors stated that she was plagued by the restless ghosts of the *Lady Elgin*'s crew and passengers. During the dark night watches, motionless silent corpses were said to stare vacantly from the foredeck at her living crew. By any account, *Augusta* was not a happy ship. Sailors avoided her whenever possible.

Another old sailor remembered his father buying and later refitting a wrecked schooner in which several of her crew had drowned. The father had great trouble getting and keeping a crew. The men he could hire insisted that they heard ghosts rattling around below decks. They wouldn't stay. A more practical seaman, the father claimed that the sounds were absolutely normal. In a sailing vessel under way with a stiff breeze, anything imaginable could be heard. Regardless of explanations, the men left anyway. They would not sail on a haunted ship.[2]

The topsail schooner *U.C. Dean* was another ship supposedly infested with spirits. Built in Willow Point on Lake Ontario in about 1848, on her first trip the crew reported experiencing a strange foreboding of disaster. They were very uneasy and "knew" something bad would happen. They were right. When she reached Lake Erie, a sudden, brutal squall blew her over. Part of the crew drowned in their bunks in the flooded forecastle. Their bloated bodies where not removed until the salvaged hulk was towed to Cleveland and finally righted in the yard. After repairs, there was a long delay in finding a crew. Superstitious sailors had no desire to bunk in a foc'sle where their brethren died so horribly. To help allay fears and drive off her bad luck, the captain even nailed a horseshoe to the foremast. Eventually she got a crew and sailed out of Cleveland to resume her career. Under the circumstances, the crew was likely "crimped" from a local dive. The horseshoe did little good. The new crew reported her still haunted, especially during the dark hours of the long night watch. Some of the new men awoke with terrible nightmares of water running down the companionway. Others saw movement in still shadows. Unexplained moans were also heard, both forward and on the dark deck. Within a short time the unfortunate schooner wrecked on Lake Erie, haunted and bedeviled to the last.[3]

The *Erie Board of Trade*

It is usually accepted that the following tale of the *Erie Board of Trade* is strictly fiction, nothing more than the result of a fertile imagination. However, there are those who admit, or at least believe, that certain elements of it might be based on a true story. There never was an *Erie Board of Trade*, but there was a *Chicago Board of Trade*, and it did have a decidedly "unnatural" career.

The 588-ton, 156-foot vessel was built in 1863 as a three-masted bark in Manitowoc, Wisconsin, by George Rand. Two years later her rig was changed to that of a schooner. While never a hoodoo ship, she was never a lucky one either. Her introduction to the world of big time trouble started on Wednesday, July 29, 1874, when she sank in 13 fathoms of water about 25 miles north-northwest of Fairport Harbor on Lake Erie.

The hull, valued at $25,000, was insured for $20,000. Her hold was filled with 30,000 bushels of corn.

Captain Thomas Fountain's explanation of the sinking was vague, claiming that his schooner bottomed on some rocks while being towed in the Detroit River. At the time, no damages were apparent. But at 7:30 a.m., while booming along off Point au Pelee, it breezed up and she began to roll heavily. After a while the wind died off and the weather became quite pleasant. At 4 a.m. on Wednesday, three feet of water was discovered in her hold. The crew manned the forward pump and stroked for all they were worth. For reasons undetermined at the time, the aft pump wouldn't draw. Limited only to the forward pump, the crew's best exertions were not enough and at 8:45 a.m. they abandoned her in the yawl. Ten minutes later the schooner went bow first to the bottom. The crew safely reached Fairport Harbor.

Some of the men claimed something was "rotten on the *Chicago Board of Trade*." They stated that she never hit anything, that there was no explanation for her sudden and unholy appetite for the lake, that instead of heading for shore once the water was discovered, the captain ran for the open lake and deep water. After all, she didn't start to leak until 27 hours after she supposedly hit the rocks. She should have started taking water immediately. The underwriters were most interested to raise the schooner to see what really happened. Responding to the charges, the *Chicago Inter-Ocean* stated, "Captain Fountain is well known on the lakes and there is no man in his capacity in whom greater confidence is placed." To help solve the mystery, in August the Coast Wrecking Company was given a $10,000 "no cure, no pay" contract by the underwriters to raise and get her into port.

The insurance men had good reason to smell something fishy. At the time of the *Chicago Board of Trade* "sinking," underwriters were beset by a rash of losses. Freights were depressed and business poor. Owners were sorely tempted to "sell" their overinsured vessels to the insurance companies. Schooners insured in the spring of 1874 for $18,000 on a valuation of $25,000 had by August depreciated to a value of $17,000 to $18,000. For less than honest owners, the opportunity for some skullduggery was ripe.

A case in point is the schooner *Hubbard*. She was on the way up to Chicago from Oswego on Lake Ontario with coal when the mate and steward discovered Captain Frederick Themble below decks busily drilling holes in the hull with a large auger. The pair immediately seized him. Themble, as did Fountain, had the reputation of a "well known and experienced navigator who had the confidence of all," making the discovery all the more startling.

When the *Hubbard* arrived in Chicago, the owner, Captain D.L. McGraw, judged the captain to be insane and fired him. Themble promptly and wisely disappeared. McGraw by the way, owned both the *Hubbard* and the *Chicago Board of Trade*, a fact not missed by the underwriters. The owner claimed that the captain was driven mad by his first wife who, he said, had been unfaithful to him. McGraw had his second wife sailing with him on the *Hubbard*, but put her ashore at Port Huron before making the attempt to sink the vessel.

The *Chicago Board of Trade* proved a difficult salvage, accompanied by numerous small accidents, mistakes and delays, more than normally characteristic of such work. Despite the problems, by December the salvagers were able to raise her enough to drag her into 50 feet of water, where she was left for the winter.

Although the *Chicago Board of Trade* was resting securely on the bottom of Lake Erie, that apparently didn't stop her "ghost" from sailing again. On April 25, 1875, a phantom ship, reported to be the *Chicago Board of Trade*, was sighted on Lake Michigan. One minute she was there, all sail billowing in the fresh breeze. The next, she was gone. Old lake captains who saw it swore that she was the *Chicago Board of Trade* and none other. Regardless of what others may say, they knew what they had seen and it was this ghost ship. Was the schooner trying in some way to impart a message about her untimely end?

The following spring and summer, the wreckers were back at work. And the bad luck of the previous season continued to dog them. In late June, they had her slung in chains with pontoons ready for a lift when an unusually strong summer storm blew up. The heavy chains broke, sending the schooner sliding back to the bottom and the salvage crew scurrying into Fairport.

By early July, the wreck finally came up and was safe in Buffalo. She was a bedraggled looking trophy. The cabin was gone and both masts broken off, as was part of her stanchions and rail. Ominously, the suspicions of the insurance men were vindicated. At least six holes were discovered in the water closet pipe and a special commission determined that they were made for the purpose of sinking the vessel. The tool used to make the holes, a short piece of iron bent and shaped at one end, was also found. A small square of carpet had been placed around the pipe, as if to deaden the sound of rushing water. The aft pump was also found disabled.

The schooner's bad luck also touched her cargo. When first examined on the bottom by divers, it was pronounced in good condition. When finally unloaded it was discovered badly spoiled and caused considerable problems. The stench was so bad that city health inspectors directed the off loading out of the city limits. Eventually most of the corn was sold to farmers for pig feed. It was good for nothing more.

Even though safe in harbor, the schooner seemed to prefer the feel of the muddy bottom. First she sank at the dock, apparently as the result of split seams. Caulked with fresh oakum, she was moored, only to sink again. While the schooner awaited drydocking for more complete repair, powerful pumps were almost constantly needed to keep her off the bottom. When the big steam pumps were taken away, down she went. Some mariners always found a rational explanation for her sinking. Others thought there just might be another reason.[4]

The underwriters finally managed to keep the reluctant schooner above water long enough to sell her. But her unsavory past always haunted her. Nevertheless, she continued to sail for another quarter century. On November 21, 1900, her end finally came when she wrecked on Niagara Reef, Lake Erie. Anchored by a full cargo of iron ore, she was beaten to pieces by the powerful gale.[5]

A Classic Great Lakes Ghost Story

Many consider the *Erie Board of Trade* to be the classic Great Lakes ghost story. Others see a relationship to the *Chicago Board of Trade*.

The tale is repeated in full as it originally appeared in the *Saginaw Weekly Courier* of August 30, 1883. Whether true or false is for the reader to judge.

Down in the lower part of South Street the other day, an old sailor sat on an anchor stock in front of a ship chandler's store. He was an intelligent-looking man and was fairly well dressed for one of his calling. Other sailors were seated on a bale of oakum, on a wide-mouthed pump without a plunger and on the single stone step of the store. The ship chandler and a young friend sat in chairs just inside the store. The group were talking about ghosts. One of the young men had just told his experience.

"You're a sorry dog," the ship chandler said to him. "You were drunk and the spirits you'd taken within made you see the spirits without. It's always that way."

The old sailor threw one leg over the anchor stock, faced the ship chandler and said, "You know I never take no grog, don't you, captain?"

The ship chandler nodded.

"Well, I saw a ghost once. I saw it as plain as I ever saw anything. The captain of the schooner I was on and the man in the waist both saw it, too. There wasn't a drop of liquor on board. It was the talk of the docks all season."

"I know a Captain Jack Custer of Milan. He's the only fresh-water captain I'm acquainted with," said the ship chandler.

"He's the man. I heard him speak of you once. It was a little over 10 years ago. I was in Chicago then. I'd been through the canal from Toronto on one of those little canallers. What with tramping around the mud with a line over my shoulder and taking turns around snubbing posts every time the schooner took a notion to run her nose into the bank, I'd enough of canal schooners. I heard at the boarding house that some men were wanted on a three-masted schooner called the Erie Board of Trade. *The boys gave her a pretty hard name, but they said the grub was good and that the old man paid top wages every time, so I went down and asked him if he got all hands aboard. He looked at me a minute, then asked where my dunnage was. When I told him, he said I should get it on board right away.*

117

"The Board of Trade *was as handsome a craft as ever floated on the lakes. She'd carry about 45,000 bushels of corn. Her model had as clean lines as a yacht. As I came down the dock with my bag under my arm, I had to stop and have a look at her. The old man saw me at it. He was proud of her and I thought afterward that he rather took a fancy to me because I couldn't help showing that I liked her looks.*

"I was in her two round trips. The last trip up was the last on the lakes. Not but what times were pretty good up there. We were getting $2.50 a day for the first trip out and $2 the last. We messed with the old man and what with fresh meat and vegetables and coffee with milk, it was a first cabin passage all the way. But the old man made it hot for most of us. There wasn't any watch below in the day and we were kept painting her up on the down trip and scrubbing the paint off again on the trip up. Skippers don't handle the belaying pins quite so much up there as they do down here when arguing with men, because there is a lot of shysters around the docks waiting to get the men to the vessel. A man who's handy in fisting a mainsail will generally find pretty fair cruising.

"The first trip round to Chicago, every man but me got his dunnage onto the dock as soon as he was paid off. I'd seen worse times than we'd had and, when I got my money, I asked the old man if he'd want anyone to help with the lines when the schooner was towed from the coal yards to the elevator. He reckoned he could keep me by if I wanted to stay, so I signed articles for the next trip. When we were getting the wheat into her at the elevator we got the crew aboard. One of them was a red-haired Scotchman. The captain took a dislike to him from the first. It was a tough time for Scotty all the way down. We were in Buffalo just 12 hours and then we cleared for Cleveland to take on soft coal for Milwaukee. The tug gave us a short pull outside the breakwater and we had no more than got the canvas onto the schooner before the wind died out completely. Nothing must do but we must drop anchor, for the current settling to the Niagara River was carrying us down to Black Rock three knots an hour.

"When we got things shipshape about decks, the old man called Scotty and two others aft and told them to scrape down the topmasts. Then he handed the boatswain's chairs to them. Scotty gave his chair a look and then turned and touching his forehead respectfully said, "If you please, sir, the rope's about chafed off and I'll bend on a bit of ratlin' stuff." The captain was mighty touchy, because the jug had left him so, and he just jumped up and down and swore. Scotty climbed the main rigging pretty quick. He got the halyards bent to the chair and swung out to hoist away.

"I and the captain's nephew were standing by. We handled that rope carefully, for I'd seen how tender that chair was. When we got

118

him up chockablock, the young fellow took a turn around the pin and I looked aloft to see what Scotty was doing. As I did so, he reached for his knife with one hand and put out the other for the backstay. Just then the chair gave way. He fell all bunched up until he struck the crosstrees and then he spread out like and fell flat on the deck just forward of the cabin on the starboard side. I was kneeling beside him in a minute and so was the old man, too, for he'd had no idea that he would fall. I was feeling pretty well choked up to see a shipmate killed so and I said to the captain, 'This is pretty bad business, sir. This man's been murdered,' says I.

"When I said that, Scotty opened his eyes and looked at us. Then in a whisper he cursed the captain and his wife and children and the ship and her owners. It was awful. While he was still talking, the blood bubbled over his lips and his head lurched over to one side. He was dead.

"It was three days before the schooner got to Cleveland. Some of the boys were for leaving the boat, but most of us stayed by, because wages were down again. Going through the rivers, there were four other schooners in the tow. We were next to the tug. Just at the big end of Port Huron a squall struck us. It was too much for the tug and some lubber cast out the towline without singing out first. We dropped our bower as quick as we could, but not before we drifted astern, carrying away thread-gear of the schooner next to us and smashing in our own boat. We were a skeary lot going up Lake Huron and no boat under the stern.

"There was a fair easterly wind on the lake and as we got out of the river in the morning we were standing across Saginaw Bay during the first watch that night. I had the second trick at the wheel. The stars were shining bright and clear and not a cloud was in sight. In the northwest a low dark streak showed where land was. Every stitch of canvas was set and drawing, though booms sagged and creaked as the vessel rolled lazily in a varying breeze. I had just sung out to the mate to strike eight bells when the captain climbed up the companionway and out on deck. He stepped over to the starboard rail and took a look around, and the lookout began striking the bell. The last stroke of the bell seemed to die away with a swish. A bit of spray or something struck me in the face. I wiped it away and then I saw something rise slowly across the mainsail from the starboard side of the deck forward of the cabin. It was white and all bunched up. I glanced at the captain and saw he was staring at it too. When it reached the gaff near the throat halyards, it hovered over it an instant and then struck the crosstrees. There it spread out and rolled over towards us. It was Scotty. His lips were working just as they were when they cursed the captain. As he straightened out, he seemed to stretch himself until he grasped the maintop mast and the mizzen with the other. Both were *carried away like pipe stems. The next I knew the ship was all in the wind. The squaresail yard was hanging in two pieces, the top hammer was swinging and the booms were jibing over.*

"The old man fell in a dead faint on the quarterdeck and the man in the waist dived down in the forecastle so fast that he knocked over the last man of the other watch. If it hadn't been for the watch coming on deck just then, she'd of rolled the sticks out of her altogether. They got the head sails over and I put the wheel up without knowing what I was doing. In a minute, it seemed we were laying our course again. The second mate was just beginning to curse me for going to sleep at the wheel, when the mate came along and glanced at the binnacle.

"'What the ____ is this,' he said , 'lying our course and on the other tack?'"

The young man by the ship-chandler had listened with intense interest. Here, he said, "That story is true. I was there. I'm the captain's nephew you spoke about. I was reading in the cabin that night. As the bell began to strike, I felt a sudden draft through the cabin and my paper was taken out of my hands and out of the window before I could stop it. I hurried out of the cabin after it but, as I got my head up through the companion way, I heard the crash of falling masts. When the schooner began to go off on the other tack, I saw a bit of a waterspout two miles away to the leeward and..."

The ship chandler laughed. "Did you find your paper?" he asked.

"No!" said the young man.

"I thought not," said the ship-chandler.

"Well," said the old sailor, "This story can easily be verified. The next voyage the schooner was sunk. The insurance companies resisted payment on the ground that she had been scuttled by her captain. During the trial of the case, the story of the death of Scotty and the loss of her topmasts under a clear sky was all told under oath. Anybody who doesn't believe it can see a copy of the printed testimony by applying to Rosbury and Barker, the ship-chandlers of 1789 Central Wharf, Buffalo." [6]

Whether this story is true or mere fiction is unknown. Although there is no record of a schooner *Erie Board of Trade*, the lists can be wrong. It should also be remembered that the best stories are also based on fact. But fact or fiction, it is a rollicking good tale of the lakes.

The Black Dog of Lake Erie

One famous shipboard haunt isn't of a person, but a dog instead. The nefarious "Black Dog of Lake Erie" was blamed for many early ship disappearances on the eastern lakes. Among other vessels reputedly lost because of the black dog curse were the schooners *C.T. Jenkins*,

Thomas Home and *Mary Jane*. The dog was also said to have been seen aboard the schooner *Phoebe Catherine*. Imaginative sailors swore that they saw the chilling sight of the black mongrel soundlessly pass during the darkest hours of the night watch. It would cross the foredeck and then vanish without a trace. Disaster, great or small, soon followed.

Phoebe Catherine was also said to have suffered from a paranormal phenomena known as "doubling." During the inky blackness of moonless night watches, wherever a sailor found himself on the boat, a "shadowy form would be seen opposite him, going through his motions." The silent spectre mimicked the sailor's every action. Crews also claimed that cabin doors wouldn't stay shut or hatches secured.

Although by all accounts a fine, well-built schooner, she carried a bad luck reputation. In 1865, her second sailing season, she went ashore near Wellington, Ontario, Lake Ontario. In 1874, she stranded on Manitoulin Island in northern Lake Huron. In another unfortunate event, her captain died aboard when she was frozen in the ice during a Manitoulin winter. Trouble just dogged her.

On one occasion the *Phoebe Catherine* was haunted by a woman in white. According to one of the ship's masters, the wife of a crewman appeared, wrapped in a sheet, during a late night card and drinking party. When the husband glanced up from the game and saw her, he collapsed in a fit, breaking the party up. Scared witless, the man "took the pledge."[7]

Another reputed victim of the black dog was the 135-foot, 345-ton topsail canal schooner *Mary Jane* of St. Catherines. Just as she was being towed away from her wharf in Port Colborne, Ontario, on Lake Erie with a cargo of cedar posts, elevator workers noticed a big black Newfoundland with "eyes like coals of fire" appear on the port side of the deck cargo. The huge beast walked across the top of the deck load and jumped ashore. When he hit the wharf he was gone, vanishing into thin air. The wind was dead calm and the tug eventually dropped the schooner just outside the harbor. She lay still, without wind for sometime, just drifting and waiting … for something. By early afternoon, the dock workers noticed that she was gone, but they didn't know where. They had detected no wind to speed her on her way. Or at least this was the popular theory. She never finished her trip, being inexplicably lost with all hands.

The story of the strange disappearance largely faded into legend, including embellishments that the weather was calm but hazy and that not a clue as to her loss was ever discovered. In fact, the lake was stormy and the schooner *E.P. Door*, which later wrecked the same night, passed the *Mary Jane* head-on. In the days following, part of the missing schooner's cargo was discovered bobbing in the lake, bearing silent witness to her end. But fair weather or foul, the black dog had struck again. No real explanation of her loss was ever offered.[8]

The infamous black dog was thought to be the ghost of a Newfoundland that drowned in the Welland Canal. The story goes that the dog was knocked overboard from a vessel while it was locking through the waterway. Instead of rescuing their mascot, the callous crew left it to drown. They felt if Newfoundlands were such good salt-water swimmers then surely a little fresh water would not hurt this one. The dog took his revenge by sealing the schooner tight in the lock. The crew had to strain mightily at the capstan to haul her through. When they finally heaved her free, they discovered the dog's body jammed tight into the lock gates, preventing their proper operation.[9] It was also claimed that the dog's spirit continued to haunt the schooner and its crew. On stormy nights, the hound's unearthly howling caused the sailors to regret their wanton cruelty.[10]

Another black dog story tells of the strange vision of the wheels-man of the schooner *T.G. Jenkins*. In November 1875, the three-master was downbound on Lake Erie from Chicago to Kingston, Ontario, with grain during an especially pleasant night. The breeze was easy and the moon bright. Without warning the helmsman started yelling loud enough to wake the dead. The entire crew, including Captain John Brown, came tumbling on deck, rubbing the sleep from their eyes. Excitedly, the wild-eyed man stated he had seen the infamous black dog – that it had climbed over the weather rail and wandered across the deckload and continued over the lee rail and into the lake. There was no splash. He saw it all as plain as day. There was another black dog aboard, a smaller one belonging to the captain, but since it plainly was still aboard, the helmsman claimed it wasn't the dog he saw.

The old captain didn't believe the sailor for a split second. Quickly searching him, he discovered a bottle of "hootch" in a pocket and promptly proclaimed him to be suffering from the "d.t.s." Ordering the cook to feed him strong coffee, he shipped the helmsman below to his bunk. Before the coffee took hold, though, the man also babbled about seeing black dogs running up the rigging.

When the schooner reached Port Colborne two days later, the helmsman again got into the booze and began to repeat his eerie tale of the black dog. Disgusted with him, Captain Brown booted him off his boat, tossing his seabag after him. As the schooner worked her way down the Welland Canal, the helmsman pleaded from shore with his old shipmates to leave the cursed vessel. Every time she stopped at a lock, the man showed up to implore them to heed his warnings. Each time the crew drove him away with curses and belaying pins.

By the time the *Jenkins* reached Port Dalhousie, the end of the line on Lake Ontario, his dire warnings had achieved some effect. The worried crew spoke plainly of letting discretion be the better part of valor and quitting. To keep his men aboard, the captain didn't dally in port and quickly sailed.That night it blew hard, but fair for the *Jenkins* and she should have sped rapidly and safely on her way. But something went terribly wrong. Somewhere between Port Dalhousie and Oswego, New York, she foundered. When she didn't reach Oswego, tugs were sent out to search but found nothing; not the schooner, a single body or lonely piece of wreckage were located. Old sailors just shook their heads. They knew it was no accident, but instead the curse of the black dog. The crazy helmsman wasn't so crazy!

At Sheldons' Point, to the west of Oswego, New York, a farmer claimed to have seen a strange black dog come ashore the night the schooner went missing. His jet black hair stuck closely to his body and he dragged his rear legs as if paralyzed. The bedraggled dog was there one minute, gone the next. Where, the farmer didn't know. Townspeople claimed that it was Captain Brown's dog and the only survivor of the schooner. But then again, was it another black dog, one with a more unusual pedigree?[11]

In another tale, a captain accidentally killed a sailor in a fight. A short time later, while the captain was in the cabin, a big black dog appeared before the door, snarling and biting at the captain. It was with difficulty he prevented himself from being mauled. Without reason the dog left as quickly and silently as it appeared. On the next trip, the vessel was lost.[12]

Some schooner men took the black dog very seriously. When a drunken mate cursed the captain of the schooner *Azimuth* with the admonition, "May the Black Dog of Lake Erie cross your deck," the captain went ballistic. After smashing the man to the ground with his fists, he pulled him back to his knees with one hand and prepared to batter his face in with the other. With blazing eyes and a voice rumbling up from the bottom of Lake Erie, he yelled, "Take it off, take it off, or your own mother will never know the look of your face."

Choking on blood, fear and bile, the mate said, "It's off. I couldn't put it on anyway. I'm not a warlocky Finn."

"All right," said the captain, "But to prove what you say, you'll come along with us next trip yourself. Not as mate, but in the foc'sle. You're not worth the salt on your porridge, but I reckon you won't go so far as to drown yourself to spite me."

The mate pleaded, "I was only foolin,' Cap'n."

Looking hard at the shriveled hunk of flesh cowering in front of him, the captain said, "By cracky, if I told the boys you'd threatened the Black Dog, they'd tear you limb from tree. To think of the blather of the likes of you scattering the *Azimuth* and her crowd along the front of some man's farm some dirty night! Take shame to yourself for thinking of it."

The mate looked at the captain and said, "Honest, Cap'n. I didn't mean it. I couldn't put the Dog on ye if I tried, and I wouldn't try if I could."

The frightened mate must have spoken the truth, for the old *Azimuth* continued to sail the lakes for many more years without any evidence of a curse following along in her wake.

Stories of the black dog of Lake Erie all have one thing in common. Should it be seen crossing a deck, the vessel would be lost. If you are sailing Lake Erie, it would certainly be wise to keep a weather eye open for black dogs.[13]

The Convict Ship *Success*

The *Success*, purported to be a convict ship that toured the Great Lakes in the 1920s and 1930s, was believed by some to be haunted by the spirits of the men and women condemned to her living hell.

The popular story claims that the *Success* was built in 1790 in Burma and for a dozen years sailed the high seas as a merchantman. In 1802, she was converted into a prison ship and became part of the "felon fleet" used to transport prisoners from England to Australia. Hundreds of men, women and sometimes even children were jammed tightly into these perdition ships for a voyage that could last months. The unfortunate prisoners were treated worse than animals and death was a constant companion.

She sailed in this terrible trade for 49 years. From 1851 until 1869, she was a prison hulk moored in the harbor at Sydney, hosting the worst criminals in Australia. When public pressure eventually eliminated the practice of confining prisoners in rotting ships, she was scuttled in 1872. Five years later, she was raised by a visionary entrepreneur and refitted into a "convict ship museum," complete with prison cells, wax dummies and torture devices.

After a successful run in Australia, she sailed to England for a tour of all the major port cities. As her name, *Success,* implied, she was a great success, with tourists eager to explore her. Stories of ghostly apparitions and unearthly sounds were common to the ship since her original abandonment as a prison, but on the long sail to England they became worse. Arms were said to protrude from empty cells and low moans came from vacant cabins. Was it just wind and shadow? The crew thought not.

In 1912, she sailed to North America to make another horror tour. Ironically, she and the R.M.S. *Titanic* departed England on the same day. The same ghostly apparitions that plagued her on the run from Australia also rattled the trans-Atlantic crew. Strange shapes danced on her decks and guttural screams and moans echoed below decks. Some of the men even refused to go below.

The "convict ship," Success, had a career that more than lived up to its name, but was always felt to be haunted. K.E. THRO COLLECTION

She proved a popular attraction for many years. Her American advertising claimed, "Aboard her are now shown, in their original state, all the airless dungeons and condemned cells, the whipping posts, manacles, branding irons, punishment balls, cat o'nine tails, coffin bath and other fiendish instruments of brutality. She is the oldest ship in the world and the only convict ship left afloat out of that dreadful fleet of ocean Hells which sailed the Seven Seas in 1790. She marked the beginning and end of England's monstrous Penal System. She is unchanged after 135 years, nothing being omitted but the Human Freight."

Wherever she was, her ghostly reputation followed her. At night, when the tourists had left and darkness blanketed her, many claimed that the ghosts of her victims walked her decks.

There is confusion as to her actual history, as opposed to the colorful one her owners advertised. Another version of the "facts" holds that she was built in 1840, not 1790, and her career was not nearly as lurid as portrayed. She was never used as a convict transport but did see duty as an emergency prison.

Regardless of her true history, in 1943 she was being towed to Port Clinton, Ohio, when she grounded about a half mile out. Instead of trying to immediately pull her off, she was thought safe for the time being and left for the winter. However, the wind and waves of Lake Erie wrecked the old ship. The broken hull stayed on the bar until July 1946, when vandals burned it. The ghosts of the *Success* have been unseen ever since.[14]

"Bill's on the Masthead"

There is the strange tale of a grain schooner said to have lost her luck. She was bound for Buffalo when a sailor named Bill fell from the masthead and was killed. The following day, a second sailor died in another accident. One death was bad enough, but two was more than the crew could accept.

When they reached port, the men were immediately paid off, as was the custom. Once they had their money in hand, every man told the captain that the ship had "lost her luck" and they wouldn't sail on her again. News of the deaths reached the grain elevator men and they initially refused to work the ship.

When she was finally loaded with a new cargo, the captain tried to get a crew for a trip to Cleveland. No one would sign on. Finally, the mate was able to shanghai a crew through a waterfront dive. They all were drunken sots and, when the mate was herding them toward the foc'sle, one of them looked up to the masthead and asked why the ship had a figurehead up there. Seeing what the man was pointing at, the mate turned ghastly white and exclaimed, "Why it's Bill!" To a man, all ran for the pier and never returned to the schooner.

The captain eventually managed to ship a crew, but never made Cleveland. The schooner was run down by a steamer off Dunkirk, New York, on Lake Erie, and sank with all hands.[15]

"The Captain's on the Bridge, Again"

The old man died at midnight. At least that's the best guess they could come up with. The captain stopped up on the bridge about quarter of the hour, had a quick word with the wheelsman then left, saying he was heading below for a few winks.

By 8 a.m. the following morning no one had seen him. This was very odd. Normally he was always up on the bridge well before dawn, "just to see another one come up boys," as he used to say. Nervously the mate, accompanied by the chief engineer and cook, knocked cautiously at his cabin door. Getting no answer, he slowly turned the brass knob and entered.

The old man lay still in his bed, staring straight up at the ceiling. His mouth gaped open and left arm dangled out from his side. The battered wind-up alarm clock was on the deck, its glass face smashed and the hands frozen exactly at midnight. He must have knocked it off the small night stand at his moment of passing. None of the crew knew how old he really was, but the best guess was at least 70. In a way he was ageless, always just the "old man."

They were only a day out of port and he would keep until they docked. After a quick radio message to the owners, the mate settled down in the pilothouse for a long watch. With the old man gone, getting the ship in safe was now his responsibility.

The fall weather was excellent, a light north wind with three-to four-foot waves dancing across the surface. They would make it just fine and right on time. The old man would have liked that. He was always a stickler for keeping the schedule.

The captain had grown up on the lakes, starting in sail but moving on to steam by the turn of the century. Ambitious, he worked his way up the long ladder from deck hand until finally getting a command. He was a natural, too. He gave his orders and expected them to be followed, but always seemed to be there if help was needed. His crews worshiped him, many following from ship to ship. The mate, for example, held his own master's ticket for years, but preferred to hang with the old man as his mate rather than taking his own ship.

The lake was the old captain's life and his only real love. He never married, although he had been known to raise a little hell once in a while. In his younger days, rumor had it he actually did have a girl in every port.

His last ship was a real old-timer, built in the days when they used to make them by the mile and cut'em off to whatever length was needed. To this point the ship had an uneventful career, running coal up and ore and grain down. She faced her share of storms, ice and fog and always plugged her way through. Although a bit smallish now, she still had years of good running left in her.

After the details of the captain's death were settled legally, the company gave the ship to the mate. Long a loyal and trustworthy employee and well recommended by the dead captain in his regular reports, he had their full confidence to keep her running to schedule.

It was on her next trip that the haunting began. A day or so out, the chief engineer privately, and somewhat reluctantly, told the new captain that he had briefly seen the old captain's ghost in the engine room. The apparition didn't say anything, just seemed to look around and then, apparently satisfied, disappeared. The chief had been known to "take a nip or two," so the new captain didn't quite believe his excited report. But then again?

A few trips later when they were locking down through the Soo in the fog and rain, one of the deck hands claimed to have seen it standing silently at the bow, as if to help guide her into the lock. Afraid of being laughed at, it was only after several stiff drinks in a waterfront dive that he repeated what he saw to his shipmates.

Late one night, the captain briefly saw the ghost standing quietly next to him in the pilothouse. He was gray and kind of mistlike. The captain could see clear through him, but it was him! The wheelsman saw it, too, but since he was trying to shake off a case of the d.t.s, refused to give it any credence. But the captain knew what he saw. The old man was really back.

For many years, the old captain's ghost was periodically seen by the ship's crew. His presence never radiated a threatening feeling, but rather the reverse. If you saw the old man, you knew all was well.

In at least two instances, the ghost saved the ship from injury. Half a day before the infamous Armistice Day 1940 storm roared onto the lakes, the vessel was due to leave port upbound and light. The ghost appeared to the captain in a dream and admonished him to hold the ship in port. While not a believer in such premonitions, the captain found reason to delay sailing and avoided confronting the storm.

Another time, the vessel was running through a blinding fog off Whitefish Point, Lake Superior, when the apparition appeared on the bridge. Walking to the engine room telegraph, it grabbed the handle and rang "full astern." For a moment, the watch looked on in shock and horror, unable to react to what they saw – or thought they saw. As the steamer started to shake violently with the effort of her reversing screw, she slowed ever so slightly. Out of nowhere another freighter sliced close across her bow. Had the ghost not intervened, the unknown steamer would have struck her fair amidships. An icy death would have been the only outcome for ship and crew.

As the years passed, the old ship continued to run along just fine, making money for the owners and "keeping to the schedule." She was simply one of the legion of bulk freighters that went without special recognition, except that she had two captains, a fact not widely known.

Finally it was time to scrap her. She was too small, too uneconomical and just too old. The old man, however, wasn't finished. He made one more appearance. In mid-Atlantic as the steamer was being towed to the Spanish ship breakers, a moderate gale rolled in. It wasn't much to speak of as North Atlantic storms go, but it was enough to break the ancient steamer's back. As the old girl started her plunge for the bottom, one of the men on the tug swore that he saw a man on her bridge. The stranger made no effort to save himself. He just gave a wave as she sank silently beneath the cold waves.[16]

Ghosts Underwater

TIME: 1988
PLACE: Emperor Wreck, Lake Superior

Deep in the engine room of the long sunken steamer a form came together; from nothing it became something, although thin and wraith-like it still had a discernable shape. The eyes were dark pools of nothing, really just black holes, but still they asked the silent questions, "Why me? Where are my friends? Why am I alone?" Without disturbing the silt that blanketed the old machinery, the nameless spirit went about its business. In death as in life, adjusting this and checking that. It was all he did in life and it was all it did in death.

Our paradigm is that we "expect" to see ghosts in the surface world – in our houses, graveyards or along lonely lakeshores. But there is no reason to believe that ghosts are confined to the surface of the planet. There is anecdotal evidence that they also inhabit the underwater world.

Numerous ships have sunk on the Great Lakes with great loss of life. Many of them also have been explored by scuba divers. In turn, divers have lost their lives while exploring wrecks. In some instances, divers perished in the open water, either from equipment or physiological problems. Others met their end after being trapped within the wreck, unable to find their way out. Desperately they searched until they emptied their air tanks, finally facing a ghastly death.

If there is any truth to the belief that spirits are often the result of violent death and that such spirits haunt the site of their demise, then these death ships should be home to spirits of both their crews as well as lost divers. Their spirits are held hostage by the wreck.

There are many recreational divers on the Great Lakes. On summer weekends they eagerly explore the underwater world. Many dive on shipwrecks. Experienced Great Lakes wreck divers usually have two common characteristics:

They have little imagination and are not given to easy flights of fancy. Diving on the hulk of a long dead shipwreck is spooky enough. The water is cold and usually dark and deep. Visibility can be very

129

limited, sometimes measured in inches. They always keep a tight rein on their nerves.

The divers also tend to be "macho," in that they admit to little bothering them and prefer to just work through problems. Blown dry suit seals, balky regulators and other mechanical problems are no reason to end a dive. Neither is a small "bending" of bottom time. The macho characteristic is not exclusive to the male of the species. Female wreck divers can also exhibit "macho" characteristics. No matter the sex, few wreck divers will ever admit to feeling "uneasy" on a wreck or to getting "spooked."

But some divers will, when properly "loosened-up" with a libation or two (or six), claim that when diving some death ships, they have felt an overwhelming "presence" of not being alone, of someone or something else being with them. It is not necessarily a threatening sensation and can be somewhat comforting. Nonetheless, it is there. The reader must understand that real wreck divers generally dive alone. They may have started the dive with a buddy, but inevitably somewhere along the way they separate (by design or accident).

It is not unusual to "hear" things on a wreck, a deep groaning or almost moaning sound rumbling from everywhere and yet nowhere. When you are moving slowly though interior compartments, every sound is magnified. One diver claimed that when he rested very quietly in a particular wreck, he could hear distant and very faint voices. The murmuring conversation was too indistinct to be understood, but it was still there, just on the fringe of understanding. Another very experienced diver stated that she could frequently hear one wreck's engines running when she entered the engine room! It didn't always happen, but when it did, there was no mistaking it.

A diver on the *Emperor*, a steel ore freighter lost with 12 men in 1947 on Lake Superior's Isle Royale, had an especially eerie experience. Swimming into one of the deck hand's cabins, he was startled to see the apparition of a crewman laying peacefully in his bunk. The ghost looked blankly at the diver, who quickly determined that he had seen enough and left for the surface![17]

Another instance occurred when a diver was shooting video on a Lake Huron wreck. As he moved carefully through the old steamer, he distinctly heard a weird metallic voice say, "Die!" Startled, he looked around to assure himself he was alone. The voice repeated, 'Die!" The third time he heard it, the diver quickly left the wreck.

Old sailors, especially in the dark of night, were always worried when they sailed past areas where other crews perished. Not only did some claim to hear their death screams, but claimed that the ghosts called

The steamer Emperor, *lost in 1947 off Isle Royale, Lake Superior, has been reported to be haunted by spirits of its crew. K.E. Thro Collection*

out to them by name. Others remembered yarns of the ghosts actually climbing aboard. Silently, these very sad spirits moved to their regular stations where they slowly went about duties. Before long, they would either vanish or just climb noiselessly over the side, returning to their watery tombs. This type of haunting was especially feared on vessels that had lost crew during a previous accident and were later salvaged and returned to service. Superstitious men claimed that the dead crew always returned to their old ship. This phenomenon is not unique to the Great Lakes and was most often reported by Grand Banks fishermen. This was also particularly true of sailors from Cornwall, where the belief had long been held. And many Cornishmen crewed on the lakes.

Can it be that the souls of the lost sailors are still with the wreck and that it is their strong presence divers feel? Haunted houses frequently give this "presence" feeling to visitors. Why can't a sunken ship do the same to divers? The evidence seems to point to this inescapable possibility.

CHAPTER FIVE

Lakeside Spirits

TIME: A cold November night, 199?

PLACE: Beach west of Whitefish Point, Lake Superior

The shadowy figure slowly treads up the dark and desolate lakeshore, occasionally looking intently toward the rolling lake. The dim glow of the waning moon casts little light in the dark night. In one hand he carries a shuttered lantern. A leather pouch swings loosely at his side, its strap running across his broad shoulders. Black oilskins glisten with moisture. The gusting north wind blows cold and hard, but it doesn't bother him, not any more. The obscure figure has made the trek so many times before. He used to have company, but that was a long time ago. Now he walks alone, along the old lifesaver's sandy trail. His gaunt white face is cracked and worn, weathered by a thousand gales. After a bit, the figure just disappears, fading quietly into the storm.

As surely as ghosts were claimed to be aboard ship, they also stalked along the shore. Areas of the beach that were littered with wrecks like Lake Erie's Long Point, Lake Michigan's Death's Door Passage and Lake Superior's Shipwreck Coast were said to be haunted by the spirits of their crews.

The deep and forbidding forests, often running right to the water's edge, provided a friendly environment for wandering spirits, or at least their tales. Whether they were earthly manifestations of lost sailors, fishermen or voyagers made no difference. They were there! They haunted the lakeshore! And occasionally their spectres became visible to those who believe.

Manitoulin Island's Restless Spirit

An early and colorful story involves Manitoulin Island in northern Lake Huron. The tale in its full glory is best told in the book *Drummond Island, the Story of the British Occupation 1815-1828* by Samuel F. Cook. "The intrepid fisherman who sails nearby or ventures to land on the shore of the Great Manitoulin Island after sunset is appalled and his blood is curdled by the sight of two headless soldiers who walk to and fro, clad in the red coats and other regimentals of the early part of this country.

"And stranger still, when nights are dark and cold, the belated fisherman, lured by a firelight on the shore and thinking that friendly greeting and warmth await him there, runs his boat on the beach and hastens to the blazing logs piled high a short distance away. He finds there no fisher comrade belated like himself, but instead the two headless soldiers sitting on a log in the glow and warming themselves by the blaze made furious by the night wind. With chattering teeth, with hair erect and eyes starting from their sockets, he runs to his boat and puts out into the night regardless of the dangers of the deep, so that he may but be far away from the uncanny guardsmen of that lonely shore. And when afterward, being jeered by his acquaintances for his superstition and cowardice, he goes to the same spot by daylight, he finds the selfsame pile of logs deeply charred by fire, but not then burning. Nor does he see any trace of the two headless redcoats.

"It was in midwinter, so the tradition runs, that two soldiers of the King deserted from the post at Drummond Island. They were evidently homesick. They longed for the scenes of old England. They could no longer endure the hardships, the rigors, the lonesomeness of that little village in the northern wilds. An officer with more ample pay, and wife and children with him, had some traces of home life and enjoyment, from all of which the private soldier was cut off, he being condemned to the monotony of fatigue duty and rest, without opportunity for enjoyable recreation. They might perchance have made their way to Mackinac Island and thus been freed from military restraint; but this was not their choice. They evidently set out for home. Their hearts longed for the lands beyond the rising sun. The shores and bays of Lake Huron were frozen over, and over the bridge thus made for them across the unsalted sea, they would make their way to the farther shoe of Georgian Bay, and thence eastward to the scenes for which they yearned.

"But the post commander was wrathful when he learned of their unannounced departure, and stormed as only a Briton or a fisherwoman can storm, with swaggering bluster and volubility of oaths. Then he sat down and wrote. In his anger he had sworn to have the men or their lives. He had murder in his heart. When he arose from his desk, an orderly took the sheet which he had written and nailed it on the door of the barracks. It made an offer of twenty dollars each for the heads of the two deserters if found dead and the same for their bodies if found alive. There were whisperings about the post, but there were none who dared to express their thoughts. In the Indian camp there seemed greater quietness than usual; but before the day had passed two swift snow-shoes runners were noticed to leave the post as if on an urgent errand. A night passed. A day – a short winter day – slipped away, more quickly closed to the denizens of Drummond post by the high ridge which towered on the west of the town, and under the shadow of which they were hid. Another long night settled down, dragged its weary length across the northern ice and snow and at length was driven far away from the clear depths of Georgian Bay. For, since the days are shorter in those regions, their glorified brightness is such that it makes amends for the brevity.

"The post commandant had not yet taken his morning coffee when in walked two Indian athletes covered with frost, their breaths coming quickly, and their eyes eager and ferocious. Advancing to the center of the room, each unfastened from his girdle a human head that had dangled there and, placing it on the table, demanded the reward for the two deserters.

"The commissary was quickly summoned and soon the bearers of the heads were washing away all thought of the blood they had treacherously spilled for money in copious libations of the King's rum; *rum*, the main reliance of the British in those days for the accomplishment of their most nefarious ends; *rum*, with which they made slaves and brutes of the Indians; *rum*, under whose influence they plotted massacres and murders and, by the aid of which, these were accomplished.

"The Indian runners, as the tale is told, following hard after the deserters who, all unaccustomed to travel over the ice and snow, had made their way with difficulty, came up with them on the Great Manitoulin Island. But they did not warn them of their danger. Like beasts of prey, they skulked out of sight until a favorable moment should appear. Weary and cold, the soldiers gathered material for a fire. High they piled the logs and loud was the crackling of the frozen wood. The flames leaped high. Higher yet they piled the wood, and having eaten their scanty supper, sat them down before the fire with no thought of impending danger. However in the darkness two red men watched their every motion; even their every breath. Lulled by the warmth and dulled by their weariness, the soldiers dozed. Perchance they are dozing yet, for they never wakened in this world. Stealthily from behind came the swift swish of the tomahawks as they cleft the air, falling upon necks conveniently bending forward. The deed was done. The two heads were fastened by the scalp locks to their girdles, and back they hastened, eager for their money and their rum.

"The headless trunks remained sitting on the log and warming themselves by the fire which made the night lurid with its glare. And ever since, unburied, they wander in those shores, seeking the heads which there they lost while sleeping; and when the nights are cold, the fire burns brightly, and they sit and warm them there."[1]

South Fox Island and the Woman in Black

In the early 1920s, the son of the lightkeeper at South Fox Island, Lake Michigan, remembered seeing the spectre of a strange "woman in black" eerily floating across the island's shallow flats. The phenomenon was observed numerous times, not only by the one boy but also by his brother. The woman always dressed in black clothes from a bygone era with a short, shoulder length black cape. The ghost seemed to come right at them, only to disappear just before reaching the pair. They never knew a reason for the haunting, but that never stopped the woman in black.[2]

The Shoveling Spirit

At 10:30 Monday night, November 29, 1897, a small tendril of black smoke curled upward from the wooden steamer *Nahant*'s cargo hold. The steamer, moored to the Chicago, Northwestern ore dock number four in Escanaba, Michigan, had already received half her cargo of iron ore. The rest would be loaded in the morning. At the base of the billowing smoke column, red flames licked hungrily at the dry wood of the old steamer. Unnoticed by the crew, the fire grew at an alarming rate. Before anyone realized the danger, it had run out of control and no action by the crew could in the least contain it. Desperately they ran for their lives, jumping from the ship to the safety of the wooden dock. Several men were burned, one severely enough to require hospitalization. Two of the crew, fireman Peter Bernstein and deck hand Harold Miller, didn't get off in time. They were burned alive, cremated in the funeral pyre of the old *Nahant*.

The flames soon spread from the *Nahant* to the ore dock, destroying the greater part of the structure, despite the efforts of the Escanaba Fire Department. Had the wind been north or northwest, all of the complex of ore docks, coal docks, hoist and stock piles, plus a large part of the city's third and fourth wards, could have burned to cinders. Many locals, heedless of the danger, considered the conflagration to be

135

"indescribably grand." Regardless, the entire city turned out to watch in awe, or fear!

The following day, after the fire had burned itself out, the captain of the steamer and the Escanaba fire chief searched the smoking wreck for the remains of the two missing men. All they discovered was a small fragment of bone. Everything else was gone, obliterated in the hellish heat. Later, the harbor tug *Delta* pushed the still floating steamer away from the remains of the dock and onto a nearby beach.

The bulk freighter *Nahant* had been built in 1873 at Springwell's Yard at Clark Street in Detroit. She measured 251 feet long, 35 feet in beam and 16.2 feet in depth. Her original capacity was 909 tons. In 1880, she was sold to Milwaukee interests and rebuilt, increasing her capacity to 2,000 tons. She had been a frequent visitor to Escanaba.

The remains of the *Nahant* lay quietly along the shore until March 9, 1898. Late that night, an upstanding Escanaba citizen was rounding the corner of Ludington Street and Smith Court when he was startled to see something "dancing" on the hulk of the steamer. More curious than scared, the man carefully crept through the lumber piles of the I. Stephenson Company Mill toward the blackened hull. In the cold light of a full moon, he saw a "perfect apparition" standing on the wreck. For a short moment, the ghost stood motionless, a sad look on its ghastly face. Then it erupted with "demon-like laughter." In a flash, it moved to a distant part of the dead hulk and then vanished.

Although understandably shaken by what he had witnessed, the observer drew his overcoat tighter around his neck and huddled down in the rough shelter of a lumber pile. He wanted to see if the mysterious spirit would return. In less than half an hour, the same or another ghost reappeared in the wreckage. With shovel in hand, the silent spectre went through the motions of digging. For two long minutes it continued with its unholy task, then it unexpectedly flew off toward the ore docks, waving the shovel wildly. A hideous, shrill scream of a poor soul suffering unbearable pain echoed over the docks. This was more than the man could take and he beat a hasty retreat.[3]

Were the two ghosts those of the dead *Nahant* crewmen? Was the first the watchman and the second the coal passer? Was there anything there at all?

Manitou Island Ghosts

During the 1830s and 1840s, a tremendous number of immigrants flowed over the Great Lakes. Although some settled in the area, the majority continued on to the new western lands.

Period newspapers wrote of steamers running from Buffalo to

western lakes ports, often crowded with more than 1,000 passengers. In 1834 alone, approximately 80,000 men, women and children passed through Buffalo for points west. By 1836, the number doubled. During the same time, 1,000 immigrants a day were arriving in Detroit. Many continued on by ship, others by wagon train. At one point, it was said that westbound wagons were leaving the city on an average of one every five minutes!

Once small frontier towns boomed with phenomenal growth. Milwaukee, Chicago and Detroit quickly became cities in every sense of the word. On northern Lake Michigan, west of Traverse City, places like the Manitou Islands, and especially South Manitou Island, became important stopping points for steamers – not only as a handy place to shelter from a storm, but also to replenish the cords of hardwood that fed their voracious boiler fires.

South Manitou Island, approximately 3.5 by 3 miles in size, is 6.8 miles north of Sleeping Bear Point. Hilly, with high bluffs on the west side, it is lower and wooded on the east end. North Manitou Island, also wooded and hilly, is 3.9 miles to the northeast. A deep-water channel runs between the two. South Manitou has an excellent harbor on the southeast side, providing protection and good holding ground.

An island legend persists that immigrant ships infected with cholera occasionally stopped at South Manitou, a conveniently remote location before reaching Chicago, and used the opportunity to bury their dead in hasty mass graves at the timber line along the sandy shore of the harbor. The story is also told that some especially callous captains also included those about to die with the dead, literally burying them alive. Why wait for the inevitable? Supposedly, on the anniversary of their burial, the restless spirits of the tormented victims rise up from the graves and walk again. Whether they march in protest over their poor treatment or in a hopeless attempt to complete their voyage can only be speculated.

An old islander told of a sailing ship that sank in a storm near the entrance to the bay. About 15 Native Americans en route to logging camps in the Upper Peninsula were sheltering in her hold when she plunged for the bottom. None of the men ever got out of the death trap. They could have been cowering in fear from the cold blasts of the hell-spawned wind or, perhaps, were locked below by a captain who didn't want landlubbers running amok on his deck when he needed working space for his sailors. Reportedly, after due consideration, it was decided to leave them in their impromptu tomb. They, too, are part of the island's spirit world.[4]

Another story involves the ghost of a farm boy who drowned while swimming near the dead hulk of the *Francisco Morazon*. This steel steamer wrecked on the southwest end of the island during a roaring gale on November 14, 1960. Her rusting remains still protrude from the water and are a popular sightseeing attraction for island tourists. The tale goes that on dark and dreary nights, the boy's ghost has been occasionally seen lurking in the shadows on the beach near the wreck. For a while, the ghost was reported to the park rangers so often that they stopped logging the incidents. Why bother? Ghosts aren't part of any federal management plan!

Others talk of hearing the horrible sounds of people drowning on wrecks from long ago. But when they investigate, no one is there. Just an empty lake, bereft of sight or sound, other than the gently lapping of the waves.[5]

The first lighthouse at South Manitou was a 35-foot tower erected in 1839. The present brick keepers house was added in 1858. The redoubtable Dr. Alonzo Slyfield, the island's only physician, served as keeper for a dozen years from 1848 to 1859. Together with the North Manitou Shoal Light, the South Manitou Light helped guide ships through the infamous Manitou Passage, one of the most hazardous stretches of water on the Great Lakes. The route is a shortcut between Gray's Reef Passage and the south end of Lake Michigan. In places the deep water channel is less than two miles wide. The original South Manitou tower was replaced in 1871 by the present 104-foot brick tower, with a Third Order Fresnel lens. On a clear day, the view from the lamp room at the top is remarkable. Eight miles across the passage are Sleeping Bear and Pyramid points. To the north is Cat Head Point at the top of the Leelanau Peninsula and, to the south, Point Betsie. In between is the terrible passage. In 1958, the Coast Guard abandoned the South Manitou light station and it is presently part of the Sleeping Bear National Lakeshore.

In 1988, the passage was designated as the Manitou Passage State Bottomland Preserve. More than 50 known shipwrecks dating from 1835 to 1960 litter its bottom. And there are those that are still not discovered – ships that sailed off "into a crack in the lake," as the old-time sailors said. During the heyday of shipping, it was not unusual for a hundred ships a day to sail through the narrow passage. That as many met disaster as did is not surprising. Even today, it is a popular shortcut for the big freighters.

Strange sounds have also been reported in the South Manitou light tower. In a recent incident, two National Park Service maintenance personnel were working in the keeper's residence when they heard noises and voices in the tower. They couldn't make out what was being said, but were certain it was coming from the lamp room. Concluding someone without authority had gained entry, they climbed the winding iron stairs and checked, but found nothing in the empty tower. The only sound was the empty echo of their own footsteps. The exterior tower door was still securely padlocked. No one could have entered through the padlocked door, nor could anyone have come past the two men in the house without being noticed. No rational explanation for their unearthly experience was ever made.

The former South Manitou Island Life-Saving Service building now serves as quarters for National Park Service personnel, who have reported numerous strange encounters. AUTHOR'S COLLECTION

The old U.S. Life-Saving Service building is also reportedly occupied by other world spirits. The lifesaving station on South Manitou became operational in 1902, the one on North Manitou in 1877. Together they provided vital assistance to vessels that wrecked trying to run the Manitou Passage. The facilities consisted of a boathouse to keep the various boats and other equipment and a station house as a combination office, mess and quarters for keeper and crew. As time passed, additional out-buildings were added. In 1915, the U.S. Life-Saving Service and U.S. Revenue-Marine were combined to form the new U.S. Coast Guard. The mission of the South Manitou station continued largely unchanged until the station was finally abandoned in 1958. North Manitou station was abandoned 20 years before. Both are presently used as seasonal quarters for National Park Service personnel.

When the haunting first started isn't clear, but several National Park Service employees have heard loud footsteps pacing the upstairs floor of the station house. The footfalls were so distinct to one man that he was absolutely certain another park employee was upstairs. When he looked, there was no one there – at least no one he could see. When he related the experience to his supervisor, he was told others had heard the strange sounds too, but there was no real explanation for it, other than ...[6]

A female ranger showering in the upstairs bathroom of the North Manitou station was startled to hear male voices coming from the old crew room. Knowing she was alone in the house, the ranger listened closely and could clearly hear the men discussing the upcoming day's drill activities. Whether the voices seemed to resonate from the old life-saving days or the newer Coast Guard era wasn't known. On other occasions, the sounds of someone knocking at an exterior door are heard. When the door is opened, no one is there.[7]

Neither of the Manitou Islands have any year-round residents. Park personnel only live on the island from May through October. However, before the park took over the islands, there had been a number of small farms, as well as some lumbering and fishing conducted on the island. Residents were few, perhaps numbering slightly more than 100 people. Peak population now might reach as high as 320 souls on a warm summer day. The rest of the year, it's desolate, without human habitation. Most of the warm weather visitors undoubtedly have no idea of the other side of these seemingly peaceful islands, the spiritual one. On the Manitou Islands, ghosts still walk.

Three-Fingered Reilly

During the heyday of Great Lakes commercial navigation, the number of vessels wrecked annually was astounding. Between 1870 and 1871, an estimated 1,167 vessels wrecked with the loss of 214 lives! To help rescue the passengers and crews, between 1876 and 1914, 62 U.S. Life-Saving Service Stations were established at especially dangerous points along the coasts of the Great Lakes. Normally manned by a crew of eight and operated during the April to November navigation season, the lifesavers spent countless hours patrolling the lonely, desolate lakeshore looking for both shipwrecks and their victims. To improve efficiency, in 1915 the lifesavers merged with the Revenue-Cutter Service to form the U.S. Coast Guard. The lifesavers' mission, however, and the lonely beach patrols continued.

Of all the Great Lakes stations, the four along Lake Superior's Michigan Shipwreck Coast stretching west of Whitefish Point for 40 miles were the most desolate. For the crews and families that lived there, they were at the end of the earth. The string of four stations, all built in 1876 and operational the year following, were at Vermilion

Point, Crisp's Point, Two-Hearted River and Deer Park. Each was approximately nine miles from each other. The dead space between the stations was faithfully patrolled by the lifesavers. The night patrols were the worst, especially those during dark and stormy weather. When the north wind whipped the lake into white froth, it was easy for the imagination to run wild, not to mention when the wolves in the ever present forest howled at the moon or followed quietly behind the walking lifesaver, their footfalls barely audible to a sharply tuned ear.

Veteran surfmen always made it a point to teach the new men the gory details of the ghost of Three-Fingered Reilly. They wanted them to know that when they walked the lonely night patrols, they were not alone!

The story of the ghost starts with the loss of the steamer *John Owen* on November 13, 1919. The 281-foot, 2,127-ton composite steamer was downbound from Duluth with wheat when she sank in a terrific gale, taking her entire crew of 21 men and one woman down with her. The location of the sinking was never determined, but was thought to have been somewhere northwest of Whitefish Point.

The following March, a Coast Guardsman running the mail with a dog sled team discovered a body frozen in the shore ice to the west of Crisp's Point. After great effort, the remains of the man, later identified as the *Owen*'s assistant engineer William J. Reilly, was chopped out of the ice. Loaded on a sled, the body was returned to the station and stored frozen until instructions regarding its disposition came from the Lake Carriers' Association. The body was in excellent condition, except for two missing fingers supposedly accidentally chopped off when the body was being freed from the ice. Due to the inability to get the body out to a proper undertaker and a spell of warm weather preventing further "storage," the body was eventually buried in the station cemetery.

If the old lifesaver's stories are to be believed, however, Reilly's spirit was not so easily disposed of. Hoary old surfmen always warned new men about the ghost of "Three-Fingered Reilly." His restless shade is said to wander the lonely shore still searching for his missing fingers. More than one patrolman is said to have come back to the station white and shaking from either hearing Reilly's footsteps just behind him or seeing his ghostly form outlined against the surf. His body may be forever buried in a long forgotten grave, but his ghost marches on.[8]

Some believe Reilly's restless spirit has company. Several dozen vessels wrecked along this dangerous section of coast, many with terrible loss of life. The lost souls of their passengers and crews were also claimed to wander the beach, as did the restless shade of at least one old lifesaver.

141

The White Horse of Yeo Island

During the 19th century, mariners reported seeing the ghost of a white horse on Georgian Bay's Yeo Island. As they sailed past under reefed foresail during dark and blustery fall nights, the supernatural beast was seen to gallop up and down the shingle beach. How the equine ghost arrived on the island is a tale unto itself.

It seems there once was a white saddle horse named Louie owned by a farmer on Drummond Island at the southern end of the St. Marys River down from Lake Superior. In 1828, the British decided to evacuate the island's fort and move to Penetanguishene at the south end of Georgian Bay. To that end, in late September two vessels, the brig *Wellington* and the schooner *Alice Hackett,* arrived at the island. The soldiers loaded on the *Wellington* and soon departed. The *Hackett* later followed with the rest of the inhabitants, including 25 settlers. Among them were the tavern keeper, Pierre Lepine, his wife, Angelina, and their 10-year-old daughter, Therese. The *Hackett* also carried four horses, including Louie, eight head of cattle, some sheep and pigs and, perhaps most important, 13 barrels of good drinking whisky.

As the schooner sailed blissfully down Lake Huron, the tavern keeper did a fantastic business with his liquid stock. All the men aboard, including the crew, got thoroughly besotted. Good navigation became, at best, questionable, with the result that under full sail on the night of October 1, the schooner fetched up hard on the south tip of Fitzwilliam Island, just off the south end of Manitoulin Island. Pushed by the north wind, the *Hackett* heeled sharply to one side, presenting a steeply angled deck.

Absolute panic reigned supreme. The single yawl was hurriedly launched and all of the passengers and crew tumbled into it. In the general stampede, all the animals, except Louie, also went flying over the side. After paddling aimlessly about in the dark, the farm stock drowned. Overloaded to the point of being nearly awash and manned by a crew too drunk even to row, the yawl drifted before the wind. It finally washed ashore on nearby Yeo Island. The only people who didn't participate in the bedlam of the alcohol-fueled abandon ship drill were Mrs. Lapine and her daughter. Both were left behind in the chaos. Thinking more clearly than the rest, she tied her child and herself securely to the mainmast and waited for daylight and a hoped-for rescue.

When the cold light of day finally broke, the survivors returned to the wreck in the yawl to salvage whatever they could. It wasn't until the men reached the schooner and found the mother and daughter nearly dead from the cold that they realized the two were forgotten during the wild panic. Louie the horse was also waiting patiently for rescue. The salvagers took both humans aboard the yawl and carefully guided the horse safely to the shallow water off Yeo Island. From there he was able to clamber to shore. Several days later, a small vessel from Penetang rescued the *Hackett* survivors. But there was neither a way to get the horse aboard nor room on the crowded vessel if they could. He was left to his fate on the desolate island.

The horse's owner solemnly promised his steed that he would not forget him and would soon return to rescue him. Unable to find a boat big enough or convince a captain of the importance of the job, he never went back for the horse. Because of Louie's occupancy of the island, it locally became known as Horse Island. Long after Louie had perished from cold, starvation or just loneliness, schooner men told of seeing his ghost prancing on the bleak shores.[9]

Louie was loyal to his grave and, if the tale is true, far beyond.

The Haunted Sands

The Great Lakes not only has haunted ships and lighthouses, but also a stretch of ghostly sand beach. According to legend, that supernatural sand was the direct cause of the loss of three vessels.

As the story goes, it was 1814 when Commodore Perry's fleet wintered in Misery Bay on Lake Erie's New York shore. To settle a dispute, two of his officers fought a duel on the beach.

Whether the duel was caused by insult or the love of a young beauty has long been forgotten. The chasm between the two officers could not be spanned by apology or reason. Only blood would do! Their seconds prepared the matched dueling pistols, carefully charging each with powder and ball. As the sun rose over the gray lake, the two men lined up back-to-back, paced off 10 measured steps, turned and fired. One ball whistled past its target, striking the sand 50 yards down the beach. The other ball found flesh, bone and blood. It was a fatal shot.

As the loser lay bleeding to death on the sand, he supposedly cursed the victor, stating that his soul would know no peace until the lake waves had washed the blood from the sand. Ever since, it is claimed, the winner's moaning ghost has wandered the lakeshore, praying for the water to cleanse the red-stained sand.

In 1909, the Ideal Company of Port Hope, Ontario, had a requirement for a quantity of molding sand to manufacture sinks, bath tubs and other plumbing equipment. Good molding sand was hard to find, but that at Misery Bay fit the bill perfectly. A shipment of it was subsequently brought to Cleveland and a steambarge dispatched from Toledo to pick it up. The steamer, however, burned to the water's edge before loading the sand. The charter then went to Captain James Peacock and the schooner *Emily B. Maxwell*. The 135-foot schooner, built in Manitowoc in 1881, had a capacity of 800 tons, just the right size for the cargo. But disaster struck the schooner when entering the Cleveland harbor. Unable to get a tug and confused by the bewildering array of cribwork and pilings, Captain Peacock crashed the *Emily B.* into some piles and wrecked her.

The third vessel to get the job was the *Sir C.T. Van Straubenzee*, under the command of Captain "Dolph" Corson. On September 25, the three-masted schooner left Toronto, Lake Ontario, bound for Cleveland on Lake Erie. She quickly locked through the Welland Canal and continued on her trip. As the *Straubenzee* sailed gracefully over the night-darkened lake, all was right with the world, at least on the schooner. But back at home things were different. During the night, the captain's wife had a nightmare so distressing that even in the morning she became nauseated. She instinctively knew that something was terribly wrong or would soon be.

The daughter-in-law of the schooner's cook also experienced an unsettling dream. In the haze of her mind, she saw two vessels collide. Both were indistinct in outline, but one was clearly a three-masted schooner. After a while, all that remained were several forlorn planks floating around on the still water. A distant voice cried out, "There lies the boat that was wrecked." The woman woke with a start when her clock struck 3. Like the captain's wife, she, too, knew intuitively something was wrong.

Driven by a reliable breeze, the *Straubenzee* sailed on through the Lake Erie night. The sky was clear and the stars winked down on the old schooner as she plowed blissfully along. Her sidelights burned luminously to mark her passage.

Eight miles off Long Point, Ontario, the watchman on the schooner spotted the lights of an oncoming passenger steamer and correctly surmised her to be the *City of Erie*. From her lights, he also guessed that she would pass very close. He burned a sputtering red flare to warn her off. But the steamer paid no attention to that flare or to the next. She continued her dangerous course. Wakened by the noise on deck, Captain Corson came topside to see what was going on. Evaluating the situation, he realized that a collision was imminent. Although it isn't known for certain, it is thought that Captain Corson recognized the extreme danger he presented to the steamer. If his vessel hit the steamer bow on, it was likely that he would sink her and cause another *Lady Elgin* disaster. If, however, he could swing into her quarter, then the steamer would escape major damage, although the old *Straubenzee* would likely not survive the crash. Without hesitation he ordered,

"Hard up, for God's sake, hard up!" The man at the wheel straightway obeyed and the steel bow of the rushing steamer plowed deeply into the old wooden hull. The schooner went down so quickly that the men on the *City of Erie* barely even knew they had hit something. Only two of the schooner's five-person crew survived the disaster. Lost were the captain, mate and the woman cook.

It was later determined that the steamer was wheeled by the pilot, who claimed that the schooner showed no lights and was, thus, invisible to him. True or not, when the fates called for the old *Straubenzee*, she came, despite a clear night, good visibility, lights and flares. The steel bow of the *City of Erie* found her and her intended cargo of cursed sand. But bad luck comes in threes and the *Straubenzee* was the third vessel lost. The sand was eventually safely delivered by the steambarge *Ida E*.[10]

Long Point's Headless Ghost

Ontario's Long Point at the top of Lake Erie has been a notorious ship trap since the earliest days of navigation. It is said that when upbound, LaSalle's *Griffon* barely missed smashing into it.

The story goes that sometime in the 1880s a downbound steamer off Long Point encountered a screaming gale. Battered by the waves, the vessel began to break up. To try to save his crew, the captain turned for Long Point with the hope of putting his vessel safely on the beach. But the steamer was disintegrating too fast. They weren't going to make it. In an act of desperation, the crew lowered the yawl, but in their hurry, a man caught his head in the falls and was decapitated. The bloody head crashed into the wild lake and the headless torso thumped into the yawl. In a minor miracle, the crew struggled through the roaring surf and safely reached shore. After recovering from their ordeal and out of loyalty to their fellow shipmate, they searched the breakers for the missing head. They never found it and eventually were forced to bury the corpse without it.

According to legend, on nights when the moon beams full, the thin wraith of a ghost is seen wandering along the shore, ever searching for his still missing head.[11]

Gros Cap Spirits

Two great Indian battles occurred in the Gros Cap area of northern Lake Michigan. In the first, the Ojibway and Ottawa fought the Iroquois in the general locality between Gros Cap, St. Ignace and St. Helena Island. In the second clash the Ojibway and Ottawa massacred the Menominee who were camped in West Moran Bay, on the southeast side of Gros Cap. As the result of both battles, the corpses of slain

Indians were left everywhere. When the Gros Cap cemetery was built in 1880, many Indian skeletons were plowed up during construction. More were discovered when the cemetery was later expanded. This stretch of lonely shore is another place where spirits walk. Some in dreadful agony, others wandering aimlessly, they still search for something on the haunted beach.[12]

The Woman in White

Just south of Parry Sound on the eastern shore of Georgian Bay is a lovely old vacation cottage. Built in 1890 and tucked neatly into the lakeshore, it's a wonderfully restful place to spend a weekend, a week or forever.

This lovely vacation property on Parry Sound, Georgian Bay, is also home to the ghost of a young woman in white. AUTHOR'S COLLECTION

The wilderness cottage is also home to the restless and mysterious ghost of a young woman. As far as is known, the apparition was first sighted in the summer of 1980. The owner had guests in for the weekend and one of them, a young woman school teacher, clearly saw the ghost, dressed in an old-fashioned long white dress and wide brimmed hat, disappear into the woods behind the house. The image was very detailed and there was no doubt in the teacher's mind that it was a spirit manifestation!

Some years later, another house guest, the holder of a doctorate in engineering without an ounce of imagination in his soul, saw the same ghost. The engineer, standing outside as the owner closed the cabin door, was startled to see the pale figure of the woman watching intently from a window. It vanished when he called attention to it.

The young woman has never been seen by the owner, his wife or their two children. They have been unable to find any clue to the reason for the haunting or who the spirit is. Previous owners of the cottage deny any knowledge of it. Instead of being scared or even uncomfortable with their supernatural guest, the family is very accepting of it. During storms, they say it provides a calming influence over the old house. No matter how hard the wind blows or how close the lighting bolts strike, there is never a feeling of danger.

Is the young woman a kind of guardian spirit, watching over "her" cottage, protecting it from harm? Was she a victim of a shipwreck, perhaps a soul lost on one of the many Georgian Bay disasters? Or is she a wandering spirit that has just found shelter in the friendly old cottage?[13]

Whose Ghost is it, Anyway?

Another stretch of haunted coast is that along Weller's Beach, on the Canadian side of eastern Lake Ontario. Before the turn of the century, local residents reported seeing strange, unexplained lights moving along the deserted shore. Many believed that they were seeing ghosts of men killed in shipwrecks.

There are two tragic wrecks considered most likely as spawning the restless spirits. The first was that of the schooner *Belle Sheridan*, lost in a roaring gale on November 7, 1880. By the time the crashing waves subsided, all of her crew save one had perished in the grasping seas.

The second vessel to wreck on Weller's Beach was the 107-foot, 209-ton schooner *Garibaldi*, stranding only 10 days after the *Belle Sheridan*. The *Garibaldi* was bound for Toronto from Fairhaven, New York, with 350 tons of coal. She sailed the length of the lake under storm canvas, blown by the screaming, ice-laden wind, finally dropping her hook outside the harbor to wait for better weather before trying to enter Weller's Bay. For 15 terrible hours the *Garibaldi* safely rode out the howling gale. After her anchor cable finally broke, the crew tried to sail the beleaguered vessel into the harbor, but their efforts were in vain. Driven by a screeching west wind, the schooner blew hard onto an offshore sandbar. Battered by the waves, the old schooner soon began to break up. The ship's yawl was smashed to kindling by a massive boarding sea preventing any effort to abandon her. Some of the crew were eventually taken off by local men using an old lifeboat, but the boat was too rickety to make another trip through the surf, leaving the rest stranded on the dying schooner. All of the remaining crew, except for one, climbed high into the frozen rigging and lashed themselves tight in the hope of surviving the storm. The mate, Louis (or Lewis) Stonehouse, doubtlessly muttering curses against the fury of the lake, went below deck. For the men aboard the old schooner, the long night was filled with horror. Towering waves crashed into the hull, sending freezing spray flying over the ship. Ice formed heavy on the deck and caked thick on the rigging. Hour by hour, the ice built up higher on the *Garibaldi* until, when the cold dawn finally broke, she was more ice than wood.

When a rescue party eventually made it out to her, they found the men in the rigging still clinging to life, but only barely. Louis Stonehouse was a different story. Down below they discovered the old mate standing silently in the cabin, frozen solid in a block of translucent ice. His boney hands were raised high over his head, as if in a last desperate effort to ward off the shimmering ice demons. For want of a good boat, he died a truly horrible death.

Afterward, local citizens claimed that his ghost haunted the desolate beach. Was he alone or did the spirits of the *Belle Sheridan* crew march with him? What were they looking for? Were they searching for a way home to loved ones left so long ago?[14]

Garibaldi was hardly a lucky name. Also lost in the fall of 1880 was the propeller *Garibaldi*, smashed ashore just south of Harrisville, Michigan, on Lake Huron. A 164-foot schooner *Garibaldi* was lost at Port Elgin, Ontario, in November 1887. Earlier, in 1865, the 120-foot schooner *Garibaldi* foundered in Georgian Bay with the loss of four lives.[15]

Cries in the Night

During a dark autumn night in 1906, a party of hunters on Georgian Bay's White Cloud Island huddled together around a blazing campfire. As hot drinks warmed their chilled bones, stories of the day's hunt filled the air. Suddenly something else permeated the cold night. Cries were plainly heard coming from somewhere out in the black lake. "Help me" and "God save us" echoed weakly over the waves. Although desperate to help, the hunters were powerless. The night was too dark and stormy to launch their small boat and the cries seemed to come from everywhere and yet nowhere.

The following day the men went out and searched for the source of the night's wretched shrieks. They found nothing – not a trace of man nor beast. Whatever the source of the pleas was long gone.

When the story was repeated ashore, knowledgeable "old salts" just shook their heads, knowing full well that the hunters had experienced a recreation of the terrible loss of the steamer *Jane Miller*. The *Miller* was a small coastal steamer built in Little Current on Manitoulin Island at the north end of Georgian Bay. Only 78 feet in length, she was 18 feet in beam and 210 tons. The steamer was no thing of beauty. Her lines were square rather than graceful, but for her designated role in life she was efficient enough, regularly handling passenger and freight traffic between Collingwood, Meaford, Owen Sound and Wiarton at the south end of the bay and in and out of all the ports on the east side of the Bruce Peninsula and Manitoulin Island.

The steamer Jane Miller *was lost in November 1885, but may have been the spectre that startled hunters in 1906.* RUTHERFORD B. HAYES LIBRARY

The steamer's last trip started on the morning of November 25, 1881, when she departed Owen Sound for Meaford, where she loaded freight and passengers before turning west for Wiarton. Although a strong southwest gale punished the *Miller* all the way, she safely reached the mouth of Colpoys Bay, where she loaded wood at Big Bay. At 8:30 p.m., she pulled away from the fuel dock bound, she thought, for Wiarton, a dozen or so miles to the west. Heavily loaded with both cargo and passengers, as 28 souls had entrusted their fate to the small steamer, she pushed on. All during the long dark night, the southwest storm blew hard and the *Miller* battled dead into it. What happened to her remains a mystery. The steamer never reached Wiarton, or any other location of the living. What little wreckage was later discovered was on White Cloud Island at the mouth of Colpoys Bay. And it was really very little – a flag staff, smashed lifeboat, oars and some of the crew's uniform caps. The hull was never found.

Marine people speculated on numerous reasons for the loss. Perhaps the gale disabled her rudder, the cargo shifted, storm stress sprang a plank or the engines failed. In any case, the storm would have quickly overwhelmed her, sending her to the bottom and those aboard to a "better world."

What did the hunters hear 25 years later? If old sailor superstitions that waters where ships sink are haunted by the restless ghosts of crew and passengers are true, then what happened was obvious. The *Miller* wreck re-created itself; the agony of an icy death was replayed. The souls of those aboard the doomed vessel have no rest.[16]

McCoy's Ghost

Just to the northwest of Parry Sound is an especially rugged set of islands known as the McCoy Islands. Surrounded by reefs, rocks and shoals, it is a dangerous area to be in. Big McCoy is the site of the ghost of an old trader known to history only as McCoy. His reputation is a vile and black one. It was said he swindled both Indian and white man alike. No man called him a friend. Life has a way of evening the score with such misbegotten men, however, and McCoy didn't escape his just reward. Late one September night, someone, whose identity is unknown, dealt with McCoy in a very permanent and appropriate fashion. He never cheated anyone again, unless it was the devil in the very bowels of hell.

Supposedly every September when the moon is full, two unearthly screams can be heard echoing from the depths of the island woods. Some say it is McCoy protesting his murder. Others that it's the trader celebrating his beating of the devil in some unholy deal.[17]

The Body on the Shore

The fury of the storm battered away at the old light tower. Torrents of scalding rain seemingly tried to drive into the very granite of the blocks. The wind howled around the ancient tower and, on the rocks below, huge breakers smashed into shards of steel-like spray. Thunder rode above the clouds and lightning flashed across the sky. It was blowing a real "gagger." High on the walkway surrounding the lamp room, the lightkeeper hung on gamely to the rail as he peered out to the distant horizon. It was miserable, cold and wet, but God, he enjoyed the storm!

He was alone at the island light, his assistant keeper having gone ashore the day before and the unexpected blow preventing his return. It was of no matter. He'd faced other storms alone and would doubtless make it through this one. He just had to work harder to care for the beacon.

Something caught his eye in the water below. It was just a spark of movement, but it was out of harmony with the storm. There it was again, about 50 yards out, just beyond the surf. Incredibly, it was a man clinging desperately to a wooden hatch cover. Periodically, a wave would sweep over him, but when it passed he was still doggedly hanging on. Inexorably, he was being driven toward the rocky shore. There was only one chance in a thousand that he would survive the rocks. Quickly the keeper ran down the winding tower steps. He had to be there to help, just in case.

Carefully the keeper worked his way down the slippery rocks, getting as close to the wild surf as he dared. The man was still visible, still clutching the hatch cover. When a quick succession of larger waves, the infamous Three Sisters, bore down upon the poor soul, the keeper knew that the man was a goner. Although he had played his cards well to have made it this far, fate held the joker.

The first wave broke hard over the hatch cover. When its wash cleared, the hatch was broken into splinters and the man was left flailing helplessly in the churning water.

The second wave buried both the splintered cover and the drowning man in a sea of white foam. The man didn't surface again. The keeper knew that he had witnessed the cold hand of death.

The third wave, larger than the first two, broke solid, roaring its way up the rocks, knocking the keeper head over heels. Its grasping fingers nearly dragged him back into the boiling surf. Dazed by the shock, the keeper slowly regained his senses as he scampered up the rocks towards the light station. He had taken only a few steps when he stumbled over something laying on the beach. It was the man who had been on the hatch. Although unconscious, he was still alive! Looking closely, the keeper saw that he was middle aged and his head topped with silver hair. Dressed well, he plainly was no common sailor. Maybe he was a captain or even an owner. Whoever he was, he was a lucky soul indeed. When the keeper bent down to start to drag him to the lighthouse and warmth, he noticed something else. Around his waist was a fat money belt!

Curious, the keeper opened the belt and found more money than he had ever seen. He also thought of his own hard struggle to make a living – the difficult work of keeping a light on this lonely forsaken island; of his wife and children ashore that he only got to see on his few days off. It just wasn't fair. This man, who would surely soon be dead from his injuries, had so much. He had so little. In a fit of rage, jealousy or madness, he removed the heavy belt and strapped it around his own waist. Grabbing the man by the feet, he dragged him back to the surf and rolled him into the surging waves. No one would ever be the wiser. When the body would be found, if it would ever be found, it was just another gristly victim of a shipwreck.

Returning to the light, he hid the money belt in his battered steamer trunk, brewed a cup of strong coffee and then climbed back up to the lamp room. It was almost sunset and time to light the wick for another long night. Later he would think of his new found wealth and what to do with it.

The next day the storm blew itself out and just before dark the assistant returned to the island. For a while everything was normal, back to the deadly dull routine of lightkeeping. Every night, when he was certain he was alone, the keeper carefully removed the belt from the bottom of the trunk and counted out the money. When he finished, he quietly returned it to the hiding place.

After a month or so, though, the keeper started having terrible nightmares. Waking up screaming and covered in sweat, he vividly recalled seeing the man crawling up out of the surf and over the rocks, moving toward him and asking, "Where is it?" Fearful of sleep and his terrible dreams, he fought against it constantly. Rest was not his to have.

He also began to see things – things that no one else admitted seeing. Sometimes at night, when he was high in the tower, he saw the ghostly image of the shipwrecked man moving slowly along the rocks as if it were looking for something. When he pointed the figure out to his assistant, the man said he saw nothing. Several times the ghost's anguished face appeared peering in the station window as the keeper sat in his chair smoking a late night pipe.

One night, when the keeper was scurrying for the outhouse, he ran headlong into the ghost. Pale and sad faced, it stared hard at the keeper before asking, "Where is it?" Shaken to his soul, the keeper ran back into the house, slamming and bolting the door behind.

The keeper's performance as lightkeeper decreased markedly. Always tired from lack of sleep, jumping at his own shadow, he developed an extreme case of nerves. At times, he shook uncontrollably. Other times he broke down in a fit of sobbing. Even alcohol had no effect. The lighthouse inspector, an old friend of the keeper, finally was forced to tell him that either he must resign or be fired. He could not continue. The keeper resigned and returned to live with his family on the mainland.

The change in scenery did him no good. The terrible dreams came every night and his health continued to deteriorate. He ate almost nothing. He never left the house after dark and insisted that all the shades be drawn when the sun went down. Day by day, his face grew more gaunt and his hollow eyes became deep pits of bottomless black. Finally, sick and fevered, he couldn't even leave his bed. When the day came for his death, his family dutifully gathered around, waiting for the end.

Overcome by guilt, the keeper closed his eyes and slowly began to speak in a low, barely audible whisper, relating his sad tale. All eyes riveted on the dying man. Those present, who knew him so well in better days, were unable to believe what was being said. When the dying keeper finished speaking, he opened his eyes and gave a fearful scream! Standing at the foot of the bed for all to see was the ghost of the shipwrecked man. Gray and wraithlike, it transfixed everyone in the room. Talking in a thick and hoary voice, it asked, "Where is it?" The only answer was the keeper's death rattle. In an instant the apparition vanished, as if it were never there. All that remained was a puddle of water on the wooden floor. The stain of that water remained as long as the house stood.

The story doesn't end here. There are details still undiscovered. The name of the keeper and his light, the identity of the survivor and his vessel all are still unknown and can't definitely be determined. At this late date, the true details will probably always remain shrouded in mystery. What happened to the money is also unknown. Some of the family, believing in the money but not the ghost, returned to the island to search for it, thinking that since it wasn't found among the keeper's scant belongings he must have hidden it there before he left. They never reported finding it, but they did claim to have briefly seen the wandering apparition searching for it too.

Whether this tale is true or not is, of course, questionable, but parts of it do have the pure ring of reality. For obvious reasons, family members conspired to keep it quiet. There was no reason to spread the shame of murder and theft. However, over generations, some of it invariably leaked out. It is speculated that the lighthouse itself is almost all gone, abandoned by the government when shipping patterns changed and new facilities were built. Later ravaged by vandals, little enough of it remains today to provide even a faint image of its old glory.

But on the rocky beach, when the storm waves roll hard and fast and the wind screams high, there are those who say the restless spirit still walks, looking, ever looking.

Belle Isle's Indian Princess

There are, of course, many Indian legends on the lakes. A number involve spirits from the world beyond. One old legend involves the ghostly image of an Indian maiden periodically sighted on the shores of Belle Isle in the Detroit River.

It seems that long ago an Ottawa chief had a daughter so beautiful, he hid her along the shore in a boat covered with a heavy cloth. The chief wanted no one to gaze on her extreme comeliness, afraid she would be stolen from him. The wind gods, however, caught a glimpse of the maiden and, captivated by her beauty, blew hard enough to ripple the cover off the boat and force the craft into the river's current. Ashamed at their action, they blew it back to shore and asked the chief not to hide her from view, but to allow them to gaze forever on her magnificence.

This the chief agreed to do and he took her to Belle Isle for safe keeping. To protect her from mortals, the Great Spirit surrounded her with many rattlesnakes. The reptiles eventually also succumbed to her charms and soon came to worship her. In recognition of her radiance, the great spirit made her immortal. Her spirit would live on Belle Island forever. To this day, some claim her wandering ghost still haunts the island.[18]

A False Light

"There it is! It must be the light," said the wheelsman. The captain agreed and ordered the *Mary Ward* swung to starboard. It was November 24, 1872, and the 120-foot steamer was bound east from Owen Sound for Collingwood, Ontario, normally an easy 45-mile run. But visibility was very poor and both men were straining hard, looking for the Nottawasaga Light. When they saw a faint glimmer through the dark just where they thought the light should be, they assumed it was the light. It wasn't! The glow they saw was from a lantern at a boarding-house at Craigleith, five miles short of Collingwood. With a shudder and crunch, the steamer ran hard up on a reef three miles or so offshore.

Since the weather was still calm and there was no reason for immediate panic, the captain sent a lifeboat to Collingwood to get a tug. They were eventually successful in arranging for the services of the 86-ton tug *Mary Ann*.

November, though, is never quiet for long and during the delay the water turned ugly. The captain, with seven others, launched another boat and headed for the now visible lighthouse for help. The waves were so roiled, the small boat just made it to the beach.

The *Mary Ann* reached the area of the stranded steamer the day after she went on the reef, but the combination of storm and shoal water prevented her from getting close enough to assist. She could neither remove the passengers and crew nor get a line to her. Helpless, she steamed back to the safety of Collingwood.

The power of the rising storm and the sight of the tug abandoning them was too much. Those left aboard the *Mary Ward* panicked. Eight of the men launched another boat. Disdaining other passengers, they headed for the nearby beach. They never made it. Capsizing in the crashing waves, the deserters "fed the fishes" the hard way. They should have kept to the steamer. The 24 souls left aboard the *Mary Ward* survived the battering of the gale. The following day, when the weather cleared, they were rescued by fishing tugs from Collingwood and the lighthouse keeper in his boat. Although much of her cargo and fittings were later salvaged, the vessel itself was a total loss. The shoal is now known as *"Mary Ward* Ledges."

But the ghosts rose from the wreck of the *Mary Ward* and for years afterward it was claimed that the boardinghouse, whose light caused the loss of the vessel, was haunted by the spirits of the men drowned in the wreck. It was their revenge for the lantern that led them to their deaths. The haunting only stopped when the old structure was demolished.[19]

Shelldrake's Spirits

By some accounts, the ghost town of Shelldrake could be considered the most haunted village on the Great Lakes. Although it still has some living, breathing residents and therefore isn't technically a ghost town, it is only the faintest image of what it once was.

Shelldrake is located on the west shore of Whitefish Bay, Lake Superior, about midway between Paradise and Whitefish Point. The town was named after the river Shelldrake, which in turn was named by the early French voyagers. The Shelldrake River is indicated on the oldest French maps, some dating from the 1630s.

When built in the 1890s, Shelldrake's fortune was based on lumbering and commercial fishing. Located between the two branches of the Shelldrake River, it was an ideal spot to capitalize on the area's extensive forests. The village included a sawmill, hospital, school house, ice house, a hotel called the "Ishkabibble Inn," as well as 40 to 50 worker's houses. In its heyday, it consisted of 155 separate buildings, including sheds, mills and barns. Unusual for the times, indoor plumbing was the norm, as was piped hot water brought in from the mill's sawdust burner.

At one time a dozen lumber camps fed the Shelldrake Mill. Both branches of the Shelldrake were thick with logs. Accurate population figures are hard to capture, but it wasn't unusual for a thousand people to be in town for the winter. When the inevitable fire destroyed the mill in 1916, Shelldrake's permanent population stood at 350. Since the timber was not exhausted, the mill was quickly rebuilt. Another blaze in 1925 again destroyed the mill and spelled the end of the village. Without mill work and with the forests largely depleted, the men left and Shelldrake slowly declined into a ghost town.

The actual history of the area is far older than that of the town. Native Americans, French explorers and fur traders all passed through or camped at the present day townsite.

In the recent past one of the old waterfront houses was occupied by a retired sailor. A long-toothed veteran of the lakes, his new purpose in life was to gaze at the wide expanse of Whitefish Bay and the freighters plowing their way over the water. Hour after hour and day after day, he sat in his ancient rocking chair in front of a large picture window and watched the bay. It was his "duty" station. The water was his great love and he would let nothing obscure his view. Frustrated by the trees growing on a neighbor's lot that partially blocked that view, he waited until the family had gone to church, then went onto the property and cut them down. Nothing would stop him from watching the lake. Nothing!

But even vigilant sailors need to rest and, when he went off his self-imposed watch, he lowered a large shade over his window. The neighbors always knew when he was up and about. The shade would be up.

Eventually the old sailor died and the house was willed to his brother's family, who promptly changed the front window, installing new shades. Once they returned to their home downstate, the shade would quickly fall off the wall and stay down until they returned weeks or months later and put it back up. This strange phenomenon happened every time they left.

In one spectacular incident some neighbors were working in their yard when they saw the shade start to shake violently. " ... to actually see that shade start shaking inside the house – it was almost like he did it purposely. We could actually see it, we were there. It started to shake, then shake some more, then fell right down. It was stunning!" Afterward, there was little doubt in anyone's mind that the old sailor wanted to see his bay and he would not be denied, in life or death.

But the Shelldrake hauntings are more extensive than this single instance.

Another house had a more visual manifestation of the supernatural. Known locally as the "green house," it was rented to a bank manager and her husband, a deputy sheriff. A small house, one bedroom was located in a wing running off the main structure like the foot of an "L." The wife was in bed one night when she plainly saw a figure of a man standing off to one side of the room. She thought it was her husband until she saw it walk through the solid wall that connected the bedroom to the main building. Startled, she rolled to the side and saw her husband sleeping soundly next to her.

Both husband and wife had similar sightings on different occasions. The mysterious figure would appear briefly, then disappear through the wall. There was no doubt that their house was haunted. However, considering their positions of responsibility within the community, neither mentioned anything of their unusual experiences.

The house was later rented to a school teacher and his wife. One night she was lying peacefully in her bed when the strange figure appeared. Also thinking it was her husband, she called to him. The ghost turned around, looked at her for a brief moment and proceeded to walk through the same wall. In another experience, the husband heard a voice, looked up and saw the figure. After a moment, it walked through the wall. There was no attempt at communication or threatening action.

Over a period of 12 to 15 years, four or five different families rented the house. Each had similar experiences with the wall-walking ghost, but they never told each other, or anyone else for that matter, of what they saw. After all, it wasn't the type of thing you went around and told people about if you wanted to retain your community standing. But in small towns everyone tends to come together for social events. At one such gathering, all of the house's previous renters happened by circumstance to be seated at the same table. Someone mentioned something about the supernatural and the stories quickly came out. Not only had all the couples seen the ghost walking through the wall, but also witnessed other supernatural experiences in the "green house."

There is a postscript, of sorts, to the story. In later years, the owner of the house needed to do some plumbing work. Working in the low and dark crawl space under the building he discovered the remains of an old double-bitted axe, an empty whisky bottle, a small triangular poison bottle complete with diamond shaped indented surface and some unidentified bones. Whether they were animal or human was never determined. The objects were found directly under the wall that the ghost always walked through. Was there a connection? Speculation could be endless. Was there a long forgotten murder? Was it by axe or poison? Were the bones those of a hastily hidden victim?

Another Shelldrake house suffered for a time from periodic visits from the "lady in blue." At various times and in different locations, this very strange apparition appeared without apparent reason. It was seen clearly by the owner, his wife, mother and children. The unscheduled manifestations were getting on everyone's nerves. Eventually, the ghost was traced to an antique dresser, circa 1850, that was brought over from the "green house." When the dresser was moved to an empty house used as a storage building, the "lady in blue's" appearances ceased. When the dresser was brought back, the ghost came, too! At present, the dresser has been removed for good.

Recently a college professor brought a group of students to

Shelldrake to examine various historical sites. The group was also interested in legends, ghosts and paranormal activities, but at the time they had no particular knowledge of the village's supernatural activities. One of the members of the group was an Indian woman reputed to have powers of extrasensory perception. She also had never been to the area and knew nothing of its history or legends. When she walked onto the porch of the "white house," she was literally overcome with the force of a "presence" within it. Others in the group had to assist her back to a safe area away from the structure. She was positive that there was a spirit in the old house. What was inside for certain was the antique dresser! The college group tried to videotape the house, but the camera and recorder refused to work. Earlier the equipment had worked fine, but not at the white house!

In another of the houses the owner inadvertently left his tape recorder on overnight. When he woke the next morning, he realized his error, rewound the tape and turned off the machine. Giving in to curiosity, he played the tape just to hear what was recorded. What came out of the speakers shocked him to his very fiber. "It was like a voice from hell. It was so scary I got goosebumps and all the kids were terrified and went away screaming. This moaning, groaning voice right out of hell. We destroyed the tape. It was the scariest thing you have ever heard in your life!"

Shelldrake may well be the most haunted village on the Great Lakes. These tales are only some of many. Pictures jumping off walls, slamming doors, unidentified sounds, bumps and groans, all echo through the old ghost town. Why the spirits walk in Shelldrake isn't known, but walk they do![20]

The Sacred Rock

One Indian legend old Lake Huron sailors were well aware of, and perhaps the more superstitious of them had reason to fear, was that of the infamous Sacred Rock. The rock, about 10 feet in diameter and five feet high, is located near the water's edge, approximately six miles north of Rogers City, Michigan.

The Sacred Rock, composed of Engadine-dolomite from Lake Superior country, doubtlessly was dragged down by the tearing glaciers that so sculptured the whole Great Lakes region. To the north of the rock are the famous sliding banks, a full 80 feet high.

The old rock was always a place of special importance to Native Americans. Passing travelers often left distinctive offerings of tobacco, pipes or other expressions of veneration. Sometimes dogs were even sacrificed on its cold surface, the fresh blood staining the sides.

Located about six miles north of Rogers City, Michigan, is the Sacred Rock of the Ojibway people. AUTHOR'S COLLECTION

Legend claims that where the rock is located was the boundary marking the hunting grounds of two tribes. The chief of one was especially aggressive, always violating the border, resulting in trouble and sometimes even bloodshed between the tribes. At last, the two chiefs met at the exact spot the rock now marks. Both argued invidiously, threatening a terrible war. Disgusted with their behavior, the Great Spirit Kitchie Manitou, who was traveling on Lake Superior at the time, seized a nearby rock and with a mighty heave threw it down, smashing both offending men beneath. The shock of the impact was so terrific that the nearby hills began to shake and slide, a phenomenon that continues to this day. The rock therefore became a unique place of significance and worship.

In another version, the two chiefs were fighting on the rock when the Great Manitou send a powerful bolt of lightning crashing into them, sending both quarrelers into the next world. It is said when rain washes the rock, the red blood of the slain chiefs can still be seen.[21]

CHAPTER SIX

Sea Serpents and Other Creatures

Sea serpents have long been reported roaming wild in the seven seas. In Roman times, the poet Virgil described them during the siege of Troy. In the Middle Ages, they were accepted as fact and so noted in ancient manuscripts. During the age of exploration, they continued to be reported and feared by sailors.

The first reported American sea serpent was seen off the Massachusetts coast in 1639 and, for years to come, the area was a hot bed for sea monster sightings. In 1817, one was even described entering Gloucester Harbor. Witnesses said it was 45 to 50 feet long with a head the size of a horse's. Two years later, 200 people sighted a similarly sized sea serpent off Nahant, Massachusetts. One author identified the years 1817-47 as the peak of American sea monster sightings.[1] The creatures were undoubtedly as much of the American culture as they were of the European.

Tales of sea serpents and other strange creatures were also prevalent on the Great Lakes. Some were accepted as factual, others were treated more humorously. Many of the stories go back to the European's first exploration of the inland seas. Others are as recent as the last several years. Whether the sightings were factual or not is, of course, subject to debate. But there certainly is no doubt that the lakes are the home to many yarns of strange and unknown serpents, monsters and fantastic creatures.

Lake Champlain

Although not one of the Great Lakes, but connected to the St. Lawrence Seaway vicariously by canal, Lake Champlain on the New York-Vermont border was the frequent site of many monster and sea serpent sightings. In addition, the reports were similar to those on the lakes. A July 29, 1873, issue of the *Buffalo Express* carried the story of a 20-foot-long, 20-inch-wide serpent seen by a gang of railroad workers. It must have been part whale since "occasionally it would spout water from its nostrils as high as 20 feet above his head ... eyes, small and piercing; mouth, broad with two rows of teeth. Moved off at the rate of 10 miles an hour." The tail was like that of a fish. The monster suddenly disappeared in front of the observers. A few days afterwards, "calves, sheep and fowls" were reported as having disappeared from the local area. Unidentified tracks gave the impression that they were dragged to the lakeshore, then off into the water.[2]

A subsequent edition of the paper claimed that the serpent was killed. A group of local men chartered a tug and armed with shotguns and rifles went to the locale where the monster was most frequently seen. After firing their guns into the water, there was a terrific bubbling and unearthly noise. The dying snake rose out of the water, eyes blazing "like coals" and after briefly struggling violently, sank into the stygian depths.[3]

The local paper editorialized that all the monster sightings were the result of either alcohol or hoaxes.

Seeing Sea Snakes and Monsters?

While on an excursion to Middle Bass Island north of Sandusky, Ohio, in Lake Erie in 1793, a party of explorers from the sloop *Felicity* reported many large rattlesnakes. The island was infested with them! The captain, who had ventured away from the main group to shoot ducks on a nearby pond, suddenly came running back, out of breath and gasping for air. It seems he had walked to the water's edge and, seeing some ducks, had fired his gun at them. Startled by the roar of his gun, a monstrous snake, more than a rod (16½ feet) in length, rose out of the grass and chased him for more than 100 yards.[4]

Another monster serpent was reported by a schooner's crew on July 3, 1817, swimming three miles offshore in Lake Ontario. A foot in diameter and 35 to 40 feet in length, its skin was almost black. One naturalist, unsure of whether it was fish or reptile, tentatively identified it as a great eel.[5]

On July 3, 1880, 30 miles from Erie, the crew of the schooner *General Scott* reported a sea serpent 35 to 40 feet long. As the creature swam close aboard the schooner, sailors were able to estimate its neck at 10 to 12 inches in diameter. Its skin was a dull mahogany, nearly black. The lake was nearly flat and the crew was able to observe the serpent for more than a minute.[6]

In July 1892, the crew of the schooner *Madeline*, bound from Buffalo to Toledo, sighted a huge serpent. A local newspaper carried the tale: "Captain Woods saw the waters of the lake lashed into foam about a half mile ahead. Drawing near, to the surprise of the captain and all aboard, a huge sea serpent was seen wrestling about in the waters, as if fighting with an unseen foe. It soon quieted down and lay at full length on the surface of the water. Captain Woods' estimate is that the serpent was about 50 feet in length and not less than four feet in circumference of body. Its head projected from the water about four feet. He says it was a terrible looking object. It had viciously sparkling eyes and a large head. Fins were plainly seen, seemingly sufficiently large to assist the snake in propelling itself through the water. The body was dark brown in color which was uniform all along."[7]

On the evening of May 5, 1896, four people at Crystal Beach, near Fort Erie, sighted another serpent. At first, they thought the commotion on the surface was caused by a school of fish, but on closer examination realized it was a single "fish." For 45 minutes the four watched in awe as the creature swam "to and fro." At times its whole length was visible. The head was like a dog's and the tail pointed. One observer estimated the creature's length at 35 feet. Just before dark it disappeared.[8]

During the intervening years, Lake Erie sea serpents continued to be reported. For example, during the summer of 1993, there were three separate reports of the creature. One sighting by a family of four placed it close ashore near Lowbanks, Ontario, in the eastern lake. It was moving rapidly through the water. The witnesses identified a 30-foot snake-like creature. Earlier, a fisherman sighted the serpent near Kelleys Island. Five days later, other fishermen observed it in the same general area.

On August 24, 1993, the *Weekly World News* reported that a 38-foot sailboat was "crushed like an eggshell" by a 200-ton sea monster. The five occupants of the boat escaped without injury. The front page of the paper carried an action photo of the attack taken by a low flying plane that just happened to be overhead with a camera at the ready at the precise moment of the attack.

A group of Huron, Ohio, businessmen offered a reward of $102,700 in cash and prizes for anyone who could prove the monster existed. It has never been collected.[9]

Some serpents may have been more "real" than others. An October 24, 1890, story in the *Detroit Free Press* described a monster snake that occasionally appeared along the waterfront at the F.E. Bradley mill. The monster normally was sighted at night, scaring the wits out of several mill workers. It was said the dead glow in its eyes shook the men to their souls. Some claimed it was 12 feet long and had a head shaped like an ox. A more rational explanation was that the creature was a large anaconda that had escaped a fire at a local museum.[10]

A group of Detroit men came face to face with a monster off Sarnia in the summer of 1897. They were fishing about three miles offshore in 145 feet of water when their boat began moving away at a very rapid speed. Suddenly a "black mass, a swiftly moving ribbon-shaped monster, dashed to the surface. One of the party began firing with his revolver (and) four rods away the water was lashed into bloody foam. The monster was at least 88 feet long, was flexible as a snake (with) a double row of fins ... it had long whiskers." As quick as it came it left, leaving the group to wonder at what they had witnessed.[11]

In early October 1938, six Sarnia fishermen claimed to have been forced to run their boat ashore by a sea serpent. Estimated at 30 feet in length, it undulated in and out of the water as it swam. A menacing tail swished back and forth. The year before, a similar serpent was reported near Southampton, 100 miles distant.[12]

Georgian Bay commercial fishermen occasionally reported encounters with sea monsters. Locations varied and included Manitoulin Island, northwest of Parry Sound at the Limestone Islands and Gull Island.

Unlike the serpent-like creatures sighted elsewhere, Georgian Bay monsters tended to be on the small side. One was said to be approximately four feet long with four feet and fins. Another was a larger version of the Lake Superior merman with fins and a tail. (See later story.)[13]

After a series of sea monster reports in Lake Michigan in 1867, a Milwaukee saloon owner offered a reward of $1,000 for its capture. It was said he intended serving it as a barroom lunch.[14]

A 1908 sea monster scare in Grand Traverse Bay was finally cleared up in 1938, when a newspaperman admitted that he paid a photographer to fake the photo of the beast. After sketching the monster on a picture of the bay, the man rephotographed it, producing a very believable "monster" that was widely circulated.[15]

In the early 1930s, another mystery was solved when the remains of a 30-foot wooden serpent were discovered on a Ludington, Michigan, beach. Made in numerous sections and wired together, it gave the appearance of swimming when pulled through the water. It was effective enough to scare many local swimmers and spawned monster stories for years to come.[16]

During fur trading days, a boat from Toronto returned unexpectedly after those aboard sighted a "great snake" 20 miles from Niagara, Ontario. An English traveler wrote, "A boat that had sailed from York, unexpectedly returned again; the people on board relating, with great terror, having seen a great snake, at least 30 feet long, which, from its rearing its head and fore-part of its body out of the water, they conjectured meant to attack them! All this they deposed on oath before a Magistrate. The Indians present, who have always a corroborating story ready, asserted that their people had seen three such snakes and had killed two!"[17]

An August 5, 1829, publication reported another serpent encounter. Several children were playing near the mouth of Ten Mile Creek in western Lake Ontario where they claimed to have seen a monster snake, 20 to 30 feet long, with a head 10 to 15 inches in diameter. After only a brief observation, the children fled one way and the creature the other. The paper noted that this wasn't the first sighting in Lake Ontario and, doubtless, that such serpents lived in the lake.[18]

The area off Kingston, at the foot of Lake Ontario and the start of the St. Lawrence River, is a hot bed of sea monster sighting. Locals have come to name "their" serpent "Kingstie."

The first sighting was reported in September 1881 by the passengers and crew of the steamer *Gypsy*. Estimated at 25 to 40 feet long, it had small legs and a large tail. Apparently the serpent and steamer raced for a while, with the creature proving the faster.[19]

In June 1888, two men sailing in the channel between Wolfe and Simcoe islands briefly sighted another serpent, reported large enough to "carry off a baby."[20]

A man and his wife were sailing in a skiff near Brakey's Bay in July 1892 when they were attacked by a huge serpent with " … eyes like balls of fire." The husband was able to beat it off using his fishing pole.[21]

In August 1931, "Kingstie" appeared again. Two medical doctors sailing from Alexandria Bay to the yacht club (Kingston) sighted a creature they thought was 30 feet long. It had a single eye in the middle of his head as well as two antler-like horns.[22]

Mike Finn and the Monster of Lake Ontario

Researched and adapted by Rosemary Nesbitt, courtesy of the H. Lee White Marine Museum, Oswego, New York.

Once upon a time, a hundred years ago, there lived in the city of Oswego a man whose name was Mike Finn. Now, Mike was an easy going, fun-loving Irishman who liked to drop in at his favorite tavern of an evening and tell stories. There wouldn't have been anything wrong with that, except that the stories were always about himself. Mike Finn, the hero of Gettysburg; Mike Finn, gold prospecting in California; Mike Finn, Pony Express rider; Mike Finn, killing a grizzly bear with his bare hands, and on and on and on. Mike's regular cronies at the bar

164

had learned to turn a deaf ear when Mike got going and didn't even bother to joke with him about his tall tales.

One evening in the early spring, however, a stranger happened into the tavern. As usual, Mike was holding forth, this time telling how nothing ever frightened him and that there wasn't a thing in heaven or earth that he couldn't handle. The stranger listened quietly for a while and then asked, "How about monsters?"

"Monsters!" Mike shouted. "Monsters! Well now, my friend, there be no such thing, but if there was, I wouldn't be afraid of them."

"How do you know there's no such thing?" the stranger persisted.

"Why, why, because there just isn't," Mike said, "Only in fairy tales be there giants and ogres and monsters."

"That isn't the way I heard it," the stranger continued. At that, all of the men standing at the bar set their glasses down and turned to look at him and at Mike.

"No sir, that isn't the way I heard it at all," the stranger went on.

"Tell us how you heard it," one of the men said.

"Well, it was this way. You all know where Rome swamp is?" There was a murmur of assent.

"Well, there's a monster that lives in the Rome swamp. Come down from Canada with the French Canadians. They call him 'The Carcagna,' but the folks around Rome just call him 'The Monster.'"

"What does he look like?" one of the men wanted to know.

"He has a big head, like a dragon, with terrible red eyes. His body is like a big snake all covered with slimy seaweed that never stops dripping. And he has huge orange wings with awful black and brown feathers sticking out of them. But the most terrible thing about him is his cry. They say if you hear it, you will go mad and never will be the same again."

Some of the men laughed, but the rest looked a little uneasy and several of them gulped their drinks and ordered another.

Mike Finn led the unbelievers. "Oh, 'tis a great story," he roared, "but that's all it is. Just a story. And anyway, even if it wasn't, what has it got to do with us? The thing lives way over in Rome," And he turned to order another draft.

The stranger smiled and set his glass down on the bar. "He used to live over in Rome, but two nights ago he left the swamp and was heard wailing and crying out over the lake just south of Port Ontario. And last night a fishing boat heard him just off the shore at Scriba. By tonight, he ought to be here in the Oswego Harbor. Nobody has ever seen him and stayed sane to tell about it. I guess that's because there has never been anybody really brave enough to go out and face the monster."

The stranger turned and looked at Mike. So did all the men in the tavern.

"What about you, sir?" the stranger said. "If there ever was a brave man, it is yourself, at least so you say."

The others looked at each other. Here it was, the opportunity they had all been waiting for. Then a chorus of voices roared out across the bar.

"Yes, how about you, Mike?"

"That's it, Mike, here's your chance!"

"Now we can all see how brave you are!"

"Come on Mike, we'll get your boat ready!"

"You don't want to miss a chance like this!"

Mike was trapped. There was nothing he could say or do. There was no way out. And so, at 7 o'clock that night, Mike Finn set out in his little rowboat to spend the night on Lake Ontario, just outside the Oswego Harbor, or so he told his friends. What he really intended to do was row out past the lighthouse, wait until it was dark and then row back and hide until morning. But, the men had anticipated that. Two of them followed in their boat until Mike was out of sight of land. Then they told him that they would patrol the mouth of the harbor all night, just in case he needed help. The last the two men saw of Mike was his little boat, bobbing like a cork, far out on the eastern horizon. The others all went back to the bar, laughing and joking and taking bets on how long Mike would stay out there.

And so, the night passed. At first light, about 6 o'clock, they all gathered on the dock, sure that their two guards would have Mike in tow by this time. But the two men who had volunteered to watch were already tied up and there was no sign of Mike. He had not tried to come back during the night, they said. Somebody else said he had probably sneaked in somewhere over by St. Paul's Cemetery. There were a lot of little coves over there. The men were just about to leave and go back to the tavern to wait for Mike and hear his story when somebody shouted, "Look, look!"

They followed his pointing finger, and there, far out on the horizon was a small black dot, bobbing up and down in the morning swell.

"That looks like Mike's boat!" someone shouted. Immediately four or five men jumped into two boats and started rowing toward the speck. The others gathered at the end of the pier to watch. They saw the men reach the little boat and attach a line to it. Then they started to tow it in.

"Mike's too tired to row himself," somebody said.

"Yes, I'll bet he's asleep in the bottom," another voice chimed in.

But, the jokes were halfhearted, and an air of uneasiness began to creep into their voices. Finally the talk stopped altogether, and they waited silently as the boats reentered the harbor and slowly approached the dock. The men in the two boats weren't talking either, and they weren't looking in Mike's boat. Their eyes were set straight ahead and their faces were grey and set. Slowly they warped the boats up to the dock, got out and turned to tie Mike's boat to the stanchion. Then, the others got their first look into the boat. Mike was there alright, or what passed for Mike. He was curled up in a little ball in the bottom with his arms wrapped around his shoulders. His eyes were fixed and his lips were drawn back in a terrible grin that revealed his chattering teeth. His hair had turned snow white.

Everyone stood in stunned silence. Finally, one of the men said, "Mike, is that you, Mike? Come on now, quit your play acting. The joke's over."

And, indeed the joke was over for Mike Finn. From that day forward, he never spoke another word. He never changed his expression, and his eyes never closed. Mike Finn had gone stark, raving mad. The men stood staring at him for what seemed like an eternity. Then, finally somebody said, "Poor Mike, it was his imagination that got him. All alone out there in the dark, he really thought he saw that thing."

"Yes, your imagination can run away with you when you are out on the lake alone at night," somebody else said.

They pulled poor Mike from the boat and started to carry him up the dock. Then, somebody remembered that they had better take Mike's boat out of the water. One of the men went back to secure it. Suddenly, the others heard a shout and, turning, saw the man staring, horrified, into the boat. They ran back just as he sank in a dead faint onto the dock. There was something lying in the bottom of the boat on the spot where Mike had been found. It was a single, long, thin, slimy, black-and-brown feather.

Lake Superior's Giant Sturgeon

Lake Superior Chippewa believed that the lake was inhabited by a giant sturgeon, reportedly big enough to "hold an entire ... village in its mouth."[23] When an Indian failed to return from the lake, the loss was attributed to the monster fish.

When early schooners disappeared, the whites blamed savage squalls or other weather problems. The Ojibway knew better. The giant sturgeon probably just eyeballed the strange interloper and flicked his massive tail in mild annoyance. Scratch one schooner.

Even large steel vessels had encounters on the lake that could best be explained by the giant sturgeon. In 1909 the 250-foot, steel-hulled

Leafeld was steaming in midlake on a perfect summer day. Lake Superior was flat calm and not a cloud dotted the sky. Suddenly the lake broke into a foaming maelstrom. Waves boiled at the *Leafeld* from every quarter, punishing her unmercifully. For 20 to 30 minutes she was pounded by the strange windless storm. As quickly as it started, the bizarre disturbance stopped. The only evidence that it ever existed was the battered deck gear. When they reached Fort William, the crew read of an earthquake and thought their adventure may have been a weird offshoot. Old-timers just shook their heads. The spot where they were pounded is more than 1,000 feet deep! Earthquakes weren't the answer. Something else was.

Sometime later, the 504-foot steamer *James E. Davidson* was downbound in a snowstorm from Slate Island in the same area. Without warning, a single massive wave roared down on her, striking her bow like a thunderbolt. The shock knocked some sailors off their feet. The huge weight of the water released both forward anchors from their pockets, plummeting them into the depths. Behind rattled hundreds of feet of rusty chain. The inertia of the anchor and chain was so great, the hawse holes were damaged and water flooded into the forward hold in torrents. Down several feet forward, the battered steamer barely made port. Later, when the behemoth was safely in a drydock, marine men were shocked to find a 10 foot dent under the bow. All they could do was shake their heads and mutter, "What the hell?" But the Native Americans knew what happened.

The steamer *Emperor* was upbound from the Soo when she had another odd experience. She was firing with some coal that had earlier been recovered from a wreck. It was still wet and wasn't burning very well. When it became necessary to clean the grates, the captain stopped in midlake. To prevent her from rolling excessively, some water ballast was added. Suddenly, the *Emperor* bumped on something solid, then slid off. Again, the charts showed more than 1,000 feet of water!

In 1928, the big steel steamer *Midland Prince* reported striking an object in the same neighborhood. No explanations were given. Mariners just couldn't understand what was happening.

When Superior Shoal was discovered in 1929 in the same general area, it was surmised by some that this was the mysterious "thing" struck by the vessels.[24] But a shoal didn't cause the *Leafeld* "storm" or *Davidson* "wave" and something as shallow as 18 feet would have been visible in terms of water coloration, even in the excitement of bumping it. The question remains, What was it? Were the Indians right? Did a giant sturgeon roam the lake?[25]

The God of Lakes and Waters

In a statement sworn before two judges of the Court of the King's Bench in Montreal, Quebec, on November 13, 1812, Venant St. Germain, a North West Company voyageur, reported that shortly after sunset on May 13, 1782, he and four others saw a "merman" near Pie Island in Lake Superior's Thunder Bay. They were traveling from Grand Portage to Mackinac Island in a canoe when they camped at the south end of the island for the night. Coming ashore after setting some fishing nets, the travelers saw "an animal in the water, which appeared to him to have the upper part of its body, above the waist, formed exactly like that of a human being. It had half of its body out of the water, and the novelty of so extraordinary a spectacle excited his attention and led him to examine it carefully. The body of the animal seemed to him to be about the size of a child of seven or eight years of age with one of its arms extended and elevated in the air. The hand appeared to have the exposed fingers exactly similar to that of a man." The voyageur also swore that he " … distinctly saw the features of the countenance which bore an exact resemblance to those of the human face. The eyes were extremely brilliant; the nose small but handsomely shaped; the mouth proportional to the rest of the face; the complexion of a brownish hue, the ears well formed and corresponding to the other parts of the figure." The creature looked curiously at St. Germain and his companions and they in turn looked back. For three or four minutes each studied the other.

St. Germain raised his musket to shoot, but an old Indian squaw traveling with him knocked it away and warned him that this was the god of the lakes and waters. Further, that because they had all looked at it, all were doomed.

The creature disappeared back into the depths. Shaken badly, the squaw refused even to walk the beach back to camp, afraid of the terrible storm she was certain would be coming. The waves would wash her into the water and drown her. Instead she carefully climbed a steep bank and from there proceeded to the camp. That night a furious storm struck the area. For three days the travelers were forced to wait out the blow.

The old voyageur added that the local Indians believed the area was home to the "god of the waters and lakes," known as Manitou Niba Nibais. He also stated that another voyager had seen a similar creature swimming from Pie Island to Thunder Cape.[26]

The Serpent of Whitefish Point

Another lake serpent was sighted in July 1895 off Whitefish Point by the steamer SS *Curry*. Captain George Robarge, the second mate

169

and a watchman all saw what they later described as a "hideous creature." It was a mere 400 yards away and all were able to get a good look with binoculars. The serpent appeared just before sunset and stayed in view for five minutes. At times it seemed to race with the *Curry*. The men later said it had a neck 15 feet in length and a jaw at least a foot wide. It swam with a strange undulating motion. As quick as it appeared, it disappeared, leaving the mariners bewildered.[27]

The previous September, Captain Owen and the crews of the steamers *George F. Williams* and *H.A. Hawgood* claimed that halfway between Whitefish Point and Copper Harbor they came across a massive sea monster. The creature was swimming with an undulating motion, its back out of the water six to eight feet. Since it was twilight, the color could not be determined.

Duluth's Giant Squid

In the summer of 1897, a party of Detroit yachtsmen told of being attacked near Duluth by a giant squid-like monster. "We were bowling along in about 10 feet of water, when we struck a rock…. General confusion filled the air. I ran forward to see if we had stove a hole, when I stumbled over a rope's end and fell overboard. I felt … sucked down by some undertow … the boat was carried out to sea. Then I caught the gleam of two giant eyes that shone like bullet eyes … a dark lantern … and I felt a sickening sponginess around my waist. It flashed on me that I was in the coils of a frightful sea serpent or monster of some sort and I decided to sell my life as dearly as possible. But he was in shoal water and I got a footing on the bottom. The serpent kept tightening its coils until I felt myself lost. All around me for 10 to 15 feet, the waters were threshed into pinkish foam. It … was at least 75 feet long … a livid green color and had great scales and a forked tail." After a desperate struggle, the victim fought his way free and survived to tell the tale.[28]

Pictured Rocks

In the middle 1930s, two Munising fishermen reported seeing an unknown sea creature swimming along Lake Superior's Pictured Rocks. It looked like a snake and made a strong wake. The men estimated its speed at 8½ to 9 miles per hour. They didn't get close enough to make a more positive identification.[29]

It Ate the Whole Thing

The summer of 1897 was a very active period for sea monster sightings on Lake St. Clair. In one instance a horse was supposedly devoured by a monster. It seems some men left their horse on the shore of the lake and rowed out to do some fishing. They were startled to hear "blood curdling whinnies from the spot where they left the horse." Returning to the beach, they discovered that their steed was gone. A local fisherman told the bewildered men that a sea serpent had slithered ashore and dragged it out into the depths.

In July 1897, a sea serpent was seen in the St. Clair flats by a man in the upper stories of the Riverside Hotel. It was observed to move at a terrific rate of speed then disappear only to reappear in a few seconds. After a while, the monster completely vanished from view.[30]

Sandwich Point

August 6, 1897, a sea serpent was sighted off Sandwich Point, in the Detroit River. Reportedly it was 87 feet long, with a bull-like head and a "magnificent pair of antlers." In addition, a single eye sat squarely in the center of its forehead. The serpent was last seen heading for Lake Erie. Although there was talk of organizing a posse, the serpent "made good its escape into the green waters of Lake Erie."[31]

Harpooned at Belle Isle

On August 16, 1897, it was claimed that a lake captain captured a sea monster at Belle Isle, near the foot of Joseph Campeau Avenue.

"Its mouth was as large as a coal stove, and the monster was sputtering and hissing through the water with the speed of a trolley car after midnight." It was coming directly at the captain and, when two men from a nearby barge saw what was happening, they ran toward him. Unshaken and with a courage of a Nantucket whalerman, the captain stepped onto a float, grabbed a boathook and made a stab at it. "The serpent ... jaws distended, turned and swam toward the captain, his tail lashing the water." The self-made harpooner drove his trusty boathook again deeply into the "carcass of the ugly beast." The captain's efforts proved successful and when the monster was hauled on the dock it measured out at 17 feet in length and two feet wide. The gaping mouth was large enough to swallow a man's head. The beast was to be stuffed and presented to the Detroit Scientific Research Association.[32]

Whether it ever was is not recounted.

CHAPTER SEVEN

Messages from Beyond

Many old sailors, and some not so old, believe that ships talk, communicating clearly their wants and needs. They also can impart their experiences, helping the present captain make it through difficult situations. One veteran Coast Guard master recalled sitting in his wardroom and hearing the previous captains talk, telling him of his ship and their experiences with her in dangers faced and overcome.

The methods that ships use to communicate can be unique. When coming around Manitou Island in Lake Superior, the U.S. Coast Guard Cutter *Woodrush* always rolled one captain out of his bunk and into the open drawer beneath. The same thing happened when the *Woodrush* ran for the *Fitzgerald* on that terrible November night in 1975. This simple act told the old man that the ship had everything under control and not to worry. They would get there safely.

Captains able to listen to their ships were (and are) able to do remarkable things, to take their vessels places where supposedly they couldn't go. But the ship knew how, if only the captains listened!

One master remembered running a perfect course in a blinding fog, right through an island. He knew where he started from and where he finished, but had no idea how he got there. Unless he went through the island. Impossible, don't tell him. His ship did it!

More than one master has been helped out of a tight spot by an innate instinct, a certain knowledge of the proper command at exactly the right time. It wasn't trained and was beyond his experience, but somehow he just knew what to do. Some men firmly believed they were reincarnations of past captains. It was the only explanation for how they "knew" so much beyond their training and experience.

Ships also develop their own personality. There were and are "good" and "bad" ships. Seasoned captains could tell which was which the minute they stepped aboard. The ship spoke to them in a language seamen understood.

Ships are not inanimate objects, mere creations of iron, steel and wood. Ships are in themselves strange and wondrous creatures. They seem to absorb experience like a sponge. If you are willing to listen, just to stand quiet and with an open mind, they will tell you vividly of the past. A door will silently open. Stand in a museum ship like the old *Valley Camp* in Sault Ste. Marie long after the rush of visitors have left for the day, when the lights are off and all is quiet. Just listen. Step back from the modern world and allow your senses full rein. Forget what you think you know and open your mind completely. The ship will speak of storms and gales, of fog and dancing ice devils. You will hear the roar of iron ore loading into her holds and the crashing of waves against her bow. The old crew will murmur to you of the past, of what they did and know – there is life in the old girl yet. Is it just imagination or an open door to another world?

Bottled Messages from the Dead

Spiritualists may use ouija boards to receive messages from beyond the grave, but on the Great Lakes the favorite method was the "message in a bottle." Long a tradition on the high seas, placing a last message in a handy bottle just before a ship sank was a favorite method of communicating a last desperate word to the outside world. While some messages were undoubtedly hoaxes, others were assuredly genuine.

During the turn of the century, brass "message tubes" were provided to bulk freighters for the purpose of saving a final crew list or other "last" messages in the event of loss. The tubes were kept in the pilothouse, ready for quick use, just before the ship settled beneath the waves.

The practice of writing a message in a bottle continued as late as November 10, 1975, and the tragic loss of the *Edmund Fitzgerald*. When one of the crewmen on the *Arthur M. Anderson* learned his ship was turning around to go back out and look for the *Fitzgerald*, he recorded his last words on an audio cassette tape and sealed it tightly in a jar. If it looked like the *Anderson* was going down, he was prepared to throw the jar overboard!

In July 1880, the schooner *Picton* foundered with all seven hands in a vicious Lake Ontario gale. Months later, a fisherman's son in Chaunmont Bay noticed a bottle floating in the water. But he did nothing about it. In fact, for three days running he saw the same bottle before finally becoming curious enough to row out and recover it.

Although it was nothing more than an old ketchup bottle capped with a cork, inside was a message. "Have lashed Vessey to me with heaving line so will be found together – J. Sidley, *Picton*"

Sidley, one of the lake's legendary hard driving sailors, was the owner and master of the schooner. Vessey was his 12-year-old son. There is no record of either body being recovered. They remained together forever, as the father intended.[1]

One of the great mysteries of Lake Michigan was the October 16, 1880, loss of the Goodrich side-wheeler *Alpena*. Bound from Grand Haven to Chicago, she foundered in a hell-bender, with the loss of an estimated 70 to 80 souls. As with most wooden vessels, a large amount of wreckage washed ashore. Tightly wedged into a section of cabin woodwork was a note, "This is terrible. The steamer is breaking up fast. I am aboard from Grand Haven to Chicago." The water soaked signature was almost illegible, but seemed to be that of a George Conner or Connell.

The following year, the lightkeeper at Point Betsie discovered a bottle with a message sealed within. "October 16, 3 o'clock, on board the *Alpena*. … she has broke her port wheel; is at mercy of seas; is half full of water; God help us, Capt. Napier washed overboard – George A.N. Moore, Chicago, Ill."

On the reverse was a despairing request, "The finder of this note will please communicate with my wife and let her know of my death."[2]

A bottled note found in Chequamegon Bay, Ashland, Wisconsin, in May 1885, purported to come from the propeller *Manistee*, was considered by some marine men to be authentic. The captain's brother, however, was also a lake master and thought it a hoax. "This is of the *Manistee*, in a fearful storm. May not live to see morning. Ever yours to the world. John McKay, Captain."

On the evening of November 15, 1883, the 184-foot wooden steamer left Bayfield, Wisconsin, bound for Ontonagon, Michigan, 74 miles to the east. Later that night, a real Lake Superior "gagger" boiled in from the north. The *Manistee* never made Ontonagon, or anywhere else.

Much wreckage eventually drifted ashore on the western beaches of the Keweenaw, but none solved the mystery. None of the bodies of the 19 crew and four passengers was ever recovered, with the possible exception of one. The following August, some *Manistee* wreckage was located on Point Mamainsee on the north shore. Just yards away was the skeleton of a man wearing a badly deteriorated fur-trimmed coat. Was he a passenger or a member of the crew? Did he even belong with the wreckage from the *Manistee*? As old pirates used to mutter, "Dead men tell no tales."

It is also interesting to note that, in an apparent premonition of disaster before the *Manistee* departed Bayfield, some of the passengers transferred to the propeller *City of Duluth*. Whether they knew something of the future or just had great luck is, of course, speculation. But they lived. The ones that stayed on the *Manistee* didn't.³

On September 19, 1901, the steamer *Hudson* sank will all hands off Eagle Harbor, Michigan, in Lake Superior. For months afterward, the bodies of many of her crew slowly drifted ashore, but it wasn't until three years later that a corked bottle was found, bearing the last message from the ill-fated steamer. Incredibly, the message was discovered drifting in the shallow water just off Point Iroquois, 182 miles to the east. Brief in the extreme, it simply said, "Captain of steamer *Hudson*. Steering engine gave out, we are all going, Good-by."⁴

For many years, the schooner *Rouse Simmons* would finish her season by carrying a cargo of Christmas trees from the Lake Michigan shore of Michigan's Upper Peninsula to Chicago where they would sell the trees from the ship. On November 26, 1912, she was downbound with trees when a powerful northwest storm overwhelmed her off Kewaunee, Wisconsin. The ship foundered with the loss of all 17 hands. Ever since, her story has been a Lake Michigan favorite.

After the famous "Christmas Tree Ship" foundered, several messages were eventually discovered. The first one, found soon afterward, stated, "Friday. Everybody goodbye. I guess we are all through. Sea washed over our deckload Thursday. During the night the small boat was washed over. Ingvald and Steve fell overboard Thursday. God help us. Herman Schuenemann." Fifteen years later, another message was found, "These lines are written at 10:30 p.m. Schooner R.S. ready to go down about 20 miles southeast Two Rivers Point between 15 or 20 miles offshore. All hands lashed to one line. Goodbye. Charles Nelson." Nelson was one of the crew.⁵

When the hurricane of November 1913 roared down on *Lightship No. 82* anchored off the entrance to Buffalo, it completely overwhelmed the small ship in a maelstrom of wind and waves. The ship and her six man crew just vanished. Later a message from the captain, Hugh M. Williams, to his wife was discovered written on a weathered board.⁶

The disappearance on Lake Superior on the big steel steamer *Henry B. Smith* in the same storm also provided a message from the grave. Found by a fisherman near Coppermine Point, it reportedly stated that the ship broke in two at the #2 hatch 12 miles east of Marquette. The actual text was never released by the shipping company.⁷

The loss of the *Andaste* with all hands on September 9, 1929, in

Lake Michigan resulted in another "boarded" message. Signed only "A.L.A.," which presumably were the initials of Captain Albert L. Anderson, it said, "Worst storm I have ever been in. Can't hold up much longer. Hope we're saved."[8]

The last words from the carferry *Milwaukee*, lost on Lake Michigan on October 22, 1929, with 52 souls, were provided by the purser:

> S.S. *Milwaukee*,
> Oct. 22, '29, 6:30 P.M.
> Ship is taking water fast. We have turned and headed for Milwaukee. Pumps are all working, but sea gate is bent and won't keep water out. Flickers are flooded. Seas are tremendous. Things look bad. Crew roll about same as last payday.
>
> A.R. Sadon, Purser[9]

Every message needs to be viewed in the context in which it was written – the thrashing seas and screaming wind, a deck that jumped and rolled as if in the final throes of an epileptic fit. Rain and spume falling in torrents, sometimes vertically and other times horizontally, driven by tearing blasts of ice-laden wind. Desperate searches for a bottle, pencil and paper and a means of sealing out the grasping lake. A mind numbed by both the need for action to save ship or self, yet stricken by the knowledge of cold death staring the writer bang in the eye. And then there were the words themselves. What to say? A last missive to a loved one or a simple final report to the owners? Would the bottle be found or smashed by an angry wave against the unforgiving rocks or buried by the shifting sands never to be found? But above all else, a message in a bottle was a last, desperate attempt to communicate from beyond the reaches of another world.

Sometimes the dead made other attempts – if not to get a message through, then to make it back themselves. In May 1888 on Lake Ontario, Young Captain Johnny Henderson sailed his schooner *Blanche* out of Oswego bound for Brighton, Ontario, with coal. Brighton was her home port and the whole crew was made up of local boys. Late that night, a banshee-driven squall tore into the schooner and she was no more. There were no survivors or witnesses to tell the tale of her terrible end. The following September, Captain Henderson came home, of a sorts. His body was found washed ashore at Brighton Beach. It had been so badly abused during its lonely sojourn, it could only be identified by the woolen socks on the feet. His mother had knitted them especially for him. Regardless of how or why, the son had come home.[10]

When the old 136-foot steamer *City of New York* foundered in a November 1921 Lake Ontario gale, five of the seven souls aboard, including the woman cook, made it to the safety of the lifeboat. When the boat was finally discovered by the steamer *Isabella H.*, all were dead, frozen into grotesque shapes. The only message they could pass to their loving families was one of despair and death. The *Isabella H.* didn't last very long after her gristly discovery. Within four years she sank in the same general area as the *City of New York.*[11]

Many, of course, never did come home. On December 12, 1909, the Pennsylvania State Fisheries tug *Commodore Perry* was cruising off Erie harbor when she sighted a weather beaten yawl drifting aimlessly on the slate gray sea. Sitting stiffly in the boat were nine men. Some still had their hands wrapped tight around the oars. When the tug hailed them, the only response was icy silence. None of the occupants moved or stirred. They just stared vacantly ahead. The captain ran the tug close aboard the yawl before he realized the occupants were all dead, frozen stiff from the terrible cold. The men were part of the car ferry *Marquette and Bessemer No. 2*, lost earlier in the month in the midst of a roaring gale. They, too, had tried to come home.[12]

Epilogue

There are many other cases where reputable people reported unexplained experiences with "something." According to a 1991 poll, 13 percent of all Americans claim to have seen, felt or heard what they believe to be a ghost. The figures are even higher in Europe. Italy, for example, reports an incredible 48 percent believers. You can accept the stories in this book or not. Laugh at them if you must but, to the people who experienced these strange and unexplained incidents, they were real enough.

Nor am I more superstitious than the average person. I do not willingly walk under ladders but, contrary to accepted superstition, I have purchased and renamed several boats without changing their "luck." However, the evidence shows that many early (also present) Great Lakes marine men were and are superstitious. Those superstitions affected what they did and how they acted in various situations. The Friday curse, for example, certainly affected sailing schedules for many old-timers and there are modern sailors who grow uncomfortable if they learn that *their* ship is scheduled to start the new sailing season on a Friday. To the extent that these superstitions can be documented as having been used on the lakes, I included them.

The material and stories for this book were drawn from many sources – period newspaper accounts, autobiographical notes from old mariners, the Walton Collection and similar documents and as many interviews as were available. Although I tried my best to document each story, at times I was forced to cite an "unidentified" source. For various reasons, all quite understandable, these people want their privacy respected. They don't want to be ridiculed or to be bothered by would be ghost-busters. In all instances, by the way, none of the ghosts in this book are the malevolent, misbegotten spirits depicted in a Stephen King novel. All are benign and, in some instances, very helpful.

Much of the focus of this book is on the superstitions and haunts of the lakes from the great age of sail, when the vast surfaces of the inland seas were dotted with billowing clouds of white. It was also the era from which most of the present superstitions and traditions date. As the legends and stories started and grew, they often continued into the first steamboats. Some endure to this day. The great age of sail on the Great Lakes ran from the end of the Civil War through the 1880s. The tremendous economic expansion following the war was largely floated on wooden hulls. Hundreds of schooners, barks, barkentines, sailing scows, topsail schooners and other rigs plied the lakes carrying valuable cargoes of lumber, grain, coal, copper and iron ore. As the nation's appetite grew, so did the number of vessels. Sail on the lakes lasted well into the 20th century because of the inherent economy. Engines were costly to build, buy and operate. Engine rooms and fuel bunkers required space that could be used for paying cargo on a sail vessel. Often a small schooner could be profitable, while a steamer could not.

In many instances, hoodoo ships, for example, the lineage of the belief can clearly be traced from the schooner through wooden steamers to today's behemoth steel freighters. A bad reputation knows no age! The tales of ghosts, ghost ships and superstitions have captured the imagination of generations. Undoubtedly, some were created by writers – others by museum guides and curators as a way to spark interest. But some can't be so easily explained away. Regardless of how they came to be, they are, and therefore have become part of the lakes' legend.

The sagas of the salt-water seas are well known. The great *"Flying Dutchman"* of Cape Horn fame (or infamy), the flaming ship of Ocracoke and strange disappearance of the crew of the *Mary Celeste* all elicit imaginative responses. Those of the Great Lakes are far less well known. Certainly some stories and superstitions transferred from ocean to lake. During the early days of sail, the crews consisted largely of men from the ocean ports who migrated to the lakes for the sailing season because of the better wages, food and working conditions. These sailors carried their beliefs and traditions with them. When the winter closed in, they went back to salt water to continue to earn a living. Gradually, many of the men stopped returning to the ocean and spent the winters securely berthed in boarding houses common to the lake ports. Over time, the sweet-water seas worked their special magic on the mariners and wove their own unique web of mystery and legend.

It is my conclusion that the old "sailors" were closer to the lakes, more attuned to them and their many moods and more susceptible to their haunting charms. That, on a dark and storm-tossed night with the weather rail slicing under, they might see things that weren't there is understandable – or is at least explainable to someone with the same experiences. Such visions were far more likely on a schooner's open and wind-swept quarterdeck than in a steamer's warm and closed-in pilothouse, high above the rolling waves.

In no instance do I pass judgement on the veracity of the beliefs or the material from which it was drawn. Were there ghost ships or not? Did the crews see the ghosts they claimed or was the sound of footsteps stomping their way up the light tower stairs really the spirit of the old keeper? Who knows for certain? What after all is a "true" ghost story? What counts is the tale.

What ghosts are, or even if they are, are questions that have bedeviled scientists investigating the paranormal. Some argue that the spirit of a person who suffered a gruesome fate will haunt the location where they lived. Are they tormented spirits caught in a limbo on earth, unable to find the peace of the grave? Others believe that a ghost is an energy force that remains after death, usually violent. The force can be seen as it passes, perhaps in the form of a nebulous cloud or even in human form. Sometimes it can be heard, will move objects around or touch a human. The lost spirit may range its haunt forever.

The point is not in the nature of a belief or a sighting, rather it's that there was a belief or a sighting. It is not whether what they believed was true or not. It's that they did believe it!

I must remind the reader that this book makes no pretensions of proving or disproving any of the superstitions, ghost tales or sea serpents. Its sole purpose is to document them, to capture the old legends before they are gone forever, to keep them alive before the crush of our burgeoning technology grinds them into homogenized oblivion. I am not attempting to compare such stories to show how they may have a common beginning or different variant. I am not a folklorist.

By no means should this book be considered the end-all of Great Lakes maritime superstitions and ghost stories. Although I cast a wide net, I didn't fish everywhere and the mesh was large. Many good tales certainly escaped. There is plenty of material for another book. It is my hope that readers who know other stories will contact me, so their tales can be captured for future generations. It would be a terrible shame to lose them forever.

And of course, above all, this book is intended to be fun.

Frederick Stonehouse

APPENDIX
The Name's the Same

As indicated in Chapter 2, a strong superstition about names involved the destruction of vessels of similar names. When one was destroyed, others with similar names were sure to follow. In addition to the "Washington" examples provided there, old-timers could also point to the following to "prove" the bad luck of a particular name.

The steamer *Erie* was destroyed by a boiler explosion near Malden, Ontario, in 1840 and that mishap was followed in 1841 by the burning of a steamer *Erie* on Lake Erie, with the loss of an estimated 250 people. In 1842, the sinking of another steamer *Erie* off Port Huron after ice damage was followed by the capsizing on Lake Michigan of the brig *Erie* with the loss of six lives in 1843, the burning of the steamer *Erie* in Detroit in 1844, the sinking of the schooner *Erie* by collision near Sandusky in 1851, the loss of the barge *Erie* off Hamburg in 1878 and the destruction of the scow *Erie* in 1902. In addition, the small schooner *Erie* was lost off Marblehead in 1872 as the *Lewis McLane*. If vessels with the word Erie as part of their name are included, the list is even longer. The schooner *Erie Queen* sunk in Oswego 1881, the tug *Erie Belle* suffered four persons killed in a 1883 boiler explosion at Kincardine and a schooner-barge *Erie Belle* sank in 1924 off Toronto. Earlier, as the schooner *Erie Belle*, she had burned to the water's edge, lost her mainmast on Lake Erie – causing the death of five men – and been dismasted on Lake Ontario. The schooner *Erie Stewart* ended up knocking over the lighthouse at Southampton and beating herself into kindling just outside Chantry Island, Lake Huron. It's all in a name![1]

Sometimes the name jinx struck suddenly. For example, on October 5, 1874, the propeller *Ontario* went aground on Lake Erie. The next day, the steamer *Ontario* went aground in the Detroit River. On October 8, the steamer *Ontario Queen* went aground in the St. Lawrence River. The next day, the schooner *Ontario* lost her jib boom. To cap it all, on October 3, the steamship *Ontario* was disabled at sea.[2]

Ocean Wave was another deadly name. The side-wheeler *Ocean Wave* burned off the False Duck Islands, Lake Ontario, on the night of April 30, 1853, with the loss of an estimated 33 lives. There were accusations that the *Ocean Wave* was racing and, as a result, overheated her engine. Regardless of the cause, tons of tallow in the hold soon ignited, flowing in streams of liquid fire over the lower deck. When the captain realized that his ship was on fire, he promptly threw a sawhorse overboard and jumped for safety. It was a particularly terrible event for the Prince Edward County residents, since 15 of those killed were local citizens who perished trying to rescue screaming and panicked people trapped on the steamer. Only 15 of 26 passengers lived through the fiery ordeal. The light from the flaming steamer was so brilliant, residents ran from their homes believing the end of the world was at hand. Within 30 minutes the steamer was gone. Barns had to be torn down to have enough coffin lumber to bury the victims.[3]

The bark *Ocean Wave* sank in Green Bay in 1866. The scow *Ocean Wave* was lost on Lake Michigan in 1869 and the Canadian schooner *Ocean Wave* wrecked with all hands on Lake Ontario in 1890. The last disaster was especially mystifying, since no cause was ever determined. All that was discovered was a floating field of wreckage. Her lumber cargo should have assured that at least her hull would float. There was no evidence of fire, storm or collision. *Ocean Wave* was unlucky as four vessels of the name have been lost on the lakes. Including WAVE adds another six vessels![4]

There were many other examples of unlucky names:

Seagull
1866 steamer *Seagull* burned on Lake Michigan
1869 schooner *Seagull* wrecked at Grand Haven
1888 schooner *Seagull* burned at Tawas
1890 tug *Seagull* sank in Saginaw Bay
1890 propeller *Seagull* burned at Tawas
1893 tug *Seagull* burned at Straits[5]

Seabird
1850 schooner *Seabird* sank on Lake Erie
1868 steamer *Seabird* burned off Waukegan, Illinois
1869 scow *Seabird* total loss
1883 schooner *Seabird* foundered on Lake Michigan[6]

Shepard
1863 bark *B.S. Shepard* wrecked on Lake Erie
1898 schooner *L.B. Shepard* capsized on Lake Michigan
1898 propeller *Sakie Shepard* burned on Lake St. Clair.[7]

The Smiths
1848 schooner *Jessie Smith* lost on Lake Michigan
1872 tug *H.P. Smith* burned on Saginaw River
1874 barge *Sophia Smith* lost on Lake Huron
1881 schooner *Julia Smith* ashore at Ahnapee
1883 tug *Thomas H. Smith* sunk in collision off Racine, Wisconsin.
1884 steamer *Peter Smith* destroyed by boiler explosion off Vermilion, Ohio
1887 schooner *J.A. Smith* sunk in Straits of Mackinac
1889 steam barge *Anna Smith* foundered off Cheboygan, Wisconsin
1893 tug *Thomas H. Smith* lost on Lake Michigan

1895 tug *Ella M. Smith* sunk in Georgian Bay
1897 schooner *Florence M. Smith* foundered off South Haven
1898 tug *Ira O. Smith* burned off Chicago
1901 schooner *Smith and Post* burned on Lake Erie
1906 schooner *Abram Smith* broken by gale on Lake Huron
1906 steamer *Governor Smith* sunk off Pointe Au Barques after collision with steamer *Uranus*
1908 tug *Sarah M. Smith* burned and sunk off Minnesota Point, Lake Superior
1913 steel steamer *H.B. Smith* foundered north of Marquette
1926 propeller *Joe Smith* burned at Amethyst Harbor, Ontario
1930 propeller *Smith* foundered off Long Point
1936 steel steamer *Sidney E. Smith* destroyed on the beach near Fairport
1972 steel freighter *Sidney E. Smith Jr.* sunk after collision with steamer *Parker Evans* near Port Huron[8]

Ottawa
1848 schooner *Ottawa* stranded and destroyed at Port Stanley
1851 side-wheeler *Ottawa* wrecked near Kingston, Ontario
1855 steamer *Ottawa* sunk near Brockville, Ontario
1875 schooner *Ottawa* sunk by collision off Sarnia
1909 steel steamer *Ottawa* foundered near Passage Island, Lake Superior
1909 tug *Ottawa* burned off Bayfield, Wisconsin
1910 steamer *Ottawa* burned at St.Vincent, Ontario
1911 schooner *Ottawa* foundered off Sturgeon Bay, Wisconsin[9]

Glossary

Ballast
Bulk material carried for weight to stabilize ships, usually water.

Bark (Barque)
Sailing ship with three masts, two of which are square-rigged. On the Great Lakes the term is applied to BARKENTINES.

Barkentine
Sailing ship with three masts, the FOREmost of which is square-rigged. On the Great Lakes usually called BARKS.

Bilge
In general, the bottom of a ship. Specifically, the "corner" where the bottom meets the side.

Bloom
Thick mass of iron ready for working into bars, sheets or beams.

Boiler
Steam generator. Large iron drum to create steam to drive machinery.

Boom
Horizontal SPAR used at foot of sail or for a derrick. Also, string of logs fastened end-to-end for enclosure of a log raft.

Bow
Front of a ship.

Breeches-Buoy
A lifesaving device using a harness suspended from overhead lines to lift survivors from ship wrecks. The lines are fired out to the wreck with a Lyle Gun.

Bulk Freighter
200- to 1,000-foot ship designed to carry loose cargo such as coal, ore, limestone or grain, which is simply dumped into HOLDS.

Bulwarks
Solid rail around the DECKS of a ship. Protective extension of ship's side which runs from deck to rail.

Bulkhead
Wall or partition between portions of ship's hull.

Bunker
Space for storage of fuel, such as coal or oil.

Canaller
A ship designed to pass through the locks of the St. Lawrence River canals. From 1845 to 1884 measuring 145 x 26 feet; from 1884 to 1958 measuring 254 x 45 feet; and since 1958 measuring 730 x 75 feet.

Capsize
To roll onto one side or to turn over.

Capstan
A type of winch stood vertically. Deck device used to haul on heavy lines for mooring, towing or handling sails, using several deck hands with long wooden bars.

Chains
Anchor chains, or steering chains. Used to connect steering wheel with rudder.

Companionway
Deck opening for a stair or ladder.

Composite
Method of constructing ship's hulls, using metal frames and wooden planking.

Consort
A towbarge.

CURV III
Cable Controlled Underwater Recovery Vehicle. See ROV.

Davit
Small fixed derrick used to raise and swing out lifeboats.

Decks:
Boat – Deck where lifeboats are carried, usually upper deck. Often a short one.
Hurricane – Highest deck. Can be same as weather or boat deck.
Main – Lowest full-length deck in a ship's hull.
Spar – In BULK FREIGHTERS, the upper full-length deck. Where HATCHES are located.
Weather – Highest decks, those exposed to weather.

183

Derelict
A ship which has been abandoned. Out of control.

Fore-and-Aft
Running in a front-to-back direction, BOW to STERN. Schooner-rigged as opposed to square rigged sailing vessel.

Forecastle (foc's'le)
Raised portion of a ship's BOW, used for windlass and anchor stowage in modern vessels, largely for crew quarters in 19th-century craft.

Founder
To fill and sink. To swamp.

Fresnel Lens
A large lens with a surface composed of many small lenses arranged to focus light on a single point. The orders of lenses range from First Order (largest) to Seventh Order. The Great Lakes lighthouses used Second to Fifth order lenses.

Gaff
Horizontal SPAR standing out from a mast and used to suspend top of a FORE-AND-AFT sail.

GPS (Global Positioning System)
A satellite-based navigation system for ships and aircraft, which provides accurate locational data.

Hatch
Deck opening, usually for loading cargo.

Hawser
Anchor line or towing line. Heavy rope, cable or chain.

Hold
Portion of ship's hull used for carrying and stowing cargo.

Jettison
To throw overboard.

Jib
Headsail. Small triangular sail carried forward of ship's FOREmast.

Jibboom
Light SPAR which projects out over a sailing ship's BOW to carry the headsails (JIBS), fixed on the end of the heavier bowsprit. FOREmost feature of a sailing vessel.

Keel
The backbone of a ship. A girder which runs down the centerline in a ship's bottom, from STEM to STERN.

Lighter
A small salvage vessel used to remove cargo from a ship in distress. To remove cargo.

LORAN
"LOng RAnge Navigation;" an electronic positioning system for ships and aircraft, which provides accurate locational data.

Master
Captain.

Mate
Assistant to Captain.

Mizzen
Third mast in a three-masted sailing craft.

Oilskins
Cotton garments waterproofed by repeated coats of linseed oil.

Picket Boat
Class of small, gasoline-powered patrol vessels measuring about 40 feet in length.

Port
Left side of a vessel when facing ship's BOW.

Propeller
Screw used to drive a ship through the water. Type of ship driven by a screw, usually a "passenger and freight propeller."

Purser
Ship's officer responsible for passenger tickets and ship's books.

Radar
Electronic device using transmitted and reflected radio waves to locate objects such as ships, obstructions or shoreline features for navigation.

Reef
Shallow area with rocky bottom.

Rigging
Wire or hemp rope used to support masts or to operate sails. Also stays for smokestack, etc.

ROV (Remotely Operated Vehicle)
An underwater device equipped with cameras and/or a manipulating arm, operated from the surface.

Schooner
Sailing craft with two or more masts, rigged with FORE-AND-AFT sails, 60 to 200 feet long.

Scow
Square-built vessel with flat sides, usually a flat bottom.

Scuttle
To sink a ship, usually by opening the sea cock, a water intake valve in the engine room.

Shoal
Shallow, sandy or muddy spot in a body of water.

Skiff
Rowboat.

Sloop
Sailing craft with one mast, ordinarily no more than 40 feet in length.

Soundings
Depth measurements.

Spar
A pole or mast used to support or spread sails or to carry lights or flags.

Starboard
Right side of a vessel when facing ship's BOW.

Steambarge
A small wooden ship used for carrying lumber products. Single-decked steamer of 130 to 200 feet with raised poop deck.

Stem
FOREmost portion of the BOW of a ship. The vertical member to which side plates are fastened at the BOW.

Stern
After (rear) end of a ship.

Steward
Officer in charge of passengers' meals and accommodations.

Strand
To run ashore or aground. To become stuck on an obstruction or a beach.

Superstructure
Cabins or "upper works" of a vessel. That part which projects above the hull.

Surfboat
Small rescue craft meant to be launched from a beach, carried on a beach-cart or trailer, usually horse-drawn. Powered by oars or small gasoline engine.

Tons:
Displacement – Actual weight of a ship where one ton equals 2,000 pounds.
Deadweight – Weight of cargo.
Register – One ton equals 100 cubic feet of space (not weight).
Gross – Entire capacity of ship.
Net – Capacity of ship's earning spaces.

Topmast
Upper portion of a two-piece mast.

Tow
A consort or barge towed behind a steam vessel. Act of towing or pulling a second vessel.

Trough
The low point between two waves. Being "caught in the trough" means to become helplessly out of control by swinging crosswise to the waves.

Whaleback
Unusual ship design with steel hulls and rounded DECKS introduced by Captain Alexander McDougall of Duluth in 1888. McDougall's American Steel Barge Company built whaleback barges and steamers between 1888 and 1896. Several were also built on the East Coast.

Yawl
Small SKIFF or lifeboat. In modern parlance a two-masted sailing craft with a short MIZZEN mast astern of the rudder post.

Endnotes

CHAPTER ONE

[1]John Columbo, *Mysterious Canada* (Toronto: Doubleday, 1988), p. 242; Rowley W. Murphy, "Ghosts of the Great Lakes, Part II," *Inland Seas* (Fall 1961), pp. 198-202; *Toronto Telegram*, April 19, 1926.

[2]Bruce Jenvey, *Great Lakes Cruiser*, October 1994, p. 38; interview, Rosemary Nesbitt, March 1995.

[3]Russell Floren and Andrea Gutsche, *Ghosts of the Bay* (Toronto: Lynx Images, 1995), pp. 269-271; Laura M. Gateman, *Lighthouses Around Bruce County* (Chesley, Ontario: Spinning Wheel Publications, 1991), pp. 38-39; J.B. Mansfield, *History of the Great Lakes Vol. I & II* (J.H. Beers: Chicago, 1899), p. 880; Stonehouse Files; David Swayze, *Shipwreck* (Traverse City, Michigan: Harbor House, 1992), p. 199.

[4]Interview, Pamela Kennedy, July 1, 1996.

[5]*Ann Arbor News*, December 16, 1989; Charles K. Hyde, *Northern Lights* (Lansing, Michigan: TwoPeninsula Press, 1986), p. 66; interview, Dan McGee, May 21, 1994; interview, Anna Hoge, Apr. 21, 1996.

[6]William O. Thomson. *The Ghosts of New England Lighthouses*. (Salem, MA: Old Saltbox Publishing, 1993), pp. 19, 51; interview, Anna Hoge, January 1996; interview, Dan McGee, July 1994.

[7]Hyde, *Northern Lights*, p. 93; Station file, U.S. Coast Guard Historians Office, Washington, D.C.

[8]*Detroit Free Press*, September 14, 1994; "Haunts of the Great Lakes," *Great Lakes Cruiser*, October 1995, pp. 42-43; interview, Lorraine Parris, May 29, 1994; interview, Anna Hoge, January 1996.

[9]Interview, Mr. Comtois, February 17, 1994.

[10]Interview, Ted Richardson, January 1994.

[11]Annual Report, U.S. Lighthouse Service, 1890-1903; Hyde, *Northern Lights*, p. 153.

[12]Interview, Joel Blahnick, June 1, 1994.

[13]Hyde, *Northern Lights*, pp. 66; Laurie Penrose and Bill Penrose, *A Traveler's Guide to Michigan Lighthouses* (Davidson, Michigan: Friede Publications, 1992), p. 33.

[14]ET1 Joseph P. Gilmartin, Sr. USCG (Ret.), "The Keeper's Light," *Shipmates*, October 1994, p. 7.

[15]Correspondence, Mr. Luther Barnett to Author, November 3, 14, 1994; Jack Edwards, "The Mystery of Sand Point Lighthouse," *Great Lakes Cruiser* (June 1995), pp. 20-32; *Iron Port*, Escanaba, March 5, 13; April 10, 17, 1886; *Marquette Monthly*, November 14, 1994.

[16]Jack Edwards, "Waughoshance, A Nautical Gravestone," *Great Lakes Cruiser*, October 1994, pp. 14-23; Hyde, *Northern Lights*, pp. 66, 103; Stonehouse File; Walton Collection, Bentley Historical Library, University of Michigan, box 4.

[17]Hyde, *Northern Lights*; Interview, Karen McDonnell, September 9, 1994.

[18]*Annual Report, U.S. Light-house Establishment*, 1890-1903; author's collection.

[19]Interview, Linda Gamble, June 23, 1994; *Mining Journal*(Marquette, Michigan), September 28, 1901; December 2, 1979; October 29, 1989; October 28, 1990.

[20]U.S. Department of the Interior, *1994 Inventory of Historic Light Stations*, National Park Service, Washington, D.C. 1994, p. 169; Interview, Roger Burrows, June 20, 1995.

[21]Station File.

[22]Interview, DeVerna Hubbard, June 2, 1994.

[23]Interview, DeVerna Hubbard, June 2, 1994.

[24]*Detroit Free Press Magazine*, October 2, 1994.

[25]Hyde, *Northern Lights*, pp. 192-193; Interview, Lee Radzak, October 13, 1994; *Split Rock Lighthouse* (St. Paul, Minnesota: Minnesota Historical Society Press, 1978), p.13.

[26]Interview, Captain Jimmie Hobaugh, September 12, 1994; Stannard Rock File, Don Nelson Collection.

CHAPTER 2

[1]Walton Collection, Bentley Historical Library, University of Michigan, box 4.

[2]Walton, box 4.

[3]John Harland and Mark Myers, *Seamanship in the Age of Sail* (Annapolis, Maryland: Naval Institute Press, 1985), pp. 24-25, 267-269; Frank Shay, *An American Sailor's Treasury* (New York: Smithmark, 1948), pp. 287-298.

[4]*Great Lakes Vesselman*, April 1926.

[5]*Toronto Evening Telegram*, September 19, 1946.

[6]Walton, box 4.

[7]Walton, box 7.

[8]Richard M. Dorson, *Bloodstoppers and Bearwalkers* (Cambridge, Massachusetts: Harvard University Press, 1952) p. 245; Frederick Stonehouse, *Lake Superior's Shipwreck Coast* (Au Train, Michigan: Avery Studios, 1985), pp. 47-48.

[9]Walton, box 4.

[10]Walton, box 4.

[11]Shay, Treasury, p. 357.

[12]*Association for Great Lakes Maritime History Newsletter*, Volume XII, No. 3, (May/June 1995), p. 3.

[13]Walton, box 4.

[14]Walton, box 4.

[15]*Buffalo Express*, May 11, 1885.

[16]Willis Metcalf, *Canvas and Steam on Quinte Waters* (South Bay, Ontario: South Marysburgh Marine Society, 1975) p. 87.

[17]Walton, box 4.

[18]*Chicago Tribune*, April 20, 1895.

[19]Dana Thomas Bowen, *Memories of the Lakes* (Cleveland: Freshwater Press, 1969), pp. 179-180; Herald-News, nd.

[20]*Detroit Free Press*, October 20, 1888.

[21]*Detroit Free Press*, September 3, 1871.

22Dorson, *Bloodstoppers and Bearwalkers*, pp. 244-245.

23Walton, box 7.

24*Detroit Free Press*, August 17, 1888.

25J. B. Mansfield, *History of the Great Lakes* (Chicago: J.H. Beers and Co., 1899) pp. 750-751.

26Mansfield, *History*, p. 723.

27*Annual Report, U.S. Life-Saving Service, 1894*, p. 278; C.H.J. Snider, "Schooner Days," *Toronto Evening Telegram*, May 15, 1937, CCXCII; *Detroit Tribune*, May 19, 1894.

28Marion Morse Davis, *Island Stories* (Lansing, Michigan: Marion Morse Davis,), pp. 71-73; Mansfield, *History*, p. 881; David Swayze. *Shipwreck* (Traverse City: Michigan, Harbor House, 1982), p. 204.

29C.H.J. Snider, "Schooner Days," *Toronto Telegram*, August 29, 1931, XXV.

30*Duluth Evening Herald*, November 28, 1900.

31David Swayze, "Davidson Sisterships, Linked by Fate," *Modoc Whistle*, Vol. 4, No. 3, (Spring, 1994), pp. 1-2, 8; David Swayze, Ralph Roberts and Donald Comtois, *Vessels Built on the Saginaw*, Vol. 1 (Bay City, Michigan: Saginaw River Marine Historical Society, 1993), pp. 1-2, 5.

32Julius F. Wolff Jr, *Lake Superior Shipwrecks* (Duluth, Minnesota: Lake Superior Port Cities, 1990), pp. 150, 165.

33*Great Lakes Journal*, January, May 1939.

34Schooner Days, CCIII, August 24, 1935.

35Walton, box 4.

36*Great Lakes News*, August 1926.

37Walton, box 7.

38*Detroit Free Press*, July 31, 1888.

39Frederick Stonehouse, *Marquette Shipwrecks* Marquette, Michigan: Harboridge Press, 1974), pp. 20-22.

40Stonehouse Files.

41Walton, box 4.

42Walter Havinghurst, *Long Ships Passing* (New York: McMillan, 1975), p. 251.

43Mansfield, *History*, pp. 847, 862-863; Walton, box 4.

44William Ratigan, *Great Lake Shipwrecks and Survivals* (New York: Galahad, 1960), p. 99.

45Walton, box 4.

46James K. Jamison, "Captain John Parker on Lake Superior," *Michigan History Magazine*, Vol. XXIII, Spring 1939, pp. 253-254; John G. Parker, "Autobiography of Captain John G. Parker," *Michigan Pioneer and Historical Collections*, Vol. 21, 1905, p. 583.

47"Log of the Coast Guard Station at Eagle Harbor." November 30-December 10, 1926; Saralee R. Howard-Fuller, "Deliverance on Superior," *Michigan History*, Vol. 65, No. 6, November-December 1981, pp. 30-32.

48Walton, box 4.

49James Cleary, *Superstitions of the Sea* (St. Clair, Michigan: Maritime History in Art, 1994), p. 179.

50Cleary, *Superstitions*, p. 182.

51Frederick Stonehouse, *Went Missing* (Au Train, Michigan: Avery Studios, 1977), pp. 63-66.

52*Detroit Free Press*, August 25, 1889.

53Dwight Boyer, *Ghost Ships of the Great Lakes* (New York: Dodd Mead, 1968), pp. 189-211.

54Walton, box 4.

55*Schooner Days*, CLXV, December 8, 1934.

56Swayze, *Shipwreck*, p. 242; Walton, box 4.

57Walton, box 4.

58Walton, box 4.

59Walton, box 4.

60Steven D. Elve, *Bridging the Waves* (Lowell, Michigan: Steven D. Elve, 1989), p. 112.

61Interview, Tom Farnquist, September 14, 1994.

62*Detroit Free Press*, November 15, 1904; *Marquette Mining Journal*, November 16, 1904; Stonehouse Wreck File.

63*The State Journal* (Lansing, Michigan), December 4, 1938.

64Walton, box 4.

65Walton, box 7.

66Walton, box 7.

67Walton, box 4.

68Walton, box 4.

69*Great Lakes News*, August 1926.

70Walton, box 4.

71Walton, box 4.

72Walton, box 4.

73Walton, box 4.

74*Great Lakes News*, August 1930.

75*Great Lakes News*, August 1926.

CHAPTER THREE

1Cleary, *Superstitions*, p. 131; Folklore, pp. 392-394; Shay, Sailor's Treasury, pp. 242-246.

2Mansfield, *History*, p. 826; C.J.H. Snider, "Schooner Days," *Toronto Telegram*, December 14, 1946, DCCLXXIV.

3Interview, Bruce Johanson, June 9, 1994.

4Wallace J. Baker, Sr., "On Manitoulin Island," *Inland Seas*, (October 1947) pp. 211-217; Dwight Boyer, *Great Stories of the Great Lakes* (New York: Dodd, Mead, 1966), pp. 215-230; David W. Stone, *Long Point, Last Point of Call* (Erin, Ontario: Boston Mills Press, 1988), pp. 22-25; Frank A. Meyers, compiler, "The Manitoulin *Griffon* vs the Tobermory *Griffon*," *Inland Seas*, (Winter 1956), pp. 275-284. Rowley W. Murphy, "The *Griffon* Wreckage at Tobermory," *Inland Seas*, (Summer 1956), pp. 142-149; Walton, box 4.

5Daniel A. Reilly, "*Hamilton* and *Scourge*, Ghost Ships of the War of 1812," *National Geographic*, Volume 163, Number 3, (March 1983): pp. 289-313.

6Cleary, *Superstitions*, p. 134.

7Mansfield, *History*, p. 834; Charles E. Herdendorf and Sandra E. Schuster, *The First Half Century of Merchant Steam Vessels on the Great Lakes* (Put-in-Bay, Ohio: Ohio State University, 1993).

8Steven L. Barry, "Shipbuilding in Vermilion," *Inland Seas*, Fall 1993, p. 193.

[9]Stonehouse, *Went Missing II*, pp. 137-147.

[10]*Iron Agitator* (Ishpeming, Michigan), April 17, 1886; Mansfield, *History*, pp. 826, 893.

[11]Walton, boxes 4/7.

[12]Stonehouse, *Went Missing II*, pp. 155-157.

[13]*The State Journal* (Lansing, Michigan), December 4, 1938.

[14]Stonehouse, *Went Missing II*, pp. 155-161; *Great Lakes Journal*, February 1919.

[15]*Milwaukee Journal*, January 24, 1895.

[16]Stonehouse, *Went Missing II*, pp. 32-41; Hudson file.

[17]Leo C. Lillie, *Historic Grand Haven and Ottawa County* (Grand Haven, Michigan: 1931), pp. 259-260.

[18]*Blade-Crescent* (Sebewaing, MI), November 8, 1988; Boyer, *Strange Adventures*, pp. 61-73; John Kaufman, "*Hunter Savidge* Disaster Recalled," *Inland Seas* (Fall 1965), pp. 233-235; Swayze, *Shipwreck*, p. 211.

[19]Clipping, unidentified, not dated.

[20]Stonehouse, *Went Missing II*, pp. 42-53.

[21]William. H. Law, *Heroes of the Great Lakes* (Detroit: 1906), p. 45.

[22]Curwood, *Great Lakes*, p. 103.

[23]George W. Stark, "A Century of Steam on the Great Lakes," *Outlook*, July 1917, p. 404.

[24]James Oliver Curwood, *Falkner of the Inland Seas* (Indianapolis: Bobbs-Merrill, 1905), pp. 11-30, 182.

[25]Rowley W. Murphy, "Ghosts of the Lakes, Part I," *Inland Seas* (Summer 1961), pp. 91-93.

[26]Walton, box 4; Wolff, *Lake Superior Shipwrecks*, p. 173.

[27]*Cleveland Plain Dealer*, May 29, 1932.

[28]C.H.J. Snider, "Schooner Days," *Toronto Telegram*, September 20, 27, DCCCXIII, DCCCXIV; Malcolm F. Willoughby, *Rum War at Sea* (Washington, D.C.: U.S. Printing Office, 1969), pp. 40-41, 90-91, 134-135; Walton, box 7.

[29]Interview, Captain Jimmie Hobaugh, September 12, 1994.

[30]*Flint Journal*, June 29, 1995.

[31]Elizabeth F. Cutler and Walter M. Hirthe, *Six Fitzgerald Brothers, Lake Captains All* (Milwaukee: Wisconsin Marine Historical Society, 1983), pp. 189, 208; Stone, *Long Point*, pp. 61-62.

[32]Steve Harold, *Shipwrecks off Sleeping Bear* (Traverse City, Michigan: Pioneer Study Center, 1984), pp. 6-7.

[33]Law, *Heroes*, p. 45.

[34]Mansfield, *History*, p. 889; Walton, box 7.

[35]Mansfield, *History*, pp. 753, 395; Metcalf, *Canvas and Steam* pp. 44-45; C.H.J. Snider, "Schooner Days," *Toronto Telegram*, CMIII.

[36]*Detroit Free Press*, January 13, 1886; Mansfield, *History*, pp. 744, 871; Swayze, *Shipwrecks*, p. 179.

[37]Walton, box 4.

[38]Interview, Anna Hoge, March 12, 1996.

[39]Interview, Pete Linquist, November 11, 1995.

[40]Interview, unidentified couple, at Duluth "Gales of November" program, November 11, 1995.

[41]Boyer, *Ghost Ships*, p. xii; William M. Lytle and Forrest R. Holdcamper, compilers, *Merchant Steam Vessels of the United States* (Staten Island, New York: Steamship Historical Society of America, 1975), pp. 250, 274, 305; Ratigan, *Shipwrecks*, p. 144.

[42]Walton, box 4.

CHAPTER FOUR

[1]Walton, box 4.

[2]Walton, box 4.

[3]*Detroit Free Press*, June 22, 1873.

[4]Victoria Brehm, *Sweetwater, Storms and Spirits* (Ann Arbor, Michigan: 1990), pp. 85-87; Mansfield, History, p. 805.

[5]*Chicago Inter-Ocean* August 5, 11, 12, 14, 15, 26, 27, December 9, 1874; July 26, 29 1865; *Cleveland Herald* July 5, 19, 22, 24, August 3, 1875; *Toledo Blade* August 1, 28, 20, 26, October 15, 1874; April 30, 1875; Vessel File, Institute for Great Lakes Research.

[6]*Saginaw Weekly Courier* (Saginaw, Michigan), August 26, 1883.

[7]C.H.J. Snider, "Schooner Days," *Toronto Telegram*, November 2, 1935, CCXII.

[8]C.H.J. Snider, "Schooner Days," *Toronto Telegram*, May 18, 1935, CLXXXVIII.

[9]*Toronto Evening Telegram*, May 22, 1937.

[10]Walton, box 6.

[11]C.H.J. Snider, "Schooner Days," *Toronto Telegram*, May 27. 1937, CCXCIII; Walton, box 7.

[12]Walton, box 7.

[13]C.H.J. Snider, "Schooner Days," *Toronto Telegram*, September 26, 1931, XXIX.

[14]"Australia and the *Success*," *Inland Seas* (April 1947), pp. 106-112; Boyer, *True Tales*, pp. 158-176.

[15]Shay, *Treasury*, pp. 257-258).

[16]Stonehouse Collection; unidentified interview.

[17]Interview, unidentified, February 1995; Stonehouse Collection.

CHAPTER FIVE

[1]Samuel F. Cook, *Drummond Island, The Story of The British Occupation 1815-1828* (Lansing, Michigan: 1896), pp. 103-110.

[2]Interview, Doug McCormick, May 21, 1994.

[3]*Iron Port* (Escanaba, Michigan), December 2, 1897, March 12, 1898.

[4]Glenn Furst, "I Remember, Mass Burials on South Manitou," Vol. 5, No. 2. np.

[5]Interview, unidentified, September 15, 1995.

[6]Interview, unidentified, August 21, 1995.

[7]Interview, unidentified, September 15, 1995.

[8]Boyer, *Great Stories*, pp. 129-135; Edward J. Canfield, D.O. and Thomas A. Allan, Ph.D., *Life on a Lonely Shore, a History of the Vermilion Point Life-Saving Station* (Sault Ste. Marie, Michigan: Lake Superior University Press, 1991), pp. 13, 35-36; Stonehouse, *Went Missing II*, pp. 118-125; Julius F. Wolff Jr.,

"A Lake Superior Lifesaver Reminisces." *Inland Seas*, Summer 1968, pp. 108-117.

[9]C.H.J. Snider, "Schooner Days," *Toronto Telegram*, Vol. CCLXXV.

[10]C.H.J. Snider, "Schooner Days," *Toronto Telegram*, February 19, 1938, CCCXXXIV; February 26, 1938, CCCXXXV.

[11]Stone, *Long Point*, pp. 55-56.

[12]Marion Morse Davis, *Island Stories* (Lansing, Michigan: Franklin Dekleine, 1947), p. 23.

[13]Interview, Dr. Bell, January 24, 1995.

[14]*Detroit Free Press*, November 29, 1882; Swayze Collection.

[15]Swayze, *Shipwrecks*, p. 94.

[16]*Great Lakes Cruiser Magazine*, October 1994, p. 45; Marine Collection, Rutherford B. Hayes Library, Fremont, Pennsylvania; Runge Collection, Milwaukee Public Library, Milwaukee, Wisconsin.

[17]Floren and Gutsche, *Ghosts*, pp. 134-136.

[18]Gundella, *The Werewolf of Grosse Pointe and Other Stories* (Detroit: Foresight Products, 1976), pp. 1-5.

[19]Floren and Gutsche, *Ghosts*, pp. 56-59; Institute for Great Lakes Research; Stonehouse Collection.

[20]Interview, unidentified, July 7, 1995; Stonehouse Collection.

[21]Frederick Denny Larke, "The Story of Sacred Rock," *Calcite Screenings* (August 1929); Rogers City Historical Society.

CHAPTER SIX

[1]Richard Ellis, *Monsters of the Sea* (New York: Alfred A. Knopf, 1994), pp. 39-54.

[2]*Buffalo Express*, July 29, 1873.

[3]*Buffalo Express*, August 16, 1973.

[4]Oliver M. Spencer, *Indian Captivity* (Chicago: R.R. Donnelly, 1917), pp. 151-152.

[5]Columbo, *Mysterious Canada*, p. 143.

[6]*Buffalo Historical Society Publication, 1880, Vol. II*, p. 366.

[7]Columbo, *Mysterious Canada*, p. 143.

[8]Columbo, *Mysterious Canada*, pp. 143-144.

[9]*Great Lakes Log*, August 9, September 7, 1993.

[10]*Detroit Free Press*, October 24, 1890.

[11]*Detroit News-Tribune*, August 8, 1897.

[12]*Great Lakes Journal*, October 1938.

[13]Floren and Gutsche, *Ghosts*, p. 195.

[14]*Milwaukee News*, August 9, 1867.

[15]*Great Lakes Journal*, October 1938.

[16]*Great Lakes Journal*, October 1938.

[17]Walton, box 4.

[18]Columbo, *Mysterious Canada*, pp. 189-190.

[19]*Toronto Globe*, September 16, 1881.

[20]*Kingston Whig*, June 11, 1888.

[21]*Toronto Globe*, July 23, 1892.

[22]*Whig-Standard* (Kingston), August 8, 1931.

[23]Boyer, *Great Stories*, p. 178.

[24]Superior Shoal, accidentally discovered in 1929 by the U.S. Lake Survey vessel *Margaret*, is approximately 77 miles northwest of Caribou

Island and 58 miles east southeastward of Passage Island. It is about 20 miles north of the present upbound course from the Soo to Thunder Bay and 14 miles into Canadian waters. It does lie directly in the track of Thunder Bay to the Soo via the Michipicoten Island channel.

[25]Boyer, *Great Stories*, pp. 178-181; C.H.J. Snider, "Schooner Days," *Toronto Telegram*, CII.

[26]David Dougald, "Mermaids: A Monster in Lake Superior, 1782," *Inland Seas* (Fall 1971), p. 218; Grace Lee Nute, *Lake Superior* (New York: Bobbs-Merrill, 1944), pp. 338-339.

[27]*Detroit Free Press*, July 31, 1895.

[28]*Detroit News-Tribune*, August 8, 1897, *Detroit Evening News*, July 31, 1895.

[29]Dorson, *Bloodstoppers*, p. 247.

[30]*Detroit News-Tribune*, August 9, 1897.

[31]*Detroit News-Tribune*, August 8, 1897.

[32]"Sea Serpent Sightings on the Great Lakes," *Historical Society of Michigan Chronicles*, October 1985, pp. 343-354.

CHAPTER SEVEN

[1]Metcalf, *Canvas and Steam*, p. 108.

[2]Stonehouse, *Went Missing II*, pp. 142-147.

[3]Stonehouse, *Went Missing II*, pp. 14-25.

[4]News clipping, unidentified, nd.

[5]C.H.J. Snider, "Schooner Days," *Toronto Telegram*, December 22, 29, 1945, DCCXXIII, DCCXXIV.

[6]Dana Thomas Bowen, *Lore of the Lakes* (Cleveland, Ohio: Freshwater Press, 1970), p. 199.

[7]Boyer, *True Tales*, p. 260.

[8]Boyer, *Ghost Ships*, p. 70.

[9]Bowen, *Lore of the Lakes*, p. 177; Boyer, *Ghost Ships*, pp. 90-91.

[10]C.H.J. Snider, "Schooner Days," *Toronto Telegram*, June 6, 1936, CLXLII.

[11]Stonehouse Collection.

[12]Hugh Wier, "Pere Marquette No. 18," *Inland Seas* (Spring 94), pp. 28-29.

APPENDIX

[1]C.H.J. Snider, "Schooner Days," *Toronto Telegram*, December 24, 1948, DCCCLXXIX; Mansfield, p. 823; Swayze, *Shipwrecks*, pp. 81-82.

[2]*Toledo Blade*, October 15, 1874.

[3]Roy F. Fleming, "The Burning of the OCEAN WAVE," *Inland Seas* (Fall 1957), pp. 226-227; C.H.J. Snider, "Schooner Days," *Toronto Telegram*, October 5, 1935, CMXIX.

[4]Mansfield, *History*, pp. 868, 899; Swayze, *Shipwreck*, pp. 174-175, 243.

[5]Mansfield, p. 886.

[6]Mansfield, p. 886.

[7]Mansfield, p. 886.

[8]Swayze, *Shipwrecks*, pp. 219-220.

[9]Mansfield, p. 870; Swayze, *Shipwrecks*, p. 180.

Bibliography

BOOKS

Baarslag, Karl. *Coast Guard to the Rescue.* New York: Farrar and Farrar, 1936.

Beaton, *From the Wheelhouse, the Story of a Great Lakes Captain.* Cheltenham, Ontario: Boston Mills Press, 1979.

Bowen, Dana Thomas. *Lore of the Lakes.* Cleveland, Ohio: Freshwater Press, 1970.

Bowen, Dana Thomas. *Memories of the Lakes.* Cleveland, Ohio: Freshwater Press, 1969.

Boyer, Dwight. *Ghost Ships of the Great Lakes.* New York: Dodd, Mead and Co., 1968.

Boyer, Dwight. *Great Stories of the Great Lakes.* New York: Dodd, Mead and Co., 1966.

Boyer, Dwight. *Strange Adventures on the Great Lakes.* New York: Dodd, Mead and Co., 1974.

Boyer, Dwight. *True Tales of the Great Lakes.* New York: Dodd, Mead and Co., 1971.

Brehm, Victoria. *Sweetwater, Storms and Spirits.* Ann Arbor, Michigan: University of Michigan Press, 1990.

Canadian Coastal and Inland Steam Vessels, 1809-1930. Providence, Rhode Island: Steamship Historical Society of America, 1979.

Canfield, Edward J. and Allan, Thomas A. *Life on a Lonely Shore, A History of the Vermilion Point Life-Saving Station.* Sault Ste. Marie, Michigan: Lake Superior State University Press, 1991.

Catlin, George B. *The Story of Detroit,* Detroit News, 1926, pp. 121-122.

Cleary, James. *Superstitions of the Sea.* St. Clair, Michigan: Maritime History in Art, 1994.

Columbo, John. *Mysterious Canada.* Toronto: Doubleday, 1988.

Cook, Samuel F. *Drummond Island, The Story of the British Occupation 1815-1828.* Lansing, Michigan: 1896.

Curwood, James Oliver. *Falkner of the Inland Seas.* Indianapolis: Bobbs-Merrill, 1905.

Curwood, James Oliver. *Great Lakes.*

Cutler, Elizabeth F. and Hirthe, Walter M. *Six Fitzgerald Brothers, Lake Captains All.* Milwaukee: Wisconsin Marine Historical Society, 1983.

Davis, Marion Morse. *Island Stories.* Lansing, Michigan: Franklin Dekleine, 1947.

Dodge, Roy L. *Michigan Ghost Towns, Volume III Upper Peninsula.* Tawas City, Michigan: Glendon Publishing, 1973.

Donahue, James. *Steamboats in Ice 1872.* Cass City, Michigan: Anchor Publications, 1995.

Dorson, Richard M. *Bloodstoppers and Bearwalkers.* Cambridge. Massachusetts: Harvard University Press, 1952.

Ellis, Richard. *Monsters of the Deep.* New York: Alfred A. Knoff, 1994.

Elve, Steven D. *Bridging the Waves.* Lowell, Michigan: Steven D. Elve, 1989.

Floren, Russell and Gutsche, Andrea. *Ghosts of the Bay.* Toronto: Lynx Images, 1995.

Frederickson, Arthur C. and Lucy F. *Frederickson's History of the Ann Arbor Auto and Train Ferries.* Frankfort, Michigan: Gull's Nest Publishing, 1994.

Gateman, Laura M. *Lighthouses Around Bruce County.* Chesley, Ontario: Spinning Wheel Publications, 1991.

Greenwood, John O. *Namesakes, 1930-55.* Cleveland, Ohio: Freshwater Press, 1978.

Gundella. *The Werewolf of Grosse Pointe and Other Stories.* Detroit: Foresight Products, 1976.

Harland, John and Myers, Mark. *Seamanship in the Age of Sail.* Annapolis, Maryland: Naval Institute Press, 1985.

Harold, Steve. *Shipwrecks Off Sleeping Bear.* Traverse City, Michigan: Pioneer Study Center, 1984.

Havinghurst, Walter. *Long Ships Passing.* New York: MacMillian, 1975.

Herdendorf, Charles E. and Schuster, Sandra E. *The First Half Century of Merchant Steam Vessels on the Great Lakes.* Put-in-Bay, Ohio: Ohio State University Press, 1993.

Heyl, Erik. *Early American Steamers, Volume IV.* Buffalo, New York: Erik Heyl, 1965.

Hilton, George W. *The Great Lakes Car Ferries.* Berkley, California: Howell-North, 1962.

Hyde, Charles K. *The Northern Lights.* Lansing, Michigan: TwoPeninsula Press, 1986.

Lambert, R.S. *Exploring the Supernatural, the Weird in Canadian Folklore.* Toronto: McClelland and Stewart, 1955.

Lillie, Leo C. *Historic Grand Haven and Ottawa County.* Grand Haven, 1931.

Landon, Fred. *Lake Huron.* New York: Bobbs-Merrill, 1944.

Law, W.H. *Heroes of the Great Lakes.* Detroit: 1906.

Lytle, William M. and Holdcamper, Forrest R. Compilers. *Merchant Steam Vessels of the United States.* Providence, Rhode Island: Steamship Historical Society of America, 1975

Mansfield, J.B. *History of the Great Lakes, Volumes I & II.* Chicago: J.H. Beers & Co., 1899.

Metcalf, Willis. *Canvas and Steam on Quinte Waters.* South Bay, Ontario: South Marysburgh Marine Society, 1979.

Nute, Grace Lee. *Lake Superior.* New York: Bobbs-Merrill, 1944.

Oleszewski, Wes. *Ice Water Museum.* Marquette, Michigan: Avery Studios, 1993.

Penrose, Laurie and Bill. *A Traveller's Guide to Michigan Lighthouses.* Davidson, Michigan: Friede Publications, 1992.

Pitezel, Rev. J.H. *Lights and Shades of Missionary Life.* Cincinnati, Ohio: Western Book Concern, 1861.

Prescott, R.E. *Historical Tales of the Huron Shore Region and Rhymes, Vol. I.* Alcona County Herald, 1934.

Ratigan, William. *Great Lakes Shipwrecks and Survivals.* New York: Galahad, 1960.

Shay, Frank. *An American Sailor's Treasury.* New York: Smithmark Publishers, 1948.

Spencer, Oliver M. *Indian Captivity.* Chicago: R.R. Donnell, 1917.

Split Rock Lighthouse. St. Paul: Minnesota Historical Society Press, 1978.

Staples, Larry. *Wilderness and Storytelling.* Ottawa: National Museum of Canada, 1981.

Stone, David W. *Long Point: Last Port of Call.* Erin, Ontario: Boston Mills Press, 1988.

Stonehouse, Frederick. *Lake Superior's Shipwreck Coast.* Au Train, Michigan: Avery Studios, 1985.

Stonehouse, Frederick. *Marquette Shipwrecks.* Au Train, Michigan: Avery Studios, 1974.

Stonehouse, Frederick. *Went Missing.* Au Train, Michigan: Avery Studios, 1977.

Swayze, David. *Shipwreck.* Traverse City, Michigan: Harbor House, 1992.

Swayze, David, Roberts, Ralph and Comtois, Donald. *Vessels Built Along the Saginaw.* Bay City, Michigan: Saginaw Marine Historical Society, 1993.

Thomson, William O. *The Ghosts of New England Lighthouses.* Salem, Massachusetts: Old Salt Box Publishing, 1993.

U.S. Treasury Department, Annual Report, U.S. Life-Saving Service. Washington, D.C. 1894.

Van der Linden, Rev. Peter, editor. *Great Lakes Ships We Remember II.* Cleveland, Ohio: Freshwater Press, 1984.

Williams, Elizabeth Whitney. *A Child of the Sea, and Times Among the Mormons.* Charlevoix, Michigan: John Rathburn, 1954.

Willoughby, Malcolm F. *Rum War at Sea.* Washington, D.C.: U.S. Printing Office, 1969.

Wilterding, John H. Jr. *McDougall's Dream, the American Whaleback.* Duluth, Minnesota: Lakeside Publications, 1969.

Wolff, Dr. Julius F. Jr. *Lake Superior Shipwrecks.* Duluth, Minnesota: Lake Superior Port Cities, 1990.

Woodson, Robert. *Side Launch: the Collingwood Shipyard Spectacle.* Toronto: Summerhill Press, 1983.

PERIODICALS

Association for Great Lakes Maritime History Newsletter. Volume XII, No. 3, (May/June 1995), p. 3.

"Australia and the *Success.*" *Inland Seas.* (April 1947), pp. 106-112.

Baker, Wallace J., Sr. "On Manitoulin Island." *Inland Seas.* (October 1947), pp. 211-217.

Bannister, J.A. "The White Sails of Dover, Part I." *Inland Seas.* (Spring 1949), pp. 20-21.

Bannister, J.A. "The White Sails of Dover, Part II." *Inland Seas.* (Summer 1949), pp. 18-25.

Barry, Steven L. "Shipbuilding in Vermilion." *Inland Seas.* (Fall 1993), p. 193.

Buffalo Historical Society Publication. Vol. II, (1880), p. 366.

Dougald, David. "Mermaids: A Monster on Lake Superior, 1782." *Inland Seas.* (Fall 1971), p. 218.

Edwards, Jack. "The Mystery of Sand Point Lighthouse." *Great Lakes Cruiser* Magazine. (June 1995), pp. 20-32.

Edwards, Jack. "Waughoschance, A Nautical Gravestone." *Great Lakes Cruiser* Magazine. (October 1994), pp. 14-23.

Fleming, Roy F. "The Burning of the OCEAN WAVE." *Inland Seas.* (Fall 1957), pp. 226-227.

Howard-Fuller, Saralee R. "Deliverance on Lake Superior." *Michigan History Magazine.* Vol. 65, No. 6 (November-December 1981), pp. 30-32.

Jamison, James K. "Captain John Parker on Lake Superior." *Michigan History Magazine,* Vol. XXIII, (Spring 1939), pp. 253-254.

Jenvy, Bruce. "Haunts of the Great Lakes." *Great Lakes Cruiser* Magazine. (October 1994), pp. 42-43.

Jenvey, Bruce. "The Haunting of the Oswego Light." *Great Lakes Cruiser* Magazine. (October 1994), p. 38.

Kaufman, John. "*Hunter Savidge* Disaster Recalled." *Inland Seas.* (Fall 1965), pp. 233-235.

Landon, Fred. "Otter Island Light, Lake Superior." *Inland Seas.* (Winter 1956), p. 305.

Larkes, Frederick Denny. "The Story of Sacred Rock." *Calcite Screenings.* (August 1929).

Meyers, Frank A., compiler, "The Manitoulin *Griffon* vs the Tobermory *Griffon.*" *Inland Seas.* (Winter 1956), pp. 275-284.

Morrison, Lauchlen, P. "Recollections of the Great Lakes, 1874-1944." *Inland Seas.* (Spring 1949), p. 49.

Murphy, Rowley W. "The GRIFFON Wreckage at Tobermory." *Inland Seas.* (Summer 1956), pp. 142-149.

Murphy, Rowley W. "Ghosts of the Great Lakes, Part I." *Inland Seas.* (Summer 1961), pp. 94-96.

Parker, John G. "Autobiography of Captain John G. Parker." *Michigan Pioneer and Historical Collections.* Vol. 21, (1905), p. 583.

Reilly, Daniel A. *"Hamilton* and *Scourge,* Ghost Ships of the Great Lakes." *National Geographic,* Vol. 163, No. 3 (March 1983), pp. 289-313.

"Sea Serpent Sightings on the Great Lakes." Historical Society of Michigan *Chronicles.* (October 1985), pp. 343-354.

Stark, George W. "A Century of Steam on the Great Lakes." *Outlook.* (July 1917), p. 404.

Swayze, David. "Davidson Sisterships Linked by Fate." *Modoc Whistle,* Vol. 4, No. 3 (Spring 1994), pp. 1-2, 8.

Walton, Ivan H. "Developments on the Great Lakes, 1815-1943." *Michigan History Magazine.* (Winter 1943), pp. 73-75.

Wier, Hugh, *"Pere Marquette No. 18." Inland Seas.* (Spring 1994), pp. 28-29.

Williams, W.R. "The Gale-Shattered *Waubuno."* *Inland Seas,* (Spring 1965), pp. 52-55.

Wolff, Dr. Julius F. Jr. "A Lake Superior Life-Saver Reminisces." *Inland Seas.* (Summer 1968), pp. 108-117.

PUBLIC DOCUMENTS AND COLLECTIONS

Institute for Great Lakes Research, Perrysburg, Ohio.

Light Station Files, U.S. Coast Guard Historian's Office, Washington D.C.

Marquette Maritime Museum, Marquette, Michigan.

Rogers City Historical Society, Rogers City, Michigan.

Stonehouse Collection.

U.S. Life-Saving Service Records (Coast Guard). Record Group 26. National Archives and Records Service. Washington, D.C.

Walton Collection, Bentley Historical Library, University of Michigan.

SERIALS

Blade-Crescent (Sebewaing, Michigan).

Buffalo Express.

Chicago Inter-Ocean.

Chicago Tribune.

Cleveland Plain Dealer.

Daily Mining Journal. (Marquette, Michigan).

Detroit Free Press.

Detroit News-Tribune.

Detroit Tribune.

Duluth Evening Herald.

Duluth News-Tribune.

Flint Journal.

Great Lakes Journal.

Great Lakes Vesselman.

Herald-News (Duluth, Minnesota).

Iron Agitator (Ishpeming, Michigan).

Iron Port (Escanaba, Michigan).

Kingston Whig.

Marine Review.

Milwaukee Journal.

Milwaukee News.

Mining Journal (Marquette, Michigan).

Saginaw Daily Courier.

State Journal (Lansing, Michigan).

Toledo Blade.

Toronto Evening Telegram.

Toronto Globe.

Whig Standard (Toronto).

UNPUBLISHED MATERIAL

Correspondence, Luther Barrett to author, November 3, 14, 1994.

Interview, author and Dr. Bell, January 24, 1995.

Interview, author and Donald Comtois, February 17, 1994.

Interview, author and Joel Blahnick, June 1, 1994.

Interview, author and Linda Gamble, June 23, 1994.

Interview, author and Tom Farnquist, September 14, 1994.

Interview, author and Capt. Jimmie Hobaugh, USCG (ret.) September 12, 1994.

Interview, author and DeVerna Hubbard, June 2, 1994.

Interview, author and Anna Hoge, April 24, 1996.

Interview, author and Bruce Johanson, June 9, 1994.

Interview, author and Doug McCormick, May 21, 1994.

Interview, author and Karen McDonnell, September 9, 1994.

Interview, author and Dan McGee, May 2, 1994.

Interview, author and Rosemary Nesbitt, March 1995.

Interview, author and Ted Richardson, January 1994.

Interview, author and unidentified, February 1995.

Interview, author and unidentified, August 21, 1995.

Index

194

About the Author

Frederick Stonehouse holds a Master of Arts degree in history from Northern Michigan University, Marquette, Michigan, and has authored 13 books on Great Lakes maritime history. Among them are *Wreck Ashore, the U.S. Life-Saving Service on the Great Lakes* and

 *Shipwreck of the* Mesquite, *Death of a Coast Guard Cutter,* published by Lake Superior Port Cities Inc., and *The Wreck of the* Edmund Fitzgerald.

He has also been a consultant for both the United States National Park Service and Parks Canada.

His articles have been published in *Lake Superior Magazine, Skin Diver* and *Great Lakes Cruiser* magazines and *Wreck and Rescue Journal.* He has been a member of the Board of Directors of the Marquette Maritime Museum and currently is a member of the Board of Directors of the U.S. Life-Saving Service Heritage Association, Great Lakes Lighthouse Keepers Association, Association for Great Lakes Maritime History and Lake Superior Marine Museum Association. He resides in Marquette, Michigan, with his wife, Lois, and son, Brandon.

Also by Lake Superior Port Cities Inc.

Julius F. Wolff Jr.'s Lake Superior Shipwrecks
Hardcover: ISBN 0-942235-02-9
Softcover: ISBN 0-942235-01-0

Shipwrecks of Lake Superior by James R. Marshall
Softcover: ISBN 0-942235-00-2

Shipwreck of the Mesquite by Frederick Stonehouse
Softcover: ISBN 0-942235-10-x

The Superior Way, Second Edition by Bonnie Dahl
Spiralbound: ISBN 0-942235-14-2

Michigan Gold, Mining in the Upper Peninsula by Daniel R. Fountain
Softcover: ISBN 0-942235-15-0

*Wreck Ashore, The United States Life-Saving Service
on the Great Lakes* by Frederick Stonehouse
Softcover: ISBN 0-942235-22-3

Shipwrecks of Isle Royale National Park by Daniel Lenihan
Softcover: ISBN 0-942235-18-5

Tales of the Old North Shore by Howard Sivertson
Hardcover: ISBN 0-942235-29-0

Lake Superior Magazine (Bimonthly)

Lake Superior Magazine Travel Guide (Annual)

Lake Superior Wall Calendar (Annual)

Lake Superior Wall Map

For a catalog of the entire Lake Superior Port Cities collection of books
and merchandise, write or call:
Lake Superior Port Cities Inc.
P.O. Box 16417
Duluth, Minnesota 55816-0417
USA

218-722-5002
888-BIG LAKE (244-5253)
FAX 218-722-4096